T

NEW AGE

4

A CHANNEL FOUR BOOK

THE
NEW AGE

An Anthology of Essential Writings

Edited by

William Bloom

RIDER

LONDON   SYDNEY   AUCKLAND   JOHANNESBURG

For Djwhal Khul

First published in the UK in 1991 by Rider
An imprint of Random Century Group Ltd
20 Vauxhall Bridge Road, London SW1V 2SA

Random Century Group Australia (Pty) Ltd
20 Alfred Street, Milsons Point,
Sydney, NSW 2061, Australia

Random Century New Zealand Ltd,
9–11 Rothwell Avenue, Albany,
Auckland 10, New Zealand

Random Century Group South Africa (Pty) Ltd,
PO Box 337, Bergvlei 2012, South Africa

British Library Cataloguing in Publication Data
The New Age: an anthology of essential writings.
  1. Occultism
  I. Bloom William
  133

  ISBN 0–7126–4804–6

Typeset by 🅐 Tek Art Ltd, Addiscombe, Croydon, Surrey
Printed and bound in Great Britain by Mackays of Chatham plc, Chatham, Kent

Contents

4 Human Potential

5 Gaia

6 Practical Implications

Notes on the Editor

William Bloom was a successful London novelist and publisher who at the age of twenty-five took two years' spiritual retreat in order to re-orient his life. Since that time he has worked as an author, counsellor and lecturer integrating the wisdom of the spiritual traditions with a modern approach to personal growth and social change. He has a doctorate in psychology from the London School of Economics where he teaches a course on psychological problems in international relations. He is a founding director of the New Age programme, Alternatives, of St James's Church, Piccadilly, and he has a long association with the educational programme of the Findhorn Foundation. He also works as a financial and project consultant for philanthropic foundations. His books include *Meditation in a Changing World* and *Sacred Times – A New Approach to Festivals*.

The television programmes on which this book is based were produced for Channel Four Television by Diverse Production Ltd.

Acknowledgements

I researched and put together a large portion of this anthology while teaching at the Findhorn Foundation. I need to thank the community as a whole for opening their libraries to me; particular thanks to Leslie Quilty for her research work and to Ian Cook who advised us and very generously let us borrow books from the Phoenix Bookshop. I also wish to thank everybody at Diverse Production Ltd, without whom this project would not have been possible.

The publishers are grateful for permission to reprint the following copyright material:

Roberto Assagioli: to Viking Penguin, Inc. for *Psychosynthesis* (Viking Press, 1973), copyright © 1965 by Psychosynthesis Research Foundation.

Alice Bailey: to Lucis Trust for *A Treatise on White Magic* (The Lucis Press, 1974) and *Esoteric Healing* (The Lucis Press, 1961), both copyright © Lucis Trust.

William Bloom and Marko Pogacnik: to Gothic Image for *Ley Lines and Ecology; An Introduction* (Gothic Image, 1985), copyright © William Bloom and Marko Pogacnik, 1985.

David Bohm: to Routledge, a Division of Routledge, Chapman & Hall Ltd. for *Wholeness and The Implicate Order* (Ark Paperbacks, 1988), copyright © David Bohm, 1980.

Eileen Caddy: to the author for *The Spirit of Findhorn* (Fowler, 1977).

Fritjof Capra: to Collins Publishers Ltd. for *The Tao of Physics* (Flamingo/Fontana, 1989).

Ken Carey: to Uni★Sun for *The Starseed Transmissions – An Extraterrestrial Report* (Uni★Sun, 1988), copyright © 1982 by Kenneth X. Carey.

Joseph Bharat Cornell: to Ananda Publications for *Sharing Nature With Children* (Ananda Publications, 1979), copyright © 1979 by Joseph Bharat Cornell.

Ram Dass: to Doubleday & Co. Inc. for *Journey of Awakening* (Bantam Books, 1985).

Christopher Day: to Thorsons Publishing Group for *Places of the Soul* (The Aquarian Press, 1990), copyright © Christopher Day, 1990.

Preface

In my view, the New Age is neither a movement nor a religion set apart from others. It is not something one can choose or not to join. It is essentially a view of the time we live in and the world we are creating. It is therefore for everyone.

I doubt that we can predict the exact nature of what is to come in the next great phase of human culture, but clearly it must emerge from the present. There are people from various walks of life who are keenly aware of the spiritual essence of this unfolding present, and the television programmes with which this book is linked brought forty of them together to discuss and if possible illuminate this process for a wider audience.

The television series was commissioned by Channel Four Television in early 1990 following several approaches to them by independent producers wishing to cover this general area. I, for example, had been pressing for some time for an opportunity to explore the phenomenon whereby many contemporary people live their lives without involvement in an established religion, but have an obvious spiritual dimension to their lives. It is to Channel Four's credit that they had the vision to fund these programmes which are about spirituality and consciousness rather than 'religion' in the conventionally accepted use of the word.

Thanks are therefore due to Bob Towler, Commissioning Editor for Religion at Channel Four Television, whose sceptical but open-minded interest resulted in my company, Diverse Production, producing the series for broadcast. Thanks also to Philip Clarke, Head of Programmes at Diverse for his interest, and to the committed team of producers, Paul ver Bruggen, Edmund Coulthard and Gillian Thomas for maintaining an energetic debate and making the programmes actually happen.

Also thanks to Deb Faith, whose enthusiasm for the subject helped develop the original idea, and William Bloom, who organised the conference event happening around the recording of the programmes and compiled this anthology.

From my perspective working in broadcast television, it is clear that all our modern media technologies have transformed the ability of people and societies to communicate with one another. Such channels have resulted in, and been an expression of, a shifting of awareness from the immediately local to the more distant. And, with mankind and cameras in space looking back, the shift has now become global. This expansion of consciousness constitutes a profound transformation of our perception of both ourselves and our world. In medicine, for example, the mechanistic approach which separated mind from body and one organ from the next is giving way to a more holistic model of the inter-relatedness of the whole. And at the frontiers of science mechanistic models of the structure of matter are giving way to models acknowledging just this same inter-relatedness.

These shifts also reflect and express more feminine modes of understanding and ways of relating to the world. Goddess archetypes are re-emerging as women play a greater role in our societies, which have been dominated by masculine attitudes and male visions of deity for tens of generations. The image of Gaia, for example, links the ancient idea of Mother Earth with a holistic vision of the inter-connectedness of the planet's life forms and its material elements.

This shift of consciousness has also expressed itself as a healthy questioning of established authorities. In the West many people have turned from established religion to a more personally experienced inward spiritual quest for meaning. Much attention has consequently turned to Eastern religions where ways of exercise and meditation have traditionally encouraged this form of personal experience. A new synthesis and balance between 'being and doing' is emerging, a New Age. These are exciting and challenging times and our children and those beyond them will be inheriting what we create now.

PETER DONEBAUER
Co-Founder and Managing Director, Diverse Production Ltd
Executive Producer, The New Age

Introduction

When I was a child, like many children, I was frightened by certain places – but I was told there was nothing there. Decades later I discovered the reality of atmospheres and energies.

When I was a child, I lay in bed observing my own thoughts, trying to understand who I, the observer, was; sometimes I panicked in a terrible anxiety, losing my identity and not understanding what was happening to me. Decades later I discovered clear maps for exploring my psyche.

When I was a child, I was sometimes overwhelmed by the beauty of the sky and thrilling atmosphere of the Earth – but where could I safely share this?

When I was a child, I imagined the spinning particles in an atom in my finger to be the cosmos of another universe. Sometimes I thought I could be like God. To whom could I confide such thoughts?

All the truths that are important to me now were denied me in my childhood. There is no blame to lay upon anyone; I was well parented and well educated. Our parents and teachers – we ourselves – have been victims of a culture and a worldview which has suppressed instinctive individual spirituality. Freud said that the major problem of civilisation was the repression of our sexuality. In my view, the major problem has been the repression of our spirituality, the repression of our instinct freely to explore the inner dimensions of our Universe and of ourselves.

We have been subject to religions and churches which allow only one kind of belief or approach to the divine unknown. We have been victims of insecurity and superstition. And we have been subject to an intellectual worldview which overthrew the power of superstition and organised religion only, in reaction, to replace it with a worldview so mechanical and so limited that it totally denied the invisible realities of existence.

I cannot ignore the fate of individualistic spiritual seekers in the past and I cannot ignore contemporary forces of repression; historical and modern reality demand new clarity when we discuss spiritual freedom.

I see the New Age phenomenon as the visible tip of the iceberg of a mass movement in which humanity is reasserting its right to explore spirituality in total freedom. The constraints of religious and intellectual ideology are falling away.

The New Age movement represents several very different dynamics, but they thread together to communicate the same message: *there is an invisible and inner dimension to all life – cellular, human and cosmic. The most exciting work in the world is to explore this inner reality.*

According to research carried out by the Gallup poll, almost fifty per cent of all people have experiences that are mystical or, at least, not scientifically explicable. The great beauty of the New Age movement is that if someone in it is approached by someone else looking for insight or counselling about the inner or religious dimension, he or she will not be told: '*Believe this! Do this! Don't do that!*' but rather: '*There are a thousand different ways of exploring inner reality. Go where your intelligence and intuition lead you. Trust yourself.*' New Age attitudes are the antithesis of fundamentalism.

Although the different dynamics which form the New Age phenomenon create a common general message, some of them make strange bedfellows. It would be a mistake to assume that all people who might come under the New Age banner get on with each other – either personally or in terms of their ideas. In fact, some who are identified as New Agers actively reject the label for fear of being associated with seemingly incompatible elements. There are divides, for example, between those of a rigorous intellectual bias and those who are dominantly instinctive and intuitive, even though they might share the same spiritual approach or work in the same field.

It seems to me that there are four major fields:

New Paradigm/New Science
Ecology
New Psychology
Spiritual Dynamics

Under *New Paradigm/New Science* come all the new theories which are reworking our intellectual understanding of the structures of life. These include the insights of sub-atomic physics, cosmology and biology. Here the mechanistic Newtonian view of the cosmos, as being made up of tangible bits and pieces following certain reliable laws of interaction, has given way to a more fluid and expanded view of reality. Matter and energy are seen as bound together, connected and formed in invisible ways that we are only just beginning to understand; according to this worldview, matter, energy and consciousness are one continuum and, like the hologram, all aspects of the whole can be contained and enfolded in a single part. All life is intimately interconnected.

Along with the new science, we are also reassessing the nature of the human body and our approaches to medicine and healing. Equally, we are reassessing the values that underpin our social structures and cultural heritage. Technological and scientific achievements appear to have brought with them many attendant ills as well as benefits. What should our priorities be? Have we, in environmental terms, paid too high a price for material progress?

Linked by a new understanding of our Earth as a complete living organism, Gaia, these questions merge with the approaches of *Ecology*, especially of the deep ecologists. The deep ecologist explores the relationship between all forms of life in its profound spiritual and philosophical dimensions. The concept of interdependence and interpenetration across all species expands to include not only our actions as consumers and workers, but also *the total energy effect of our actions and attitudes*. Not only our supermarket purchases but also our moods create our global environment. This is spiritual ecology taking responsibility for the total state of our planet. Situation by situation, moment by moment, we confront our moral and social responsibilities.

The third thread is the *New Psychology*. Freud pointed out the invisible world of the unconscious, but the new psychology demonstrates not only the repressed and primitive areas of the unconscious, but also the extraordinary dynamics of the supraconscious and transpersonal. A core concept of new psychology is that *all* people are capable of becoming integrated, fulfilled and completely loving human beings.

But for me the hallmark of the New Age is the power of its *Spiritual Dynamics*. Certain weights – repression, fear, power interests, materialism – have been holding down this dynamic; but these weights are shifting.

The new science and psychology show the severe limits of apparent scientific logic.

The new psychology demonstrates no limits in human potential.

The ecological crisis has shown the failure of unfettered industrialisation, science and commerce. Technology becomes the servant of ethics.

The vision of our planet from space and the Gaia hypothesis show us our beautiful and inescapable interdependence. The sense of impotent post-industrial isolation and alienation is disappearing.

And the slumbering spiritual mammoth, like Gulliver released from the many strands, is beginning to awake.

In the New Age movement there is an enthusiasm, humour and release. It draws its lessons and inspirations from many sources. One of its major characteristics is its honouring of all the esoteric religious traditions and of the mystic traditions of native peoples. A remarkable renaissance of the wisdom traditions is taking place, both those within the major religions and those of indigenous peoples. Within the major religions, for example, are the gnostic tradition of Christianity, the Qabalah of Judaism, Sufism in Islam, and Zen and meditation techniques of Buddhism. The native traditions include those of Celtic Europe – such as Wiccan and Druidism – north American Indians, Australian Aborigines and African medicine people. And there is a powerful rebirth of the female aspects of deity, as the Goddess resumes her crucial role in our lives.

At the same time, as people use various mystical techniques to explore their own psyches and consciousness, they have tapped great reservoirs of spiritual knowledge and awareness. Much of this has come through in new teachings and much of it has also come through in inspirational and lyrical prose, as well as music, art and movement. But a common theme resonating through all the new inner awareness is that we are entering a New Age and that human consciousness is going through a transformation that is cosmically significant. Perhaps this understanding of the New Age is vainglorious egotism; that is for you to decide. Less glamorous is the notion that we are passing out of 2,000 years of Piscean astrological influence into the influence of Aquarius, which will affect all aspects of our culture as we move away from Piscean structures of hierarchical devotion to more fluid and spontaneous relationships that dance to an Aquarian rhythm. Also less glamorous is the notion that the problems facing our post-industrial global village with its sophisticated electronic awareness on the one hand and its gross social injustices on the other, are forcing humanity into a new consciousness.

I began this introduction with words about my childhood and the lack of response to my most serious inner questions. I then repressed my spiritual enquiry as an adolescent, but many circumstances drew me back to it in my early twenties. On my own I meditated and read in depth, exploring inner dimensions, an exploration whose beginning I continually re-experience, whose end I cannot now even begin to sense.

As a young person, and now older, I want and need maps to help me. At the very least and to its great credit, the New Age movement, in all its various facets, gives us maps, insights, friends, techniques, inspiration and strength in our exploration of the inner world. May we and all our children, wherever upon the planet, have the freedom always to pursue this exploration.

This anthology in its six sections exactly parallels the themes of the six programmes of Channel Four's series, *The New Age*. Section by section I have attempted to include extracts which give a genuine taste of the depth and breadth of New Age thinking. Without exception, section by section, I have had to exclude, for lack of space, many authors and insights which I would have dearly loved to include. I apologise now for what is missing.

Nevertheless it is, I think, an extraordinary feast of wisdom and stimulation, and it has been an honour and pleasure to select and edit it. Working with this material has moved me and renewed my faith. I hope that it also touches you.

What is the New Age?

Barbara Marx Hubbard
Marilyn Ferguson
Peter Russell
Willis W. Harman
Alice A. Bailey
David Spangler
Sir George Trevelyan
Starhawk

Introduction

In the 1960s, along with many others, I grew my hair long, wore an earring, and surrendered to flower power. I liked the flowers and I also liked the power – the power of sensing that we were in an era of social transition and spiritual transformation. But the dynamism of the time subsided and what had felt like the growing climax of a new mass awareness evaporated. We lost our joy and we lost our naïveté, and some folk looked back with echoes of remorse and embarrassment. In many hearts, however, there had been deep changes – including my heart.

In 1972 I resigned from my job in London publishing and took two years' retreat, reading and meditating alone in the mountains of the Moroccan High Atlas. There, in my meditation, alongside my own path of change, I became increasingly certain that the sense of a global transformation, a shift in the mass consciousness of humanity, was neither romantic nor naïve.

Then books began to pass my way which spoke about this change, which spoke about 'a new age'. With no hesitation, with neither thought nor contemplation, I, who had never joined anything, found myself aligned with and part of this movement.

The most important books which first came to me were those of Alice Bailey. These books were not, in fact, hers – she had acted as secretary for a Tibetan teacher named Djwhal Khul and had drawn upon Tibetan teachings. The Alice Bailey books are not everybody's cup of tea; their language and general style are old-fashioned and remote. But they possess a depth of wisdom about esoteric philosophy unequalled in this century. Reflecting this, many of the volumes have been reprinted up to seventeen times and translated into over two dozen languages. In the English language alone over one and a half million copies have been printed. Moreover, according to the master index, there are 285 passages in them referring to the 'New Age'. During my retreat I read all the Bailey books and by the time I had completed them I had absorbed the term 'New Age'. These books are considered by many people, including antagonists of the New Age movement, to be the key inspiration for it.

Echoing Alice Bailey, but resonating in a more poetic and immediate style, David Spangler and Sir George Trevelyan also talk about the New Age in an almost purely spiritual way. David Spangler, one of the most down-to-earth, loving and amusing human beings you could ever meet, was responsible for inspiring and integrating the first educational programmes of the Findhorn Foundation community. Located in north-east Scotland, this community is thought by many people to be the most important New Age centre on the planet. The community's literature and programmes, along with David's book, *Revelation – Birth of a New Age*, brought the phrase 'New Age' into greater currency. Sir George Trevelyan, with his twinkling eyes and proudly lyrical voice, is generally accepted as the father-figure of the New Age movement in Britain.

But this section actually begins with excerpts from a social and political activist, Barbara Marx Hubbard, who recognised the transforming power of these new times and inspired much of the networking and social awareness of the movement.

She is followed by Marilyn Ferguson whose original research into the mind's potential led her to believe that the human species was undergoing a fundamental change. Her analysis was published as *The Aquarian Conspiracy* and is a classic introduction, from a more psychological and sociological basis, to the New Age phenomenon. The other introductory classic, this time from a more scientific and ecological perspective, is Peter Russell's *The Awakening Earth*. Both Marilyn Ferguson and Peter Russell have been instrumental in making New Age thinking respectable, as has the academic and futurist, Willis Harman.

This section ends with a powerful passage from Starhawk proclaiming the rediscovery of the Goddess and the female power in mystery and divinity. Starhawk was only in her mid-twenties when she wrote *The Spiral Dance* from which this extract is taken, but her voice spoke with a clarity and authenticity that brought an immediate response.

BARBARA MARX HUBBARD

The Evolutionary Journey

By the time I was thirty I thought I was neurotic. I had done everything I could think of to be purposeful. Love. Children. Husband. I had clean air and water, good food. I tried to make people 'happy'. And I was dying. But of what? Of meaninglessness.

Then I made three discoveries.

First, Abraham H. Maslow's *Towards a Psychology of Being*. It saved my life. He said that once your deficiency needs are relatively easily met, your 'growth needs' for a richer sense of beingness, for chosen work of intrinsic value, become imperative – as necessary as food to the hungry. If you don't grow at that stage, you get psychologically sick.

I then understood that my problem was unused growth potential. I simply had not known what to work for. I was underdeveloped, not sick! Alienation was a divine discontent driving me towards a next level of growth. I determined to learn how to be 'normal' and joyful in the twentieth century.

Maslow also pointed out that all self-actualising people feel related to a transcendent or trans-personal order beyond self-fulfilment. This too felt right to me. It explained, quite simply, my urgent reaching out towards the source of meaning, towards the divine.

The second life-saver was Teilhard de Chardin's *Phenomenon of Man*. An epiphany! There is a continuing, evolving pattern in the process of Nature which leads to greater whole systems, higher consciousness and freedom – and it's going on NOW! It's unfinished. The world is evolving, not just the individual. Not only do I have unused growth potential – so does the world – so does our species – so does the Universe! Something new is coming. The magnetic attraction was right. I could trust my intuition.

I was getting closer to the answer to the question of purpose.

Then in 1962 John Glenn penetrated our blue biosphere into outer space. I had a sense of our species at the moment of physical transformation. Not only is our consciousness expanding as the mystics have proclaimed for ages . . . so also, our bodies are transcending Earth-boundedness. When I saw the rocket rise the words FREEDOM! BIRTH! exploded into my mind. We could become a universal species! That was the purpose of our power, our technologies, our sciences. They provided us with the skills to carry us beyond the womb of our Mother Earth into a Universe in which there may be billions of life-systems comparable to our own. The Western world has been developing the technologies of transcendence commensurate with the visions of transcendence.

It was like being alive when the first fish flopped out on dry land . . . a critical evolutionary event that surely went unnoticed by that adventurous fish and his friends. Similarly we, the human family, have not yet understood the significance of present events. We are still lacking a perspective broad enough to see what's happening. However, for me, something began to change radically as I opened to a bigger vision.

In one of those flashes of insight and expanded reality that can change one's life, I experienced ourselves as one planetary body being 'born into the Universe'. In my mind's eye I was in outer space with that rocket, witnessing myself and all others as conscious cells in the body of Earth. Our whole body was struggling to co-ordinate. We were gasping for breath as pollution poisoned our biosphere. We were feeling the pain of oneness as the mass media flashed 'news' of hunger, accident, and war. And as we reached together into outer space for new life, we awakened to our oneness, we connected and we experienced total empathy, total joy. The whole planet smiled – a planetary smile!

The flame of expectancy rose to a burning intensity, motivating me to seek an expanded vocation, an 'evolutionary connection' between my need for personal growth and the needs of the world in transition. My second life began – a chosen life. I felt free within myself not by separating myself from the formative processes of the Universe, but by connecting my own growth urge to the force that is evolving the Universe. I had discovered a purpose related to the evolution of the world.

I worked with a powerful joy to try to understand the Story of Creation at the dawn of the Universal Age. I read constantly, piecing together cosmology, geology, biology, psychology, current events, futuristics, religious visions. I sought out people throughout the world working on aspects of our next step forward, feeling the attraction which Teilhard describes. All my relationships changed. I became a growing woman, a deeper mother, able to relate to my children as co-evolvers in a transforming world. In my forties I felt at the beginning of life – almost a second adolescence.

I became convinced that we stand upon the threshold of the greatest age of human history. Anyone who can see the opportunities will emancipate their own potential through involvement in the world. Personal and planetary growth are not merely parallel, they are one.

★　★　★

We live at the most marvellous moment in human history. Everyone now alive is involved in the greatest upheaval since humanity emerged out of the animal world.

We are at the dawn of 'conscious evolution', when the creature-human first becomes aware of the processes of creation and begins to participate deliberately in the design of our world.

We are the first generation to awaken to the awesome fact that we are affecting the future by our every act, from the number of children we have and the kind of food we eat to the creation of new life forms and new worlds in space.

We will either stumble blindly towards self-destruction through misuse of our new powers, or we will move consciously towards a new order of the ages. We will begin the great evolutionary tasks: the restoration of Earth, the freeing of people from want, the development of the vast untapped potential of our bodyminds, and the exploration of the unlimited frontiers of outer space.

Different people are drawn to different vital functions, often not realising they are interconnected. Environmentalists preserving the biosphere may not recognise that they are related to space scientists extending the biosphere. People exploring the inner space of spiritual growth may not see their relationship with political leaders agonising over the allocation of resources. Those concerned with freedom may not identify with others working towards greater global unity, etc. Nonetheless, all are related in one complex planetary act. A powerful movement of action for life is spreading throughout the world. Untold individuals are building a 'cathedral of action', an edifice of effort to transcend the limitations of the present and to create a desirable future for humankind. Each embodies a gift, a shining act of excellence which is incorporated into the cathedral.

There are three invisible pillars to this cathedral: Freedom – all acts to emancipate us from deficiencies in order to do our unique best; Union – all efforts to unify the world in freedom; Transcendence – all breakthroughs to relate us consciously with the universal processes of which we are a creative part.

Increasing numbers of people, experiencing the transformation with joy, rather than fear, are gathering together to ask, to listen, to learn how to take our next step into a future of immeasurable possibilities.

★ ★ ★

Nature's secret intent is union for the creation of new life. In our efforts to 'come together' in loving whole groups, we are not working alone. The laws of attraction are working with us. The power that organised the Universe is organising us! When we feel the excitement of fusion pulsing through our bodies, drawing us to other people, it is the Creative Intention, the godforce, the irresistible magnet.

This excitement is essential. A bored species will never make it! Nature put the capacity to be aroused at the centre of the act of physical creation. An unexcited man cannot procreate. And an unexcited group cannot create a desirable future. The sacrifice, the hard work, the patience that the nurturing of life calls for must be buoyed up by joyful union. We can trust the 'compass of joy'. When we are participating in the formation of a new whole, joy enters our life. Connecting is pleasurable. It is the essence of growth.

When we fuse as a group, our consciousness begins to rise to a new kind of spirituality. We crave to stay connected. This deepening togetherness stimulates a form of consciousness that does not yet have a name. Evolutionary consciousness, co-creative consciousness, may be appropriate. It is a synthesis of mystical and secular awareness emerging in this super-rich information environment under the pressure of convergence and growing responsibility.

Erich Jantsch calls it 'syntony', or super-conscious learning. We sense that there is a transcending evolutionary process which runs through the core of the spiral, a Designing Intelligence operative throughout the Universe, which we humans did not invent. 'It' invented us!

As group-connectedness and synergy increase, like a more complex radio receiving set, we are capable of attuning to the signals from the process more clearly. Perhaps through some resonance or vibratory phenomenon, like the DNA communicating the plan to the RNA messengers which gather the proteins to build the cell, we are receiving information from a planetary information code instructing us how to build a planetary whole, a new synergistic civilisation greater than the sum of the separate parts.

What has been experienced in the past as mystical insight – such as St Paul received on the road to Damascus – sudden, traumatic, blinding enlightenment, almost too powerful for the nervous system to endure, is becoming a new shared norm – the democratisation of awareness. As we interconnect as a planetary whole, each person is becoming a clearer channel to the 'Source', the Process of evolution, God.

The complexity of planning for a planetary body is too intricate to be understood by rational, empirical knowledge alone. We also need super-intuitive knowledge to survive.

It feels as though the organic process of planetary transformation is being orchestrated at a higher level.

Paradoxically, as we become more responsible for the process, we are also more responseable. We are receiving deeper super-intuitive guidance.

We 'know' that our physical bodies are hungry, sick, tired, etc., by complex means. Through our extended planetary nervous system (television, telephone, satellites, computers) and through increased 'syntony' we begin to 'know' when members of our extended planetary body are threatened – without having to read hundreds of books to understand. We feel the direction of health for Earth in our own blood and bones. Pollution is not 'out there'. It is happening to us. If people are hungry anywhere in the world, we feel it. If people are fighting each other, it's a fever in our body. All pain is ours. Mindless destruction of any part of nature is destruction of us.

MARILYN FERGUSON

The Aquarian Conspiracy

For the first time in history, humankind has come upon the control panel of change – an understanding of how transformation occurs. We are living in *the change of change*, the time in which we can intentionally align ourselves with nature for rapid remaking of ourselves and our collapsing institutions.

The paradigm of the Aquarian Conspiracy sees humankind embedded in Nature. It promotes the autonomous individual in a decentralised society. It sees us as stewards of all our resources, inner and outer. It says that we are *not* victims, not pawns, not limited by conditions or conditioning. Heirs to evolutionary riches, we are capable of imagination, invention, and experiences we have only glimpsed.

Human nature is neither good nor bad but open to continuous transformation and transcendence. It has only to discover itself. The new perspective respects the ecology of everything: birth, death, learning, health, family, work, science, spirituality, the arts, the community, relationships, politics.

The Aquarian Conspirators are drawn together by their parallel discoveries, by paradigm shifts that convinced them they had been leading needlessly circumscribed lives.

As experienced by an individual, the paradigm shift might be compared to the discovery of the 'hidden pictures' in children's magazines. You look at a sketch that appears to be a tree and a pond. Then someone asks you to look more closely – to look for something you had no reason to believe was there. Suddenly you see camouflaged objects in the scene: the branches become a fish or a

7

pitchfork, the lines around the pond hide a toothbrush.

Nobody can talk you into seeing the hidden pictures. You are not *persuaded* that the objects are there. Either you see them or you don't. But once you have seen them, they are plainly there whenever you look at the drawing. You wonder how you missed them before.

Growing up, we experienced minor paradigm shifts – insights into the principles of geometry, for instance, or a game, or a sudden broadening of our political or religious beliefs. Each insight enlarged the context, brought a fresh way of perceiving connections.

The opening up of a new paradigm is humbling and exhilarating; we were not so much wrong as partial, as if we had been seeing with a single eye. It is not more knowledge, but a *new knowing*.

Edward Carpenter, a remarkably visionary social scientist and poet of the late nineteenth century, described such a shift:

> If you inhibit thought (and persevere) you come at length to a region of consciousness below or behind thought . . . and a realization of an altogether vaster self than that to which we are accustomed. And since the ordinary consciousness, with which we are concerned in ordinary life, is before all things founded on the little local self . . . it follows that to pass out of that is to die to the ordinary self and the ordinary world.
>
> It is to die in the ordinary sense, but in another, it is to wake up and find the 'I', one's real, most intimate self, pervades the universe and all other beings.
>
> So great, so splendid, is this experience, that it may be said that all minor questions and doubts fall away in the face of it; and certain it is that in thousands and thousands of cases, the fact of its having come even once to an individual has completely revolutionized his subsequent life and outlook on the world.

Carpenter captured the essence of the transformative experience: enlargement, connection, the power to permanently transform a life. And, as he said, this 'region of consciousness' opens to us when we are quietly vigilant rather than busily thinking and planning.

Both accidentally and deliberately, people have had such experiences throughout history. Deep inner shifts may occur in response to disciplined contemplation, grave illness, wilderness treks, peak emotions, creative effort, spiritual exercises, controlled breathing, techniques for 'inhibiting thought', psychedelics, movement, isolation, music, hypnosis, meditation, reverie, and in the wake of intense intellectual struggle.

Over the centuries, in various parts of the world, technologies for inducing such experiences were shared among a few initiates in each generation. Scattered brotherhoods, religious orders, and small groups explored what seemed to be extraordinary reaches of conscious experience. In their esoteric doctrines, they sometimes wrote of the liberating quality of their insights. But they were too few, they had no way to disseminate their discoveries widely, and most of earth's inhabitants were preoccupied with survival, not transcendence.

Quite suddenly, in *this* decade, these deceptively simple systems and their literature, the riches of many cultures, are available to whole populations, both in their original form and in contemporary adaptations. Airport news-stands offer the wisdom of the ages in paperback. University extension classes and weekend seminars, adult education courses, and commercial centres are offering techniques that help people connect to new sources of personal energy, integration, harmony.

These systems aim to fine-tune the mind and body, to expand the brain's sensing, to bring the participants to a new awareness of vast untapped potential. When they work, it's like adding sonar, radar, and powerful lenses to the mind.

The widespread adaptation of such techniques and the spread of their use throughout society were predicted in the 1950s by P.W. Martin, when 'consciousness' research was first under way. 'For the first time in history, the scientific spirit of inquiry is being turned upon the other side of consciousness. There is a good prospect that the discoveries can be held this time and so become no longer the lost secret but the living heritage of man.'

All of the systems for widening and deepening consciousness employ similar strategies and lead to strikingly similar personal discoveries. And now, for the first time, we know that these subjective experiences have their objective counterparts. Laboratory investigation, as we shall see, shows that these methods integrate the brain's activity, making it less random, provoking it into higher organisation. *Brains undergo a quite literal accelerated transformation.*

The transformative technologies offer us passage to creativity, healing, choices. The gift of insight – of making imaginative new connections – once the speciality of a lucky few, is there for anyone willing to persist, experiment, explore.

In most lives insight has been accidental. We wait for it as primitive man awaited lightning for a fire. But making mental connections is our most crucial learning tool, the essence of human intelligence: to forge links; to go beyond the given; to see patterns, relationships, context.

The natural consequence of these subtle sciences of the mind is insight. The process can be so accelerated that we are dizzied, even a little frightened, by the unfolding of new possibilities. Each empowers us to understand better and predict more precisely what will work in our lives.

Little wonder that these shifts in awareness are experienced as awakening, liberating, unifying – transforming. Given the reward, it makes sense that millions have taken up such practices within a scant few years. They discover that they don't have to wait for the world 'out there' to change. Their lives and environments begin to transform as their minds are transformed. They find that they have a sane, healthy centre, the wherewithal to deal with stress and to innovate, and that there are friends out there.

They struggle to convey what has happened to them. They have no tidy rationale, and they may feel somewhat foolish or pretentious in talking about their experiences. They try to describe a sense of awakening after years of being asleep, the coming together of broken parts of themselves, a healing and home-coming.

★　★　★

In the transformative process we become the artists and scientists of our own lives. Enhanced awareness promotes in all of us the traits that abound in the creative person. Whole-seeing. Fresh, childlike perceptions. Playfulness, a sense of flow. Risk-taking. The ability to focus attention in a relaxed way, to become lost in the object of contemplation. The ability to deal with many complex ideas at the same time. Willingness to diverge from the prevailing view. Access to preconscious material. Seeing what is there rather than what is expected or conditioned.

The transformed self has new tools, gifts, sensibilities. Like an artist, it spies pattern; it finds meaning and its own, inescapable originality. 'Every life', said Hesse, 'stands beneath its own star.'

Like a good scientist, the transformed self experiments, speculates, invents, and relishes the unexpected.

Having done field work in the psychotechnologies, the self is a folk psychologist.

Awake now to the imprint of culture on itself, it attempts to understand diversity with the curiosity and interest of an anthropologist. The practices of other cultures suggest endless human possibilities.

The transformed self is a sociologist, too – a student of the bonds of community and conspiracy. Like the physicist, it accepts ultimate uncertainty as a fact of life, it senses a realm beyond linear time and blocked-out space. Like a molecular biologist, it is awed by Nature's capacity for renewal, change, and ever-higher order.

The transformed self is an architect, designing its own environment. It is a visionary, imagining alternative futures.

Like a poet, it reaches for original metaphorical truths deep in language. It is a sculptor, liberating its own form from the rock of custom. With heightened attention and flexibility, it becomes a playwright and is its own repertory company: clown, monk, athlete, heroine, sage, child.

It is a diarist, an autobiographer. Sifting through the shards of its past, it is an archaeologist. It is composer, instrument . . . and music.

Many artists have said that when life itself becomes fully conscious, art as we know it will vanish. Art is only a stopgap, an imperfect effort to wrest meaning from an environment where nearly everyone is sleepwalking.

The artist's material is always close at hand. 'We live at the edge of the miraculous,' Henry Miller said, and T.S. Eliot wrote that the end of all our exploring will be to arrive at our starting point and know it for the first time. To Proust, discovery consisted not in seeking new landscapes but in having new eyes. Whitman asked, 'Will you seek afar off? You will come back at last to things best known to you, finding happiness, knowledge, not in another place but in this place . . . not in another hour, but *this* hour.'

For too long we have played games we did not care about by rules we did not believe in. If there was art in our lives it was paint-by-number. Life lived as art finds its own way, makes its own friends and its own music, sees with its own eyes. 'I go by touching where I have to go,' wrote poet Eric Barker, 'obedient to my own illuminated hand.'

To the transformed self, as to the artist, success is never a place to stay, only a momentary reward. Joy is in risking, in making new. Eugene O'Neill scorned 'mere' success:

> Those who succeed and do not push on to greater failure are the spiritual middle classers. Their stopping at success is the proof of their compromising insignificance. How pretty their dreams must have been! . . . Only through the unattainable does man achieve a hope worth living and dying for – and so attain *himself.*

A designer-engineer advised, 'Do things in the spirit of design research. Be willing to accept a mistake and redesign. There is no failure.'

If we take the artist-scientist's view towards life, *there is no failure*. An experiment has results; we learn from it. Since it adds to our understanding and expertise, however it comes out we have not lost. Finding out is an experiment.

As folk scientists we become sensitive to Nature, relationships, hypotheses. For example, we can experimentally learn to tell our reckless impulses from genuine intuitions, getting a kind of long-range biofeedback for that inner sense of rightness.

The survey of Aquarian Conspirators asked for a choice of the four most important instruments for social change from a checklist of fifteen. More often than any other answer, 'Personal Example' was checked.

More than a decade ago Erich Fromm was warning that no great radical idea can survive unless it is embodied in individuals whose lives are the message.

The transformed self is the medium. The transformed life is the message.

PETER RUSSELL

The Emergence of a Social Super-organism

It is commonplace today to speak of the pace of life speeding up, and to look back with nostalgia at the more leisurely pace of our grandparents' time. But this speeding up is not new; it has been going on for the last fifteen billion years. In evolution each new development was able to draw upon what had already been accomplished. (The evolution of complex macromolecules, for example, was able to utilise the properties and characteristics of less complex molecules such as amino acids, aldehydes and water.) Each new phenomenon became another platform that evolution could use in its relentless movement towards yet greater complexity. The more that had already been accomplished, the broader the platform on which evolution could then build, and the greater the rate of development. This produced accelerating patterns of growth.

As a result of this natural tendency to accelerate, the major developments in evolution have not occurred at regular intervals; rather, the intervals have been shortening. When we talk in terms of billions of years, however, it may sometimes be difficult to see this happening. Such concepts are way beyond our experience. To get a more tangible image let us compress these fifteen billion years into a film a year long – the ultimate 'epic'. And so that you may fully appreciate the time-scales involved, imagine what it really would feel like sitting through this film.

The Big Bang, with which the film opens, is over in a hundred millionth of a second. The Universe cools rapidly and within about twenty-five minutes stable atoms have formed. No more significant changes happen during the rest of the first day, nor for the rest of

January (you will need plenty of popcorn): all that you are viewing is an expanding cloud of gas. Around February and March the gas clouds begin slowly condensing into clusters of galaxies and stars. As the weeks and months pass by, stars occasionally explode in supernovae, new stars condensing from the debris. Our own sun and solar system are eventually formed in early September – after eight months of film.

Once the Earth has formed, things begin to move a little faster as complex molecules start to take shape. Within two weeks, by the beginning of October, simple algae and bacteria appear. Then comes a relative lull (and more popcorn) while bacteria slowly evolve, developing photosynthesis a week later, with the consequent build-up of an oxygen atmosphere after five more weeks, in early November. Within another week, complex cells with well-defined nuclei evolve, making sexual reproduction possible, and with this stage accomplished, evolution accelerates again. It is now late November, and the major part of the film has been seen. The evolution of life, however, has only just begun.

The first simple multi-cellular organisms appear around early December, and the first vertebrates crawl out of the sea on to the land a week or so later. Dinosaurs rule the land for most of the last week of the film, from Christmas to midday on December 30th – a long and noble reign!

Our early ape-like ancestors made their début around the middle of the last day, but not until 11 o'clock in the evening do they walk upright.

Now, after 365 days and nights of film, we come to some of the most fascinating developments. Human language begins to develop one-and-a-half minutes before midnight. In the last half minute farming begins. Buddha achieves enlightenment under the bodhi tree five-and-a-half seconds before the end, and Christ appears a second later. The Industrial Revolution occurs in the last half second, and World War II occurs less than a tenth of a second before midnight.

* * *

The growing complexity within society reveals three important areas of growth in terms of evolution: a diversity of human beings, their numbers stabilising around the critical size of 10; an elaborate organisational structure, parallel to that observed in all other living systems: and a communication and information processing capability approaching that of the human brain. Thus society would appear to be completing the prerequisites for the emergence of a new evolutionary level.

What might this new level look like?

Just as matter became organised into living cells, and living cells collected into multi-cellular organisms, so might we expect that at some stage human beings will become integrated into some form of global social super-organism. (I use the word super-organism rather than organism since the term 'organism' strictly applies to biological organisms, i.e. to multi-cellular organisms, whereas we are now talking of multi-organism organisms, and these may take very different forms from biological organisms.) . . . .

Social super-organisms are not new to nature. In the animal world there are several examples of organisms that come together to form integrated social units. Thousands of bees may live and work together in a single hive, regulating the temperature and humidity of their collective 'body', the colony as a whole surviving the continual birth and death of its members. Army ants form colonies containing up to 20 million individuals. Advancing like a single organism through the forest, a colony will cross streams by forming a living bridge of ants clinging tenaciously to each other. When one army meets another they will avoid close contact, behaving like two separate entities. Termites construct complex cities housing up to several million individuals, complete with ventilation shafts and complex food-processing systems.

Similar tendencies can be found in higher animals. Many fish swim in schools, the whole acting as a single unit without any single leader. Individual fish may take on specific functions, such as that of an 'eye', reducing the need for the others to be continually on the lookout. When danger is spotted a whole school can react in less than a fifth of a second. Flocks of birds can likewise behave like a super-organism. (One of the largest ever recorded was a flock of 150 million shearwaters, over ten miles across, observed between Australia and Tasmania.) Slow-motion films of bird flocks have revealed 50,000 individuals turning in synchrony in less than a seventieth of a second. There is no indication of their following the leader; the flock is integrated into a functional whole.

But such examples, fascinating as they might be, only afford us a glimpse of the integrated social super-organism that humanity has the potential to become. Firstly, this super-organism will not contain a few million individuals, as occurs with bees, ants, or birds; rather, it will be comprised of the whole human race – billions of individuals distributed over the face of the planet.

Secondly, in all instances of animal super-organisms there is very little individual diversity. Bee and ant colonies usually contain only two or three different types (e.g. worker bee, drone, queen bee), while in fish and bird groups all the individuals are usually identical, only temporarily taking on specific functions such as an 'eye' or 'skin'. Human society, however, is extremely diverse and specialised, made up of thousands of different types, each able to make his own particular contribution to the whole.

Thirdly, a human social super-organism would not entail our all becoming non-descript 'cells' who have given up their individuality for some higher good. We already are 'cells' in the various organs that compose society, yet still retain considerable individuality. The shift to a social super-organism would essentially mean that society became a more integrated living system. As we shall see in later chapters, this is likely to lead to greater freedom and self-expression on the part of the individual, and to an even greater diversity.

Lastly, when insects and animals come together, they congregate as a single unit. But it is extremely unlikely that the human social super-organism will form itself on the physical level. From what we have seen of evolutionary trends, we should not anticipate that human beings will come together as a large conglomerate mass in some supermegalopolis. With humanity evolution has gained a new platform on which to build.

Just as earlier, after life had emerged from matter, evolution moved up from the physical level to the biological level, so it now has moved up to a new level – consciousness. We could therefore hypothesise that the integration of society into a super-organism will occur through the evolution of consciousness, rather than through physical or biological evolution. This implies a coming together of minds, which is why communication is such an important aspect of evolution today; it is a mind-linking process. Humanity is growing together mentally – however distant we might be physically.

The Fifth Level of Evolution

One philosopher who spent much of his life contemplating the integration of humanity into a single being was Pierre Teilhard de Chardin. Teilhard displayed that rare synthesis of science and religion: he was both a Jesuit priest and a geologist/paleontologist. In the 1930s he worked in China where he was closely involved with the discovery of the skull of 'Peking Man'. As a result of his study of the evolutionary process, he developed a general theory of evolution, which he believed would apply not only to the human species but also to the human mind, and the relationship of religious experience to the facts of natural science.

One of his principal conclusions was that humanity was headed towards the unification of the entire species into a single interthinking group. He coined the word 'noosphere' (from the Greek *noos*, 'mind') to refer to the cumulative effect of human minds over the entire planet. Just as the biosphere denotes the system comprising all living beings, so the noosphere denotes that comprising all consciousness minds.

Evolution, having passed through geogenesis (the genesis of the Earth), and biogenesis (the genesis of life), was now at the stage of 'noogenesis' (the genesis of mind). He saw this stage as the 'planetisation of Mankind . . . (into) a single, major organic unity. The fulfilment of the process of noogenesis Teilhard referred to as the 'Omega Point', the culmination of the evolutionary process, the end point towards which we are all converging.

Another philosopher with a similar vision was the Indian mystic Sri Aurobindo, a contemporary of Teilhard's. We also find an interesting combination of talents in Aurobindo. He was educated in classics at King's College, Cambridge, and was, on his return to India, an active political revolutionary. As a result he spent several years in Indian jails, and it was during these periods that he had some of his most significant insights into the evolution of humanity.

Sri Aurobindo saw evolution as the 'Divine Reality' expressing itself in ever higher forms of existence. Having passed from energy through matter and life to consciousness, evolution was now passing through the transformation from consciousness to what he called 'Supermind', something so far above consciousness as to be beyond our present dreams of perfection – the ultimate evolution of 'Spirit'. This new level he saw as coming through the increasing spiritual development of individual consciousness towards a final, complete, all-embracing consciousness, which would occur on both the individual and collective levels.

When Teilhard wrote of the unification of the noosphere in the Omega Point, he appears to have been talking about an integrated planetary consciousness. Similarly, Aurobindo, although he made it clear that Supermind was far above the individual mind, still generally discussed this new phenomenon in terms of mind and consciousness.

Yet the evolutionary trends and patterns we have looked at thus far suggest a further possibility: the emergence of something way beyond even a single planetary consciousness or Supermind – a completely new level of evolution, as different from consciousness as consciousness is from life, and life is from matter.

This new order of existence will be the ultimate effect of the continued integration of humanity, and in this respect humanity will be its platform. Yet it will not be happening to humanity. Rather, it will be happening at the planetary level, to Gaia. (A helpful analogy might be made with a photograph composed of many dots. The dots themselves do not contain the picture, yet they are its basis. The picture emerges from the collected organisation of the dots viewed as a whole.)

Since we do not yet have an adequate term in our vocabulary for this fifth level, I have chosen to refer to it as the 'Gaiafield' (much as self-reflective consciousness might be termed the 'human field'). The Gaiafield will not be the property of individual human beings, any more than consciousness is the property of individual cells. The Gaiafield will occur at the *planetary* level, emerging from the combined interactions of all the minds within the social super-organism.

Exactly what the nature of this new level would be is very difficult to say. The minute we begin to contemplate a fifth level of evolution, we inevitably do so in terms of human experience. But as we have already seen, each new order of existence is not fully describable in terms of the previous orders, and the Gaiafield would possess entirely new characteristics incomprehensible to consciousness.

Similarly, a single cell in your body knows nothing of the consciousness that emerges from the living system as a whole. Although it might have a very rudimentary form of awareness, it has no conception (if we may excuse the word) of your thoughts, feelings, imaginations and inspirations. It does not know what state of consciousness you are in, or even whether you are conscious or not. And it would almost certainly find it impossible to 'conceive' of what was meant by self-reflective consciousness.

Thus it is not altogether surprising if we find it equally difficult to conceive of evolutionary stages as far beyond us as we are beyond single cells. Being individuals, the collective phenomena must theoretically remain to us an unknowable. We can only know the 'cell' that we are.

The idea of a collective phenomenon generated from the activity of our individual consciousnesses may sound a little strange. How can many separate consciousnesses give rise to a single planetary phenomenon? The question is no easier to answer than the one which scientists and philosophers continually face with respect to human consciousness: how do the electrical and chemical activities of many separate nerve cells give rise to a single integrated consciousness?

All that can be said with any degree of certainty is that the consciousness of each individual human being is somehow related to the highly complex and integrated interaction of billions of living cells in the brain. Without going into the neurological arguments here, it seems probable that a particular conscious experience corresponds not to the activity of small groups of cells, but to overall patterns of activity, to the coherence of the numerous information exchanges continually taking place in the brain. In a similar manner this planetary field would emerge from the integrated interaction of the billions of conscious beings composing humanity. As the communication links within humanity increase, we will eventually reach a time when the billions of information exchanges shuttling through the networks at any one time create similar patterns of coherence in the global brain as are found in the human brain. Gaia would then awaken and become her equivalent of conscious.

How far away are we from the point in time where this might happen? Teilhard, although he spoke of evolution moving rapidly towards the Omega Point, was thinking in cosmic time-scales rather than human ones, and by 'rapidly' he seems to have meant thousands or perhaps millions of years. Sri Aurobindo, on the other hand, believed that it could happen a lot more quickly, perhaps within the next hundred years.

Yet this new level may well come even faster than either Teilhard or Sri Aurobindo envisaged. It could possibly happen within a few decades.

WILLIS W. HARMAN

Metanoia

As some activists phrased it late in the 1960s, 'The real revolution is in people's heads.' This statement explains why the use of perception-changing techniques has played such a central role. These techniques are of two types. One type is mainly self-chosen and aimed at spiritual or transcendental awareness; it includes meditation, yoga, self-awareness exercises, various group and individual psychotherapies, and psychedelic drugs. The other type is largely imposed on others and is aimed at social and political awareness, that is, at perceiving aspects of the breakdown of the industrial-era paradigm and of oppressive elements of social institutions; examples are consumer and environmentalist confrontations, black-white and student-police confrontations, and political theatre. These radicalising techniques are similar in that they jolt the person out of his habitual perceptions so that he sees – as he has not before – both his own transcendental nature and the influences of social institutions.

Taken together, these challenges to diverse aspects of the industrial-era paradigm and its institutions support the view that a societal metamorphosis could be imminent. If it is, at the core of this transmutation would be a change in our most basic views about the meaning of human experience. Furthermore, if it is successful, we can anticipate that this trans-industrial paradigm would include the following characteristics:

1. It would perceive that the fundamental *dilemmas of industrialised society* are rooted in the inadequacy of the value postulates of the

industrial-era paradigm.

2. It would recognise that *science* has been shaped by the prediction-and-control values of the industrial-era paradigm, and that a science aimed at guiding the evolutionary development of man and society will place more emphasis on understanding and less on generating manipulative technology; it would view 'explanations' (both scientific and religious) as useful metaphors and hence would see no necessary contradiction between scientific metaphors adapted to the objective physical world and the religious or metaphysical metaphors used in communicating about supra-sensory experience.

3. It would assume the existence of a *spiritual order*, discoverable and explorable, and in some sense testable, against which human value choices could be assessed; emerging from this spirituality would be a creative work ethic, placing a high value on aware participation in both individual and social evolution. The primary emphasis would be on 'to be', rather than 'to have' or 'to control'.

4. It would embody an *ecological ethic* of concern for the whole, deriving from the transcendental order and unitary perception of reality.

5. It would involve a *teleological view* of life and evolution (as having direction and purpose); hence the future would be perceived to be partly shaped by human choices, guided by supra-conscious evolutionary tendencies towards development of man's spiritual potentialities beyond the realm of his mundane experiences. Such a trans-industrial paradigm would *extend* rather than *contradict* the contemporary scientific world view, much as relativity theory extended Newtonian mechanics. Moreover, its most fundamental postulates are not essentially new. They have comprised a central stream of thought in the humanities, in Western political tradition, and in transcendentalist movements in our own nation's history. They have, however, never formed the guiding paradigm of an entire society. Popular religions, both Eastern and Western, have included ethics similar to those implied by the five aforementioned characteristics. However, these traditional ethics have typically existed in an authoritarian context, rather than as discoverable and testable propositions of an open inquiry.

Transformation Anyone?

If such a paradigm, involving a basic shift in the accepted vision of reality, were to become the basis of presently industrialised society, its institutionalisation would amount to one of the most thorough-going transformations in the history of mankind. We might apply to such a change the Greek word *metanoia*: 'a fundamental transformation of mind', as in religious conversion. This transformation is to be distinguished from other changes that are revolutionary in a social or political sense but do not involve a significant change in the basic, implicit, unchallenged, taken-as-given metaphysic of the society.

Some futurists have noted that the 1970s appear to be a time of profound change, and have likened contemporary discontinuities to one or another great transformation in the past. Comparison is made with the Industrial Revolution, which involved profound institutional changes, with accompanying value and life-style changes. As in present times, the period was characterised by apparent advance on some fronts (e.g. manufacturing technology) and temporary regression on others (e.g. quality of life in the factory cities). Changes brought about by the Industrial Revolution encountered bitter opposition and strong resistance.

Somewhat similarly, in the case of the Copernican (or scientific) revolution there were profound changes in the basic concept of the nature of knowledge, in culturally held beliefs and values, and in social institutions. Scientific laws replaced theological explanations, values became more this-worldly, and beliefs shifted from supernatural to natural explanations. Science displaced the church as the official truth-seeking system. Again, changes brought about by the Copernican revolution were strongly resisted; there was a traumatic transition period with decades of religious wars.

And yet the changes of the Industrial and Copernican revolutions, profound as they were, amounted to no more than periods of accelerated working-out of aspects of the 'basic long-term multifold trend' of Western society – becoming over at least eight centuries increasingly more secular, this-worldly, utilitarian, empirical, sensate, manipulative, scientific, innovative, industrialised, urbanised, literate, and affluent. *We may now be entering a transformation that involves a basic alteration of that trend.* If so, we probably cannot postpone its appearance.

ALICE A. BAILEY

The Way of the Disciple

Out of the darkness of time there have emerged the great religions. These religions, though diverse in their theologies and forms of worship, though characterised by distinctions of organisation and ceremonial, and though differing in their methods of application of truth, are united in three basic aspects:

1. In their teaching as to the nature of God and of man.
2. In their symbolism.
3. In certain fundamental doctrines.

When men recognise this and succeed in isolating that inner significant structure of truth which is the same in all climes and in all races, then there will emerge the universal religion, the One Church, and that unified though not uniform approach to God, which will demonstrate the truth of St Paul's words 'One Lord, one faith, one baptism, one God and Father of all, who is above all and through all and in you all.' Theologies will disappear into the knowledge of God; doctrines and dogmas will no longer be regarded as necessary, for faith will be based on experience, and authority will give place to personal appreciation of Reality. The power of the Church over the group will be supplanted by the power of the awakened soul in men; the age of miracles and the disputations as to the why and how of those miracles with the consequent scepticism or agnosticism will give way to the understanding of the laws of nature which control the superhuman realm and the supernatural stage of the evolutionary process. Man will enter into his divine heritage and know himself as the Son of the Father, with all the divine characteristics, powers and capacities which are his because of his divine endowment. But in the meantime what have we? A breaking away from old-established tradition, a revolt from authority, whether of the Church, of dogma, doctrine or theology; a tendency towards self-determination and an overthrowing of the old standards, and of old barriers of thought and the divisions existing between races and faiths.

Hence we are passing through an intermediate stage of chaos and of questioning, of rebellion and consequent apparent licence. The methods of science – investigation and analysis, comparison and deduction – are being applied to religious belief. The history of religions, the foundations of doctrine, the origin of ideas and the growth of the God idea are being subjected to research and study. This leads to much disputation; to the rejection of old established ideas as to God, the soul, man and his destiny. . . . Out of the medley of ideas, theories, speculations, religions, churches, cults, sects and organisations, two main lines of thought are emerging – one doomed eventually to die out, the other to strengthen and grow until it, in its turn, gives birth to that (for us) ultimate formulation of truth which will suffice for the next age and carry man to a high pinnacle of the Temple and to the Mount of Initiation. These two lines are:

1. Those who look back to the past, who hang on to the old ways, the ancient theologies, and the reactionary rejection methods of finding truth. These are the people who recognise authority, whether that of a prophet, a bible or a theology. These are those who prefer obedience to imposed authority to the self-imposed guidance of an enlightened soul. These are the followers of a Church and a government, who are distinguished by a pure devotion and love, but refuse recognition to the divine intelligence with which they are gifted. Their devotion, their love of God, their strict but misguided conscience, their intolerance mark them out as devotees, but they are blinded by their own devotion and their growth is limited by their fanaticism. They belong mostly to the older generation and the hope for them lies in their devotion and the fact that evolution itself will carry them forward into the second group.

To this first group is committed the work of crystallisation which will result in the complete destruction of the old form; to them is given the task of defining the old truths so that the mind of the race will be clarified, that non-essentials and essentials will be recognised for what they are, and fundamental ideas so contrasted with the formulation of dogmas that that which is basic will be seen and the secondary and unimportant beliefs therefore rejected, for only the basic and causative will be of value in the coming age.

2. The second group is as yet a very small minority, but a steadily growing one. It is that inner group of lovers of God, the intellectual mystics, the knowers of reality who belong to no one religion or organisation, but who regard themselves as members of the Church universal and as 'members one of another'. They are gathered out of every nation, race and people; they are of every colour and school of thought, yet they speak the same language, learn by the same symbols, tread the same path, have rejected the same non-essentials, and have isolated the same body of essential beliefs. They recognise each other; they accord equal devotion to the spiritual leaders of all races, and use each other's Bibles with equal freedom. They form the subjective background of the new world; they constitute the spiritual nucleus of the coming world religion; they are the unifying principle which will eventually save the world.

In the past we have had world Saviours – Sons of God who have enunciated a world message and brought an increase of light to the peoples. Now, in the fullness of time, and through the work of evolution there is emerging a group who perhaps will bring salvation to the world, and who – embodying the group ideas and demonstrating the group nature, manifesting in a small way the true significance of the body of Christ, and giving to the world a picture of the true nature of a spiritual organism – will so stimulate and energise the thoughts and souls of men that the New Age will be ushered in by an outpouring of the love, knowledge and harmony of God Himself.

Religions in the past have been founded by a great soul, by an Avatar, by an outstanding spiritual personality, and the stamp of their lives and words and teaching has been set upon the race and has persisted for many centuries. What will be the effect of the message of a group Avatar? What will be the potency of the work of a group of knowers of God, enunciating truth and banded together subjectively in the great work of saving the world? What will be the effect of the mission of a group of world Saviours, not as Christs, but all knowers of God in some degree, who supplement each other's efforts, reinforce each other's message, and constitute an organism through which the spiritual energy and principle of spiritual life can make their presence felt in the world?

Such a body now exists with its members in every land. Relatively they are few and far between, but steadily their numbers are increasing and increasingly their message will be felt. In them is vested a spirit of construction; they are the builders of the new age; to them is given the work of preserving the spirit of truth, and the re-organising of the thoughts of men so that the racial mind is controlled and brought into that meditative and reflective condition which will permit it to recognise the next unfolding of divinity.

Connected with these two groups, the reactionary doctrinaires and the subjective band of mystics, is the majority of the new generation of young people who are part of neither band and whose ideas are largely disorganised by the recognition of both. This majority do not belong to the past and refuse to accept the authority of that past. They do not belong to the inner group of Knowers who are working at the task of swinging the thoughts of men into right channels, for they have not reached as yet the point of knowledge. They only recognise two things: their need for freedom, and an intense eagerness for knowledge. They despise the tradition of the past; they reject the old formulations of truth; and because as yet they stand on no sure ground but are only in the position of seekers and enquirers, we have our present state of world upheaval, of apparent licence and disruption. It should not be forgotten that this world state is therefore the result of the clashing of the three types of force prevalent in the world of today.

1. That emanating from the holders with the old tradition, who, emphasising the forms and the past produce the destruction of those forms.

2. That emanating from the inner group of mystics, who, under the guidance of the planetary Hierarchy are building the new form.

3. That emanating from the masses who belong to neither group and who are wielding force as yet blindly and often unwisely until such time comes when they recognise those constructive channels into which it can wisely be poured.

Hence the problem of this transition period and hence the necessity for the giving out of teaching which will enable the seeking aspirant and enquirer to find himself. Hence the need for the laws of the soul and for the truth as to the individual unfolding to be made clear to those who, rejecting the old tradition, and refusing recognition to the mystic, yet seek to know themselves as liberated souls. With that knowledge will come the steady growth of the Building Mystics, for when a man has found his soul and recognises its relationship to its mechanism of expression, the threefold lower man, he automatically passes into the consciousness of the subjective life, begins to work with cause and is no longer lost in the world of effects. Then he finds himself standing shoulder to shoulder with the mystics and knowers of all time. This is the trend of the religious impulse at this time and this is the glory of the coming age.

If it is true that there is being gathered together in the background of our present world-state a group of mystics who are distinguished by knowledge, vision, and a power to work on mental levels, unseen and unrecognised by men, it could also be noted that this band is not confined to the strictly religious types. Men and women in every branch of human thought are found among this group including scientists and philosophers.

Like all else at this time, science itself is in process of transformation, and little as it is realised by many, their work with what they call matter, and their investigations of the atom, are entering into a new field. In this field the older techniques and mechanisms will gradually be discarded and a new approach and a different fundamental concept as to the nature of matter will mark the New Age. Within the next twenty-five years, emerging out of the two seemingly different ideas as to the nature of the atom, a recognition of certain energy impulses will be seen and this will be based on the discovery of those energies which (playing on the atom and on atomic forms) produce the tangible concrete shapes to which we give names in the various kingdoms of nature. The truth of certain basic premises of the Ageless Wisdom will be demonstrated, such as:

1. The soul is the form-building principle, producing attraction and cohesion.

2. This soul is an aspect or type of energy, distinguished from that of matter itself.

3. The atom has been recognised as an energy unit, but as yet the energy which sweeps atoms into aggregates which we call organisms and forms has not been isolated. This the mystics in the scientific world will sense and work to demonstrate during the next generation. It is this type of energy, the energy of the form-building aspect of manifestation which is the source of all magical work; and it is this energy in the various kingdoms of nature that produces form, shape, species, kind, type and the differentiations which mark and distinguish the myriad forms through which life itself manifests. It is the quality of the energy which produces the quantity of forms; it is the light which causes the emergence into consciousness of the race of heterogeneous shapes which aggregates of atoms can assume.

4. This type of energy which produces the shapes and forms and coherent organisms in all the kingdoms of Nature is not the life principle. The life principle will remain undiscovered and unrecognised until such time as the soul or qualifying principle, the builder of the forms, is studied, recognised and in its turn investigated.

5. This is only possible as Man steps forth into a fuller conscious possession of his divine heritage, and working as a soul and in control of his mechanism (physical, emotional, and mental) can work consciously *en rapport* with the soul in all forms.

This will be possible only as the race grasps the above hypothesis and recognises it as a possibility, and seeks to demonstrate the fact of the soul-factor lying behind its structure or body of manifestation or, equally, seeks to disprove it. All great scientists and workers in the realm of objective nature have worked as souls, and all the most amazing of the developments in the realm of physics and chemistry, as in other departments of human knowledge, have been made when the worker in any particular field has launched forth with faith in some hypothesis he has formed, and has investigated and progressed his work forward stage by stage until he has contacted an aspect of the truth hitherto unformulated by man. Then, having through the use of his intuition entered into a new realm of thought, he takes the knowledge there discovered and formulates it in such way by theory, principle, experiment and mechanical contrivance that it becomes the possession of the group, and in due time is understood and utilised by the world. But in its genesis it has been mystical work and based on a mystical intuition.

It might be noted here that three great discoveries are imminent and during the next two generations will revolutionise modern thought and life.

One is already sensed and is the subject of experiment and investigation, the releasing of the energy of the atom. This will completely change the economic and political situation in the world, for the latter is largely dependent upon the former. Our mechanical civilisation will be simplified, and an era ushered in which will be free from the incubus of money (its possession and its non-possession), and the human family will recognise universally its status as a bridging kingdom between the three lower kingdoms of Nature and the fifth or spiritual kingdom. There will be time and freedom for a soul culture which will supersede our modern methods of education, and the significance of soul powers and the development of the superhuman consciousness will engross the attention of educators and students everywhere.

A second discovery will grow out of the present investigations into light and colour. The effect of colour on people, animals and units in the vegetable kingdom will be studied and the result of those studies will be the development of etheric vision or the power to see the next grade of matter with the strictly physical eye. Increasingly will people think and talk in terms of light, and the effect of the coming developments in this department of human thought will be triple.

1. People will possess etheric vision.
2. The vital or etheric body, lying as the inner structure of the outer forms, will be seen and noted and studied in all kingdoms of Nature.
3. This will break down all barriers of race and all distinctions of colour; the essential brotherhood of Man will be established. We shall see each other and all forms of divine manifestation as light units of varying degrees of brightness and shall talk and think increasingly in terms of electricity, of voltage, of intensity and of power. The age and status of men, in regard to the ladder of evolution, will be noted and become objectively apparent, the relative capacities of old souls and young souls will be recognised, thereby re-establishing on Earth the rule of the enlightened.

Note here, that these developments will be the work of the scientists of the next two generations and the result of their efforts. Their work with the atom of substance, and their investigations in the realm of electricity, of light and of power, must inevitably demonstrate the relation between forms, which is another term for brotherhood, and the fact of the soul, the inner light and radiance of all forms.

The third development, which will be the last probably to take place, will be more strictly in the realm of what the occultists call magic. It will grow out of the study of sound and the effect of sound and will put into Man's hands a tremendous instrument in the world of creation. Through the use of sound the scientist of the future will bring about his results; through sound, a new field of discovery will open up; the sound which every form in all kingdoms of Nature gives forth will be studied and known and changes will be brought about and new forms developed through its medium. One hint only may I give here and that is, that the release of energy in the atom is linked to this new coming science of sound.

The significance of what has happened in the world during the last century in the realm of sound is not appreciated yet nor understood. Terrific effects are, however, being produced by the unbelievably increased noise and sound emanating from the planet at this time. The roar of machinery, the rumble of the transportation mechanisms in all parts of the world – trains, vessels and aeroplanes – the focussing of the sounds of men in such congested areas as the great cities, and, at this time, the universal use of the radio bringing musical sounds into every home and into street life are producing effects upon the bodies of men and upon all forms of life everywhere which will become apparent only as time elapses. Some forms of life in the animal kingdom, but primarily in the vegetable kingdom, will disappear and the response of the human mechanism to this world of sound, uproar and music in which it will increasingly find itself will be most interesting.

These three developments will usher in the new age, will produce in this transition period the needed changes, and will inaugurate a new era wherein brotherhood will be the keynote, for it will be a demonstrated fact in Nature. It will be an age wherein men will walk in the light, for it will be a world of recognised inner radiance, wherein the work of the world will be carried forward through the medium of sound, and eventually through the use of words of power and the work of the trained magician. These trained workers in substance, understanding the nature of matter, seeing always in terms of light and comprehending the purpose of sound will bring about those structural changes and those material transformations which will establish a civilisation adequate for the work of the coming race. This work will be that of the conscious unification of the soul and its vehicle of manifestation.

DAVID SPANGLER

Revelation – Birth of a New Age

This New Age has been foreseen for centuries by individuals who had learned to manifest a cosmic consciousness and could witness, freed from time and space, the unfolding patterns of development for life on this planet. They saw what this New Age would bring as the logical continuance of the unfolding of creative being, an important phase in the curriculum of consciousness. They also saw what prior development and preparation would be needed by evolving life, humanity in particular, in order properly to receive and benefit from the energies and opportunities the New Age would bring. With this knowledge, these great ones began to prepare the consciousness of mankind and of all the world.

What was their vision of the need? Towards what ends was this preparation directed? For humanity, it was seen that the Aquarian cycle would stimulate the emergence of a new kind of consciousness, an intuitive-mental awareness, attuned to a level of knowing and power unlimited by space and time. Such a consciousness would have its creative faculties greatly enhanced. This would be in contrast to the emotional-mental awareness within which man has functioned for many centuries, an awareness very much bounded by concepts of separation, time and space and thus comparatively limited in its creative powers. The unleashing of greater creativity without comparable change in the level of Man's awareness and direction would be like placing weapons in the hands of children. Because of the scope of the new powers which New Age consciousness offers to Man, these abilities can only be exercised within an environment of love, selflessness and a sensitive dedication to and awareness of the good of the whole of life. Without such a consciousness of love and that sensitive discrimination between what is appropriate in the moment and what is not (a sensitivity known as truth), these energies and the powers they would stimulate cannot be released. Therefore, it was necessary to do everything possible to unfold and nourish from humanity at least the strong seeds, if not an actual blossoming, of such a consciousness of love and truth.

★ ★ ★

The New Age is here now. This is the essential message of Revelation. Earth has entered a new phase of energy expression. It is important to realise that this new pattern of consciousness was not imposed upon this planet from outside. The cosmic energies act only as stimuli to draw forth from within the life of Earth the qualities which, when expressed actively, best complement and blend with those energies. The New Age is a result of education, a drawing out from within. It has always existed in essence, just as future ages, yet to come, now exist as unrealised potentials. Revelation is merely the educational impulse to bring the New Age potentials to the surface, to spark them into expression. There is no conflict with the past, for the past is seen as the womb of the future. The forms in which life has expressed itself in the past may have to change, to expand in order to adapt to the expansion of that life itself, but change of this nature is evolution, growth, not conflict, not opposition. Forms always change, but the essential life within those forms goes on eternally, expanding itself into greater and greater expressions of its intrinsic potentials and characteristics.

The same is true for the individual. For each of us the New Age is here now. It has always been here, our spiritual 'genetic pattern' awaiting the proper timing to unfold. Yet, for many of us, the New Age remains only a vision, a dream, something yet to come, if indeed we know anything about the New Age at all. Thus, we have the paradox of carrying around within us the seed, the reality, the life of a new world, a new culture, a new creative explosion of indwelling life, yet actually living and acting attuned to an old world, a limiting culture, and seeing that world as the only reality.

It is to break this paradox, to resolve the energies of the two worlds and to liberate the new world from within each individual, that Revelation manifests. This is the function of Revelation: to reveal, in whatever form is necessary to impress its message on to human awareness, the energies, the visions, the inspiration, the direction and the stimulus that will catalytically unleash the New Age from within the existing patterns of the world and of humanity. Unless it does this, Revelation has no value in itself. The New Age cannot be grafted on to the world; it must be unfolded from within. Mankind cannot be coerced into building a new culture. It must be inspired to do so. Because of man's free will, the higher dimensions of consciousness, from whence all true revelations flow, can only act through individuals who, in their personal, physical level aspects, have responded to the vision and have released its transforming potentials from within themselves. Each man must choose the direction and attunement which shall guide his life and development.

Thus, in the final analysis, Revelation becomes a very personal matter. Each person must decide inwardly for himself the truth of what any revelation proclaims and if he decides that it is valid, he must act accordingly. He must become the word of Revelation made flesh; he must embody the vision, the inspiration, the direction, and act to release from within himself the new world which Revelation describes. In no other way can Revelation be fulfilled. The whole being must transform itself in orientation to the new vision. Simply to consider it intellectually or emotionally, to treat it on the level of phenomena or words or pleasant hopes, is to miss the point of the Revelation. The energies of the New Age seek complete personal transformation and rebirth, nothing less. The New Age is not a spectator sport. Whatever the cosmic drama behind Revelation may

29

be, for each individual it has value or not, depending on his personal response and understanding and acceptance of a responsibility to allow the energies and visions of Revelation to live in his daily life.

SIR GEORGE TREVELYAN

Spiritual Awakening in Our Time

This note of joy is a real sign of the New Age. It seems to run through so many of the contemporary groups that characterise our era. Despite often difficult and adverse contingencies, the soul can nevertheless be flooded with joy and confidence through the vision of its eternal nature and the certainty that it is on the path to the worlds of light and oneness.

Thus the whole of life becomes sacred. And once the same divinity is seen to be working within all diversity, all aspects of daily life begin to take on something of a ritual character. Meditation becomes a necessity at some time during the day, for during this period the stilled consciousness is lifted to approach the higher worlds. It is a ritual of inner listening which leads to a blending with the Creative Intelligence.

The spiritual world-view, once experienced, cannot but permeate all our thoughts and actions. Attitudes then begin to change. Many people, for instance, both young and old, find they must change diet. It becomes essential to eat whole foods, organically grown. Many feel compelled to become vegetarian. Not only does flesh become distasteful, but it appears unthinkable to take animal life for the purpose of eating. Instead, one learns to live on the life forces within plant and fruit and grain. And the eating of fresh and uncooked food becomes both a delight and a necessity. Moreover, the need to give thanks to the beings which have produced such food becomes appropriate – a natural and sincere thing to do. The meal, then, like all else, becomes a new ritual. Partaking of the new pattern entails simplification. We must get closer to the heart of life, and too many things or too complex an existence are barriers to our exploration.

There are other dimensions to the spiritual world-view as well. Even if one is in no sense clairvoyant, one awakens to the certainty of invisible planes of consciousness interweaving with our material world – regions peopled by those we love, who have moved on through the gate of physical death. One learns that they have telepathic contact with us and – since they are beyond space and time – can respond instantly to a call sent up to them with love and thanks. This offers further possibilities of inner communion – with both our minds and our hearts.

As we have stated, the inner being in each of us is immortal. It cannot be touched by the 'death' which will break down the discarded sheath of the body. This recognition of the spiritual entity in man has immense implications. We are a creature of body, soul and *spirit* – and the spiritual being within us, the true 'I', is imperishable. It always was and always will be.

In the first centuries of the Christian epoch this was accepted, as it had been in the ancient mysteries. But in 869 AD, the Eighth Ecumenical Council at Constantinople, under Pope Nicholas I, decreed that it would in future be heresy to speak of an immortal spiritual entity. Man was to be regarded as a duality, a creature of body and soul, and all spiritual qualities were categorised as mere adjuncts of the latter. Spirit, in short, was denied its divinity, was thrown back, so to speak, into the mundane world of limited reason and the senses. Thus sundered from its source, it assumed the forms by which we recognise it today – self-consciousness, intellectual pride and arrogance. And during the last two centuries, doctrines have proliferated that even attempt to show that soul is a fallacy, that Man is a physical body and nothing more. Despite their pioneering work in fields of extra-sensory perception, the most scientists will conclude from their remarkable discoveries is that the physical body has subtle and invisible vibrations and attributes. Soul is dismissed as non-existent. The spiritual awakening in our time attempts to restore both soul and spirit to their proper status. It seeks to re-establish the realisation that the essential nature of Man is immortal spirit, and that the 'soul body' and physical body are the sheaths necessary for life on the Earth plane.

This position restores a meaning and coherence to life. Every event takes on intensified significance, and the world becomes an endless adventure, an immense opportunity for realisation of the true individuality on ever finer spheres of being. We are now, one might say, reversing the edict of Pope Nicholas I and re-instating Man as a spiritual being. The implications of this are enormous. But it is important to remember that we are not talking about a religious revival or a proselytising movement. We are talking rather about a transformation in consciousness, such as occurred at the beginning of the Christian era, at the Renaissance and at the so-called 'Enlightenment' – which, in many respects, was anything but that. We are talking about a new channelling of energies of Higher Intelligence, a recognition of guidance from the invisible and the possiblity of widening consciousness to blend with the inner worlds of light. This entails, in one individual after another, a veritable transfiguration of mankind. And it brings in turn a 'gentling' of human nature – particularly necessary in an age when so many lost souls, in apprehension and doubt, are succumbing to panic and violence.

A New Age is being born and a new society is forming, composed of those who have found within themselves the power of light and love. The spiritual within Man unites with the spiritual in the cosmos, and out of this union a new order begins to crystallise.

In this new order all living things are experienced as divine. A quite new orientation takes shape. Teilhard de Chardin called it 'homing upon the Omega point'. The soul, the human nomad, experiences internally its goal and path of re-uniting with the Divine Source from which it descended; and, like a homing pigeon, it sets its course to find the unity (or numinous) which is there to be born again within the heart. In our chaotic world this obviously offers an immense and forgotten prospect of home. And the big evolutionary picture *is* essential to us. Mankind has evolved an unprecedented degree of ego-centred self-consciousness, with all its desolating sense of aloneness and separation. He has reached the point in his evolution where he may transcend that state, may discover that his inner being is spiritual, immortal and already one with the Whole. The barriers between the worlds are beginning to crumble. Inner and outer worlds are, as we are beginning to see, intimately and inextricably linked. Release of consciousness becomes possible, so that the soul may expand beyond its bodily limitations.

★   ★   ★

We are in the second Elizabethan Age, the second Renaissance. In the first, our ancestors explored the seas and discovered new continents, new tracts of the physical world. Those who failed to master the new arts of navigation risked drowning, but the goals of Drake and Raleigh were worth the risk. In our present Elizabethan Age, we are setting out to explore the cosmos and reality. True, our rockets may reach the moon and beyond, but the spiritual awakening of our time is an exploration of inner space. And of course it is dangerous. We are approaching fields in which the soul can well be lost if it allows itself to function recklessly or irresponsibly. Yet such dangers must not deter us from exploration. And nothing will stop the contemporary surge of investigation into esoteric wisdom, just as nothing will stop Man from space exploration. We must recognise the dangers and learn to distinguish between valid and invalid paths of Enquiry. And we may be certain that we have invisible guides and helpers who can lead us through to the light.

But there is also a sense of urgency. We are approaching a crucial turning point, and this generation is involved in a great task. Either Man learns the true healing impulse of blending consciously with the powers of light, or he will plunge himself into disaster and catastrophe. Much may have to fall away in our present social structures, but a new society may then emerge in which the unifying spiritual impulse is genuinely at work. For there are springs of creative energy which can never run dry because they tap the eternal reservoirs of love and creative imagining.

If changes are imminent, it is important that as many souls as possible awaken to their spiritual nature and be able to discern what is happening. In consequence, the immediate present is a time of profound growth and mind–opening – a resurgence of the spirit linking individuals and injecting fresh impulses into man's under-standing. And as the pressure of inner and outer change increases, all who have touched their spiritual realities will comprehend what is occurring. We are truly involved with a Second Coming. Essentially, all is well, despite the ostensibly proliferating difficulties. But we need the courage to see that something tremendous is upon us – the majesty of a New Birth on a planetary and a cosmic scale – and that we are all a part of it. The only *real* anxiety is that we may not be awake and aware when our moment comes.

STARHAWK

The Rebirth of the Goddess

'The Goddess is reawakening,' I say to Laurel, in a moment of probably lunatic optimism. 'What do you mean by that?' she asks.

I say, 'A mode of consciousness that has been dormant for thousands of years is now coming to the fore; we are beginning to see holistically; our model of the cosmos has been changed; we are beginning to value the feminine, the life-generative principle, to value humanness, and the existing world.'

I look at what I have written.

'In circles, in cities, in groves, in streams, in waking and sleeping dreams, in words, in motion, in a flow of music, in poetry, in an opening art, in a day and a night, in struggle, in hunger, in joy, in quickening, in milk, in wine, in the blink of an eye, in a breath, in love, a seed is planted.'

But I am forced to consider the question, 'Will it have time to take root and grow?'

If we accept the responsibility of claiming the future for life, then we must engage in the demanding task of recreating culture. A deep and profound change is needed in our attitude towards the world and the life on it, towards each other, and in our conceptions of what is human. Somehow, we must win clear of the roles we have been taught, of strictures on mind and self that are learned before speech and are buried so deep that they cannot be seen. Today women are creating new myths, singing a new liturgy, painting our own icons, and drawing strength from the new-old symbols of the Goddess, of the 'legitimacy and beneficence of female power.'

A change in symbols, however, is not enough. We must also change the context in which we respond to symbols and the ways in which they are used. If female images are merely plugged into old structures, they too will function as agents of oppression, and this prospect is doubly frightening because they would then be robbed of the liberating power with which they are imbued today.

Witchcraft is indeed the Old Religion, but it is undergoing so much change and development at present that, in essence, it is being recreated rather than revived. The feminist religion of the future is presently being formed. Those of us who are involved in this re-formation must look closely at the culture context in which our own ideas about religion were formed, and examine the many regressive tendencies present in society today. Otherwise, the new incarnation of the Goddess will be subtly moulded on the very forms we are working to transcend.

★ ★ ★

The paradox, of course, is that we are the Goddess: We are each a part of the interpenetrating, interconnecting reality that is All. And, while we can't stop the Earth from turning, we can choose to experience each revolution so deeply and completely that even the dark becomes luminous. To *will* does not mean that the world will conform to our desires – it means that *we* will: We will make our own choices and act so as to bring them about, even knowing we may fail. Feminist spirituality values the courage to take risks, to make mistakes, to be our own authorities.

We need to win clear of the belief that only a few individuals in history have had a direct line on truth; that Jesus or Buddha or Mohammed or Moses or Freud or Werner Erhard know more about our souls than we do. Certainly, we can learn from teachers, but we cannot afford to give over our power to direct our lives. A feminist religion needs no messiahs, no martyrs, no saints to lead the way. Instead, it must validate us in discovering and sharing our experiences, inner and outer. Its goal should be that impossible task of teaching ourselves – because we have no models and no teachers who can show us the way – to become human, fully alive with all the human passions and desires, faults and limitations, and infinite possibilities.

Many forces today are shaping the genesis of new myths. I have discussed the changes science has brought to religion, and the impact of the East–West dialogue. Our growing awareness of ecology, the impending environmental apocalypse, has forced on us a realisation of our interconnectedness with all forms of life, which is the basis of Goddess religion. Our changing cultural attitude towards sexuality is also influencing our spirituality.

Feminists have quite rightly pointed out that the so-called sexual revolution has too often meant the open marketing of women's bodies and the objectification of women. But this is because we are not yet sexually free. Pornography, rape, prostitution, sadomasochism simply bring out into the open the theme that underlies asceticism, celibacy, and Christian chastity – that sex is dirty and evil, and by extension, so are women. Under patriarchy, sexuality provides the rationale for violence against women – the stoning of adulteresses, the burning of Witches, the snickering probe into the conduct of rape victims.

Goddess religion identifies sexuality as the expression of the creative life force of the Universe. It is not dirty, nor is it merely 'normal'; it is sacred, the manifestation of the Goddess. Fortunately, this does not mean you have to be ordained before you can do it. In feminist spirituality, a thing that is sacred can also be affectionate, joyful, pleasurable, passionate, funny, or purely animal. 'All acts of love and pleasure are My rituals,' says the Goddess. Sexuality is sacred because it is a sharing of energy, in passionate surrender to the power of the Goddess, immanent in our desire. In orgasm, we share in the force that moves the stars.

The strongest mythogenic force at work today, however, is feminism. Women have dared to look through the acrostic eye, and the moulds have shattered. The process of cultural change is a long and difficult one. The laws, the language, the economic and social system do not yet reflect our vision. We are discovering and creating myths and symbols and rituals that do. We need images that move us beyond language, law, and custom; that hurl us beyond the boundaries of our lives to that space between the worlds, where we can see clear.

The feminist movement is a magico-spiritual movement as well as a political movement. It is spiritual because it is addressed to the liberation of the human spirit, to healing our fragmentation, to becoming whole. It is magical because it changes consciousness, it expands our awareness and gives us a new vision. It is also magic by another definition: 'the art of causing change in accordance with will.'

If we are to reclaim our culture, we cannot afford narrow definitions.

And when we have won clear, 'we must return to the circle'. The circle is the ecological circle, the circle of the interdependence of all living organisms. Civilisation must return to harmony with Nature.

The circle is also the circle of community. The old family structures, the networks of support and caring are breaking down. Religion has always been a prime source of community, and a vital function of feminist spirituality is to create new networks of involvement. Community also implies broader issues of how equitably power, wealth, and opportunities are shared among different groups, and the issues of who cares for children, the aged, the sick, and the disabled. When the Divine becomes immanent in the world, these are all areas of spiritual concern.

The circle is also the circle of Self. Our view of the Self – what it is, how it perceives, in what modes it functions – has changed greatly. Feminist spirituality is also an inner journey, a personal vision quest, a process of self-healing and self-exploration.

To return to the circle does not necessarily mean to embrace Witchcraft specifically. I hope the religion of the future will be multi-faceted, growing out of many traditions. Perhaps we will see a new cult of the Virgin Mary and a revival of the ancient Hebrew Goddess. Native American traditions and Afro-American traditions may flourish in an atmosphere in which they are given the respect they deserve. Eastern religions will inevitably change as they grow in the West – and part of that change may be in the roles they assign women.

But there are valuable underlying concepts in Witchcraft, on which other feminist traditions can draw. The most important is the understanding of the Goddess, the divine, as immanent in the world, manifest in Nature, in human beings, in human community. The All-That-Is-One is not now and never has been separate from this existing physical world. She is here, now, *is* each of us in the eternal changing present; is no one but you, is nowhere but where you are – and yet is everyone. To worship Her is to assert, even in the face of suffering and often against all reason that life is good, a great gift, a constant opportunity for ecstasy. If we see it become a burden of misery for others, we have the responsibility to change it.

Because the Goddess is manifest in human beings, we do not try to escape our humanness, but seek to become fully human. The task of feminist religion is to help us learn those things that seem so simple, yet are far more demanding than the most extreme patriarchal disciplines. It is easier to be celibate than to be fully alive sexually. It is easier to withdraw from the world than to live in it; easier to be a hermit than to raise a child; easier to repress emotions than to feel them and express them; easier to meditate in solitude than to communicate in a group; easier to submit to another's authority than place trust in oneself. It is not easy to be a Witch, a bender, a shaper, one of the Wise; nor is it safe, comfortable, 'laid back', mellow, uplifting, or a guarantee of peace of mind. It requires openness, vulnerability, courage, and work. It gives no answers: only tasks to be done, and questions to consider. In order to truly transform our culture, we need that orientation towards life, towards the body, towards sexuality, ego, will, towards all the muckiness and adventure of being human.

Witchcraft offers the model of a religion of poetry, not theology. It presents metaphors, not doctrines, and leaves open the possibility of reconciliation of science and religion, of many ways of knowing. It functions in those deeper ways of knowing which our culture has denied and for which we hunger.

The world view of Witchcraft is cyclical, spiral. It dissolves dualities and sees opposites as complements. Diversity is valued; both poles of any duality are always valued because between them flows the on-off pulse of polar energy that sustains life. That cycle is the rhythm of the dance, to which the Hunter, the seeker, is always drawn back.

Finally, the Craft provides a structural model: the coven, the circle of friends, in which there is leadership, but no hierarchy, small enough to create community without loss of individuality. The form of ritual is circular: We face each other, not an altar or a podium or a sacred shrine, because it is in each other that the Goddess is found. Every Witch is Priestess or Priest: there are no hierophants, no messiahs, no avatars, no gurus. The Goddess says, 'If that which you seek, you find not within yourself, you will never find it without. For I have been with you from the beginning.'

When we return to the circle, when we win clear, what will we be? I have snatches of visions; perhaps they are the memories of future lives:

> The children awaken in the middle of the night, to watch the moon rise. They are taught nothing about the moon until they have lived with her for a cycle, arising with her rising, sleeping when she sets. They are not taught about the sun until they have watched it for a year, following its movements along the horizon. Their teachers encourage them to make pictures, stories, and songs about the moon and sun.
>
> When they are older, they are shown a model of the solar system. They are not told about it, they are simply left with it for a time each day, to observe it, with an open mind. For some of

37

them, understanding will come in a moment's illumination. For others, it will not. It doesn't matter. After a time, they are encouraged to ask questions. After a time, they are answered.

When they are older yet, they may make a pilgrimage to the moon. Some may live for a time in the Shrine of the Bright Face, watching the Earth wax and wane. Some may prefer the Dark Shrine, which always faces the stars.

The path is sometimes steep, but not hard to follow. Aradia knows her uneasiness comes only from being alone. Like all the other children, she has hiked and camped in these mountains many times. But never before alone.

She stops for a moment in a high meadow, to soak up the sun. Three days. She will live off the land, or fast. Already the Feast of First Blood, the celebration, the ceremonial dishes of red food, the gifts wrapped in red paper that she will not use for a year, are memories of a past life. Now she is passing. She has given away her dolls and toys. Along the high ridge, she follows the trail to the Lake of Women.

Anna waits by the lake. It lies cupped in the hollow of the mountains like a teardrop in the hand. She drinks the silence: after all the years of noise, children, work, demands. After years of drawing plans for buildings, it is good to look at trees and rocks, to take her Year of Repose. When the young girls come, she and the other women teach them things about their bodies, about wind and rock, fire and water. They learn to spin and weave, to bring flame without matches, to understand the speech of animals. At night, they are taught the mysteries and songs that women remember. And they work magic. . . .

It is the night of the Winter Solstice. In San Francisco, there are bonfires everywhere: strung along the beaches, blazing on Twin Peaks, on all the high places. In the parks and on rooftops small groups gather around cauldrons. There are no mass meetings, only circles.

They begin with a very old custom: walking the land and searching for papers or foreign objects. The Elders have debated discontinuing the custom: it is outdated. There is never any trash to find. Nothing is made to be idly tossed away; nothing is wasted.

From the hilltops the city is a coloured mosaic set in green. Everywhere are gardens. The last rays of the sun gleam rose in a thousand solar collectors.

The Witches take hands around the fire. The wind rises, rattling the eucalyptus branches. Across the city, thousands of gaily painted windmills spin to life, flashing the coloured lights with which they are decorated at Midwinter. Candles are blown out;

altars topple over. No one minds. They have all they need to make magic: their voices, their breath, each other.

Through the long night, they chant each other's names. They sing hymns to the newborn sun, to the eternally revolving Goddess. They pour libations and give thanks – especially the very old ones, who remember when it was different:

'I am thankful that in this city no one goes hungry.'

'I am thankful that in this city no one is left to die alone.'

'I give thanks that I can walk the dark streets without fearing violence.'

'I give thanks that the air is clean, that life has returned to the waters of the bay, that we are at peace.'

'I give thanks that everyone has work to do.'

In the morning there are parades down Market Street, and the neighbourhood groups and unions present their elaborate floats, the creation of the city's finest artists. Gorgeously arrayed figures of the Virgin arrive from the Mission District, followed by a glittering Wheel of Lights from the Electrical Worker's Union, and a Sun Child made of yellow flowers from the Midwives' Guild. There are clowns, jugglers, marching bands – people pour out of their houses to dance in the streets. Later, there will be concerts, parties, masquerade balls, and special theatre performances.

The last day of celebration is quiet and peaceful. People visit each other's homes, exchanging food and simple gifts. Families and covens eat together.

At night, they return to the hillsides and rekindle the fires. They join together to earth the power of the season, and slip between the worlds. Beyond time, in touch with past and future both, with all possibilities, they speak to us. We can hear them. They say to each one of us:

'Wake up! You are it. You are a part of the circle of the Wise. There is no mystery that has not already been revealed to you. There is no power you do not already have. You share in all the love that is.'

> When we return to the circle
> we have won clear.
> Return the dance to the pulses of the Hunt.

The Goddess awakens in infinite forms and a thousand disguises. She is found where She is least expected, appears out of nowhere and everywhere to illumine the open heart. She is singing, crying, moaning, wailing, shrieking, crooning to us: to be awake, to commit ourselves to life, to be a lover in the world and of the world, to join our voices in the single song of constant change and creation. For Her law is love unto all beings, and She is the cup of the drink of life.

May life thrive, now and always!
The circle is ever open, ever unbroken.
May the Goddess awaken in each of our hearts.
Merry meet, and merry part. And blessed be.

2

Inner Voice

Liz Greene
C.G. Jung
Ram Dass
Corinne McLaughlin
Agni Yoga
Eileen Caddy
Ken Carey
A Course In Miracles
Jane Roberts

Introduction

If we accept that all life and that we ourselves are multi-dimensional, then a journey of investigation into this invisible world begins. But how are we to know it, how are we to understand it?

More than that, if we genuinely sense our multi-dimensionality, how do we then get clarity about our purpose and the nature of our inner journey through life?

Since human beings first started asking these questions, there must have been people – sincere and authentic, cunning and charlatan – ready to communicate messages from the invisible reality. 'You can't see the truth. Well, I can. Give me some gold, give me your devotion, give me your soul, and I will tell you.' My own intellectual background and sense of individuality made me suspicious of all oracles, psychics and interpretive systems. My own path was that of meditation, white magic and self-reflective psychology. But as I became more sure of my own self, psychological and spiritual, so I became more relaxed, tolerant and open, and I began to appreciate the value of oracles, psychics and interpretive systems. Why not, with one's eyes open, accept help, reflection and stimulation?

I found that a serious and psychologically wise astrology existed. Perhaps the most influential contemporary astrologer integrating the insights of modern psychology is Liz Greene who opens this section. I also found the extraordinary wisdom of the Chinese oracle, the *I Ching*, and cannot resist including an extract from Jung's introduction in which the pioneering psychologist makes a relationship with this oriental oracle.

To cover an aspect of the inner energies of meditation, there is a portion from Ram Dass, the academic turned mystic whose book *Be Here Now* became the unofficial bible of flower power and hippy New Agers.

We then come to the more tricky subject of channelling and psychics. Channelling is when a person allows their own mind to go still and clairvoyantly or telepathically picks up and communicates the messages and thoughts of another consciousness. Of all areas of the New Age, this one aroused the deepest suspicion in me, a suspicion that only finally disappeared when I married my partner, Sabrina, who was born psychic, has a deep instinctive understanding of human character, and uses these skills in counselling – often me! The extracts from channellings are, however, preceded by some wise words from Corinne McLaughlin on how to evaluate channelling.

Some channelling, especially done by psychics in counselling, is purely personal. Other channelling discusses philosophy and metaphysics with great sophistication; some is also very sweet and poetic. The first channelled extract is from *Heart*, one of the *Agni Yoga* series written by Helena Roerich; its dynamic beauty is extraordinary. Then comes an extract from Eileen Caddy, part of which describes her experience of channelling, as does the extract by Ken Carey. Eileen is the co-founder of the Findhorn Foundation where she still lives, daily meditating an inner presence into the community.

The next extract is from *A Course in Miracles*. Channelled through Helen Shucman, *A Course* is divided into three sections: an address to students; 365 lessons; and an address to teachers. It is thought by many to be the most powerful transformatory course currently available. Its style is based in Christian devotion, but it possesses a wry wisdom.

The final reading is from Jane Roberts who channelled a consciousness named Seth. The Seth books, for my and many other people's money, are the most insightful, intelligent and amusing books on transpersonal psychology available. In this extract he speaks about the dream world. Seth, incidentally, is responsible for bringing the term 'multi-dimensional' into common usage.

LIZ GREENE

The Planetary Map of Inner Potential

Any understanding of the language of astrology must commence with a realisation of what the birth horoscope can and cannot tell us. The horoscope is a highly complex astronomical map, based not only on the date of birth but on the time, year and place as well. We must first, therefore, discard all preconceptions and prejudices based on popular magazine astrology, which has virtually nothing to do with the real study.

The birth map does not plot the fate of the individual in a predestined way. Rather, it symbolises the basic lines of his character's potential development. It takes a minimum of thought to realise that a man will act and shape his life according to his needs, fears and abilities, and that these needs, fears and abilities stem from his inherent disposition. In this sense character is fate, and if we are ignorant of our own natures – as most of us are who have never explored the unconscious – then the stars cannot be blamed for the fact that we run headlong and blind along the course we ourselves have chosen. This fundamental point is critical to an understanding of the entire study of astrology. The more shallow interpretation of fate and free will – fate is what I am 'destined' to do, while free will is what I 'choose' to do myself – makes it impossible for us to see the subtle paradox that these two opposites are one and the same.

We know that behind all life, whether psychic or material, lie the archetypal patterns, the bare bones of the structure of existence. We do not yet know whether there is any material basis for the fact that astrological data correlate with human behaviour, although through our research on biological clocks and sunspot cycles it will not be long before we have our evidence. Michel Gauquelin's laborious and thorough statistical research has demonstrated in a dramatic way that such correlations are valid, but the reason for their validity still eludes us. The material facts pertaining to astrology, however, such as the possibility of energy emanations from the planets which affect the energy field of the sun, are only one end of the spectrum of the archetype. The other end is symbolic, and the positions of the heavens at a particular moment in time, by reflecting the qualities of that moment, also reflect the qualities of anything born at that moment, whether it be an individual, a city, an idea, a company or a marriage. One does not cause the other; they are synchronous, and mirror each other.

So far as the reason for this synchronicity is concerned, we are left, on the one hand, with Jung's archetypes of the collective unconscious and, on the other, the teachings of esoteric doctrine. These two viewpoints seem to disclose the same truth, which the findings of quantum physics and biology in the last twenty-five years are beginning to affirm. Life is really one organism, and the various parts of that organism, although different in form and apparently separate, partake of the same whole and are interconnected with every other part.

Paracelsus, writing on astrology in the sixteenth century, says:

> If I have 'manna' in my constitution, I can attract 'manna' from heaven . . . 'Saturn' is not only in the sky, but also deep in the earth and in the ocean. What is 'Venus' but the 'artemisia' that grows in your garden? What is 'iron' but 'Mars'? That is to say, Venus and artemisia are both the products of the same essence, and Mars and iron are both the manifestations of the same cause. What is the human body but a constellation of the same powers that formed the stars in the sky? He who knows what iron is, knows the attributes of Mars. He who knows Mars, knows the qualities of iron.

The solar system is not only an arrangement of physical sun and planets bound together by the force of gravity and orbiting through space. It may also be seen as the symbol of a living energy pattern, reflecting at any moment the smaller forms of life which are contained within it.

In attempting to understand the symbolism of the birth horoscope, it is useful to consider what we know of the psyche, for the chart at birth is really a model, in symbolic terms, of the various energy patterns or psychic components which make up the individual. We know that the ego, as the centre of the field of consciousness, is a regulating centre which serves the function of illuminating those areas of the unconscious, both personal and collective, which are striving for light; and we know as well that the ego is the surrogate or reflection of that mysterious centre which Jung calls the Self, and which esoteric teaching calls the Soul. We know too that as an individual develops it is likely he will block from his field of awareness those aspects of his nature which in reality belong to him, yet which for one reason or another are incompatible with his values or with the values of his family or society. Finally, we know that it is extremely important, if one seeks self-fulfilment and a meaningful life which fulfils also the larger purpose for which one has been born, to bring these aspects of his own nature to light, rather than condemning them to the perpetual darkness of the unconscious. As it is ideally projected from the early days of childhood, the personality is almost never fully expressed; only a part is enacted, and for many people this part is far smaller than that which constitutes their real birthright. In such cases, we say that a man has not really fulfilled his potential, that he has wasted opportunities or talents, or that he has never really been 'true to himself'.

The birth chart is a seed or blueprint of all that potentially belongs to a man's personality – if it were in full flower, and fully conscious. It is a road map in the truest sense, for the object of studying it is not to 'overcome' the 'influences' of the planets, but rather to allow room in one's life to express all those qualities and drives of which the chart is a symbol. Only then can the individual approximate the original plan for his life's development as it is 'conceived' – for we must in the end infer intelligent, purposeful development – by the Self.

If this seems too abstruse or lofty a definition of the birth horoscope, it is pertinent to remember that astrology, before it became the property of popular magazines and newspaper columns, was once a sacred art. Through it, the student had access to an intuitive perception of the workings of the energies behind life, which no other ancient system – except perhaps its Eastern equivalent, the *I Ching* – could offer. The great is reflected in the small, and the fact that astrology can also be used to illumine more mundane problems is not a repudiation of its deeper psychological value. It is only a reflection of the fact that even in the minutest details of our lives, we reflect that which is our essence.

When seen in this light, it will be apparent that an understanding of the birth horoscope affords a new dimension to the understanding of one's life path. Likewise, the comparison of two horoscopes will provide considerable information about the interworkings of two lives; and it is from this art of chart comparison that synastry – the use of chart comparison to explore and evaluate relationships – has developed.

Astronomically, the birth horoscope is simply a map – accurately calculated so that it cannot be faulted by the most pernickety astronomer – of the heavens as they appear from the exact time and place of the individual's birth. The circle of the twelve zodiacal signs is a symbol of totality, and in its totality it represents all life's possibilities. In this respect, the zodiac is like any other universal symbol of wholeness, such as the egg, or the urobouros (the serpent devouring its tail), or the equal–armed cross. It is a mandala, and as Jung has shown, mandalas are the symbolic expression of the potential wholeness of life and of the human psyche. They are at the same time symbols of the Self, and symbols of God, for these two are, in terms of human perception, the same.

Against the backdrop of this circle of the zodiac (which is called the ecliptic and which is in fact the apparent circle of the sun traversing the heavens) lie the sun, the moon and the eight known planets. The positions of these planets as they are placed around the zodiacal wheel at the moment of the individual's birth form the internal pattern of the birth chart. Thus we have a symbolic picture, with the wheel of wholeness around the outside and the individual combination of psychological components on the inside. Every chart is made up of the same ingredients: twelve zodiacal signs, eight planets, and the sun and moon. Yet every chart is different because at any given moment the arrangement of all these factors is different, both within the planetary pattern and in the relationship between the planets and the horizon of the earth itself.

In other words, human beings are built of the same raw stuff, the same drives or energies, needs and possibilities; but there is an individual arrangement of these energies which gives the stamp of uniqueness to the pattern. The same forces are present in all of us, a fact with which one is confronted endlessly in any work involving counselling or therapy. But there is a creative individuality which makes of these basic energies a unique work of art, which is the individual life. This creative shaping does not, we must assume, stem from the ego, which is hardly capable of such a feat; it stems from the Self, and the Self, as such, is not mapped out on the birth chart. It is the entire zodiac. Nor can the chart show the individual's decision at any point in his life to voluntarily cooperate with his own psyche's endeavour to achieve greater consciousness, and therefore to make fuller use of those potentials which are his from the beginning. In this decision lies the deepest meaning of individual free will.

C.G. JUNG

Foreword to the I Ching

The axioms of causality are being shaken to their foundations: we know now that what we term natural laws are merely statistical truths and thus must necessarily allow for exceptions. We have not sufficiently taken into account as yet that we need the laboratory with its incisive restrictions in order to demonstrate the invariable validity of natural law. If we leave things to nature, we see a very different picture: every process is partially or totally interfered with by chance, so much so that under natural circumstances a course of events absolutely conforming to specific laws is almost an exception.

The Chinese mind, as I see it at work in the *I Ching*, seems to be exclusively preoccupied with the chance aspect of events. What we call coincidence seems to be the chief concern of this peculiar mind, and what we worship as causality passes almost unnoticed. We must admit that there is something to be said for the immense importance of chance. An incalculable amount of human effort is directed to combating and restricting the nuisance or danger represented by chance. Theoretical considerations of cause and effect often look pale and dusty in comparison to the practical results of chance. It is all very well to say that the crystal of quartz is a hexagonal prism. The statement is quite true in so far as an ideal crystal is envisaged. But in Nature one finds no two crystals exactly alike, although all are unmistakably hexagonal. The actual form, however, seems to appeal more to the Chinese sage than the ideal one. The jumble of natural laws constituting empirical reality holds more significance for him than a causal explanation of events that, moreover, must usually be separated from one another in order to be properly dealt with.

The manner in which the *I Ching* tends to look upon reality seems to disfavour our causalistic procedures. The moment under actual observation appears to the ancient Chinese view more of a chance hit than a clearly defined result of concurring causal chain processes. The matter of interest seems to be the configuration formed by chance events in the moment of observation, and not at all the hypothetical reasons that seemingly account for the coincidence. While the Western mind carefully sifts, weighs, selects, classifies, isolates, the Chinese picture of the moment encompasses everything down to the minutest nonsensical detail, because all of the ingredients make up the observed moment.

Thus it happens that when one throws the three coins, or counts through the forty-nine yarrow stalks, these chance details enter into the picture of the moment of observation and form a part of it – a part that is insignificant to us, yet most meaningful to the Chinese mind. With us it would be a banal and almost meaningless statement (at least on the face of it) to say that whatever happens in a given moment possesses inevitably the quality peculiar to that moment. This is not an abstract argument but a very practical one. There are certain connoisseurs who can tell you merely from the appearance, taste, and behaviour of a wine the site of its vineyard and the year of its origin. There are antiquarians who with almost uncanny accuracy will name the time and place of origin and the maker of an *objet d'art* or piece of furniture on merely looking at it. And there are even astrologers who can tell you, without any previous knowledge of your nativity, what the position of sun and moon was and what zodiacal sign rose above the horizon in the moment of your birth. In the face of such facts, it must be admitted that moments can leave long-lasting traces.

In other words, whoever invented the *I Ching* was convinced that the hexagram worked out in a certain moment coincided with the latter in quality no less than in time. To him the hexagram was the exponent of the moment in which it was cast – even more so than the hours of the clock or the divisions of the calendar could be – inasmuch as the hexagram was understood to be an indicator of the essential situation prevailing in the moment of its origin.

This assumption involves a certain curious principle that I have termed synchronicity, a concept that formulates a point of view diametrically opposed to that of causality. Since the latter is a merely statistical truth and not absolute, it is a sort of working hypothesis of how events evolve one out of another, whereas synchronicity takes the coincidence of events in space and time as meaning something more than mere chance, namely, a peculiar interdependence of objective events among themselves as well as with the subjective (psychic) states of the observer or observers.

The ancient Chinese mind contemplates the cosmos in a way comparable to that of the modern physicist, who cannot deny that his model of the world is a decidedly psychophysical structure. The microphysical event includes the observer just as much as the reality underlying the *I Ching* comprises subjective, i.e. psychic conditions in the totality of the momentary situation. Just as causality describes the sequence of events, so synchronicity to the Chinese mind deals with the coincidence of events. . . .

I submitted two questions to the method of chance represented by the coin oracle, the second question being put after I had written my analysis of the answer to the first. The first question was directed, as it were, to the *I Ching*: what had it to say about my intention to write a foreword? The second question concerned my own action, or rather the situation in which I was the acting subject who had discussed the first hexagram. To the first question the *I Ching* replied by comparing itself to a cauldron, a ritual vessel in need of renovation, a vessel that was finding only doubtful favour with the public. To the second question the reply was that I had fallen into a difficulty, for the *I Ching* represented a deep and dangerous water hole in which one might easily be mired. However, the water hole proved to be an old well that needed only to be renovated in order to be put to useful purposes once more.

These four hexagrams are in the main consistent as regards theme (vessel, pit, well); and as regards intellectual content, they seem to be meaningful. Had a human being made such replies, I should, as a psychiatrist, have had to pronounce him of sound mind, at least on the basis of the material presented. Indeed, I should not have been able to discover anything delirious, idiotic, or schizophrenic in the four answers. In view of the *I Ching*'s extreme age and its Chinese origin, I cannot consider its archaic, symbolic, and flowery language abnormal. On the contrary, I should have had to congratulate this hypothetical person on the extent of his insight into my unexpressed state of doubt. On the other hand, any person of clever and versatile mind can turn the whole thing around and show how I have projected my subjective contents into the symbolism of the hexagrams. Such a critique, though catastrophic from the standpoint of Western rationality, does no harm to the function of the *I Ching*. On the contrary, the Chinese sage would smilingly tell me: 'Don't you see how useful the *I Ching* is in making you project your hitherto unrealised thoughts into its abstruse symbolism? You could have written your foreword without ever realising what an avalanche of misunderstanding might be released by it.'

The Chinese standpoint does not concern itself as to the attitude one takes towards the performance of the oracle. It is only we who are puzzled, because we trip time and again over our prejudice, viz. the notion of causality. The ancient wisdom of the East lays stress upon the fact that the intelligent individual realises his own thoughts, but not in the least upon the way in which he does it. The less one thinks about the theory of the *I Ching*, the more soundly one sleeps. . . .

As to the thousands of questions, doubts, and criticisms that this singular book stirs up – I cannot answer these. The *I Ching* does not offer itself with proofs and results; it does not vaunt itself, nor is it easy to approach. Like a part of Nature, it waits until it is discovered. It offers neither facts nor power, but for lovers of self-knowledge, of wisdom – if there be such – it seems to be the right book. To one person its spirit appears as clear as day; to another, shadowy as twilight; to a third, dark as night. He who is not pleased by it does not have to use it, and he who is against it is not obliged to find it true. Let it go forth into the world for the benefit of those who can discern its meaning.

Zurich, 1949

RAM DASS

The Energies of Meditation

As your mind quiets more and more in meditation your consciousness may shift radically. With quietness can come waves of bliss and rapture. You may feel the presence of astral beings; you may feel yourself leaving your body and rising into realms above your head; you may feel energy pouring up your spine. You may have visions, burning sensations, a sharp pain in your heart, deep stillness, stiffening of your body. You may hear voices or inner sounds such as the flute of Krishna, a waterfall, thunder, or a bell. You may smell strange scents or your mouth may be filled with strange tastes. Your body may tingle or shake. As you go deeper you may enter what the southern Buddhists call *jhanas*, trance states marked by ecstasy, rapture, bliss, and clarity of perception. You may have visions of distant places or find you somehow know things though you can't explain how.

These experiences may seduce you. If you cling to them, fascinated – whether the fascination be out of attraction or repulsion – you invest them with undue importance. When you've had this kind of seductive experience, its memory can be an obstacle to meditation, especially if you try to recreate the experience. To keep going in meditation, you've got to give up your attachment to these states and go beyond. If these experiences come spontaneously, fine. But don't seek them.

I remember taking a fifteen-day insight meditation course. On the twelfth day I experienced a peace that I had never known in my life. It was so deep that I rushed to my teacher and said, 'This peace is what I have always wanted all my life. Everything else I was doing was just to find this peace.' Yet a month later I was off pursuing other spiritual practices. That experience of peace wasn't enough. It was limited. Any experiential state, anything we can label, isn't it.

★   ★   ★

Meditation is like diving deep in the ocean. To allow you to go to the depths and come back up smoothly your body must acclimatise at each stage. As you adjust to each new level, you are filled with a greater energy. The predicament is that as you receive greater energy during meditation, it carries over to the times you are not meditating, when your old habits of mind to which you are still attached hold sway. The temptation is to use these new energies to strengthen your old habits, to use the meditative energy in the service of your ego. For example, you may find that these new energies enhance your sexual excitement, enthusiasm, and proficiency or your social power or charisma. This undoubtedly is one of the attractions of meditation.

But if your yearning is to go to the depths of your own soul – if your journey is to seek what Buddha had, what Christ had, what Ramakrishna had, what Abraham had, what Mohammed had – then you must beware of dissipating these energies through your old habits. You must channel them to go deeper. The energies that come from going near God can take you even nearer to God.

The ego is designed to survive in the midst of this energy. It's like a spacecraft with walls of thick steel to protect it from the incredible bombardment of the high energies of outer space. The art of meditation, however, is to work gradually with these new energies to free awareness from ego without destroying it.

If your mind and heart are not open enough, the energies that

50

surge into you can take negative forms. They may feel like raw power that causes you fits of violent shaking. You may feel edgy, nervous, unable to sleep, speedy, excited, or agitated. You may feel a paranoia because you are having insights that no one you know understands.

To prepare yourself to handle these energies positively, purify your mind and strengthen your body. Then you will be ready when the boundaries between you and the larger sources of energy become thin. As this intense energy courses through your being, you will be able to handle it, though you may notice symptoms such as shaking or nervousness. When this happens to me, I focus on my heart, breathe in and out of it, filling with love on each breath. Great force can come to you, but when it is balanced with love you won't feel overwhelmed. With love, you are more open to the energy. Then you will grow in power – the power of love. You are on the way home.

★ ★ ★

In the first part of your journey you may be quite eclectic, trying out many methods. Don't consider these changes from one method to another a weakness. Nor is it a weakness to stay with one method if it feels right to you. But it is a weakness to stay with a method that doesn't feel right, or to shift methods to avoid going too far with any one of them. How do you know when to shift, when to stay? Listen to your inner voice, your heart, and be truthful with yourself. This self-reliance and honesty will guide you not only in these early stages, but all the way to enlightenment. Each person has to be very honest and honour his or her stage of evolution. Nobody can live another's life. You've got to live your own.

CORINNE MCLAUGHLIN
How To Evaluate Channelling

Channelling or receiving guidance is not a new phenomenon at all, as many major religious traditions have examples of those who received information from non-physical sources – from shamans among native and aboriginal peoples, to the Delphic oracles of ancient Greece, to Abraham and Moses in the Hebrew tradition, Joan of Arc in the Christian, and Joseph Smith in the Mormon tradition. One of the best-known psychics of this century was Edgar Cayce, who channelled health remedies and information on past lives for over 8,000 people.

But why is so much channelling happening today? Why so many psychic channels? Some spiritual teachings say it's because of the shift into the Age of Aquarius, an astrological changing of the ages, which happens every 2,000 years or so, and the incoming of energies termed 'the seventh ray'. Others say it's because the planetary 'etheric web' (the subtle life-force body of the earth) has been rent through wars and atomic explosions, and without this protective web there is a greater inflow of 'astral' or psychic energy, which makes communications with the non-physical worlds easier.

Many people feel that this sudden interest in non-physical communication today is definitely helping to re-orient thousands of people inward towards the spiritual life and away from the obsession with materialism. But sincere spiritual seekers also urgently caution that psychics and channels should not replace one's relationship to God, to the highest spiritual source, and that psychics should never be consulted purely out of curiosity or a need for entertainment. The highest source of guidance for anyone is always within each person – the voice of the soul, the inner Divinity.

But if someone insists on consulting another person, a psychic or 'channel' for counselling, how can he or she derive benefit and avoid all the pitfalls and distortions? First of all, it is important to recognise the relative nature of channelled information. Depending on where someone is on his or her spiritual path, any given channelling may represent either a next step, or something that is totally regressive and inappropriate (or somewhere in between). If, for instance, someone is very materially oriented and thinks that money and possessions is all there is to life, then to suddenly experience a channelling might open him up to the possibility that there are other levels of reality beyond the purely physical. On the other end of the spectrum, if someone has been following a spiritual discipline for many years and listening to the voice of his own soul or inner Divinity to guide him, then the same channelling for him might offer no new spiritual inspiration or wisdom, and to become dependent on it for guidance might set him back many years (or lifetimes) spiritually.

What is most curious about the current fascination with guidance is that many people believe that anything from a non-physical source must be 'truth from on high'. They mistake the non-physical worlds for the truly spiritual worlds. No one makes the mistake of accepting as authority everything a typical man-in-the-street in our physical world has to say on a given subject. Similarly, the non-physical worlds are populated with beings who have varying degrees of wisdom and authority relating to spiritual matters, and so it is best to not just listen to anyone who is non-physical but to seek out the wisest.

Also, why should it be just because Aunt Sally is dead that suddenly she is any wiser than when she was living? If we didn't take her advice when she was living, why take it when she's dead and wanting to deliver a message as a spirit guide?

To determine the quality of the message and the level from which the message is received, it helps to look at the life of the channel to see whether he or she is applying the information received and whether it has helped him or her to live a more spiritual life. 'By their fruits you shall know them,' as the Bible says. Does the channel seem to be mainly concerned with helping others through her gift or with accumulating fame, money and power? Is she using any money received to expand her work (build a centre, train others, publish information, etc.) or is she using it merely to create a more pleasurable life for herself personally? A good test is to ask yourself whether you would go to this person for spiritual advice if she weren't channelling. Do you trust her to be wiser spiritually than yourself, or is it merely the glamour of channelling that attracts you to her? Glamour is really the substitution of the unreal for the real, of the image for the substance.

A good analogy is that of a radio receiver. A good radio picks up clear signals from nearby as well as distant places. A cheap or broken radio picks up a lot of distortion and static and only gets signals nearby. Similarly with a channel. A good channel picks up clearer messages coming from a greater distance – i.e. from the higher spiritual planes. (This is called 'higher psychism' and is relatively rare.) A lesser-quality channel picks up a lot of distortion and only gets messages from nearby sources – the planes closer to earth where 'Indian spirit guides' and other astral entities often dwell. This is the more common 'lower psychism'. The relative purity of the channel's life will attract a message on the same level through the law of resonance. An emotionally uncentred person who is motivated by ego, anger, fear, greed, etc. will probably attract a similar type of spirit guide – perhaps even a non-physical 'busybody' who is just looking for other people's lives to control. Someone who is bored or unhappy with his life will also attract a lower spirit. And negative emotions, wrong motivations, confused thinking will distort whatever message does try to come through. Drug use will also tend to attract a lower spirit or distort the message.

Unfortunately also, it can sometimes happen that a channel may start out being well-intentioned and sincerely trying to help others spiritually and so attract a helpful spirit guide. But then as increasing attention and power comes her way, her personality is not pure enough to handle it and the ego gets inflated and another spirit gets attracted. This second spirit is a lower entity who may masquerade as the first spirit and start subtly distorting the message and trying

53

to control people through guilt or threats. So if the channel doesn't work on purifying herself and use a lot of discrimination, accepting full responsibility for what comes through her, she can easily become deluded and end up deluding others and harming their spiritual life. This has happened many times and is the reason why most spiritual traditions caution against this kind of 'lower psychism', where the channel is open to any kind of spirit communicating through her, as it can also lead to possession.

One of the reasons for this lack of discrimination on the part of many channels and those who follow them is that we in the West have traditionally no background or cultural framework to interpret non-physical entities. We usually believe in God *transcendent* (the Creator who is beyond human knowing), rather than God *immanent* (within each person and within all life) as do Eastern religions. Therefore, anything non-physical is either God or the Devil, with nothing in between. But Eastern thought holds that there are many levels of reality or 'planes of existence' in between the physical reality and the ultimate reality or God consciousness.

★ ★ ★

Some researchers suggest that about 85 per cent of all guidance and channelling is from the person's own subconscious or from the astral plane (which is the emotional plane of illusion and distortion). Only about 8 per cent may be coming from the soul level and 5 per cent from spiritually advanced 'disciples', with less than 2 per cent from a true spiritual Master. Although many psychics believe they are channelling a true Master, in fact, they may only be contacting his 'astral shell' – the build-up of all the desires, longings, and devotional thoughts about higher beings and Masters, which begins to take on a life of its own on the astral plane. Or they often contact a lower astral spirit who masquerades as a Master. How can you tell which it is? An imposter behaves quite differently than any real Master, as he often lacks love and usually flatters or chastises his followers and demands obedience. A real Master always leaves his disciples free and never demands but only suggests. Also, a real Master, by definition, has mastered all the planes of earthly existence – physical, emotional and mental – and so has a highly developed mind. Channelled messages that are an insult to the intelligence of any thinking person could hardly be coming from a real Master.

★ ★ ★

The only really guaranteed way to avoid getting false information or being deceived or controlled by a psychic or channel is – don't consult one in the first place! Try the slower, but safer method – strengthening the contact with our own soul and inner Divinity, for this source is guaranteed to be both accurate and relevant.

Guidance from someone else is not meant to take the place of the person's relationship to God and to his or her soul. It is merely meant to provide helpful guideposts along the path and to help the person develop his or her own inner guidance. . . .

What techniques are most useful in seeking guidance from our soul, our higher self? The most effective technique is a regular meditation practice. Although there are many types of meditation practice that are helpful, it's always good to begin by calming the body, emotions and mind through regular, deep breathing. The most important thing is then to shift our attention and energy from the solar plexus centre (at the navel) to the heart and/or head centre (sometimes called the 'third eye'). If our energy stays focussed at the solar plexus level and we become too passive, opening ourselves to anything that comes into our awareness, we may just pick up the feelings and thoughts of others. Or we may pick up an 'astral' entity who wants to influence us, and who may not intend our highest good. It's better to stay alert and aware, not passive, and to lift our energy to a higher centre (or 'chakra' as they're called in many spiritual traditions), and then to consciously seek contact with our soul or higher self. This can be done through prayer, visualisation, mantra (repeating a spiritual word or phrase over and over), invocation, or through the focussed attention of the higher mind. The important thing is the intention of contacting the soul for guidance, and not just any non-physical entity that's nearby.

If, on the other hand, we're concerned that we never receive any guidance, no words or visions, even when we ask a question in our meditation – don't worry. Many spiritually evolved people do not receive guidance in this way. Rather, they are guided in the moment, in action. In fact, receiving guidance implies duality and separateness – a split between giver and receiver – rather than being one with all wisdom. The true goal is union with God.

In the end, the most important thing about guidance is not just receiving information. Rather, it is about learning to think as higher beings do, as wisely and as broadly, to see things from their perspective.

AGNI YOGA

The Heart of the Aum

1. To behold with the eyes of the heart; to listen with the ears of the heart to the roar of the world; to peer into the future with the comprehension of the heart; to remember the cumulations of the past through the heart; thus must one impetuously advance upon the path of ascent. Creativeness encompasses the fiery potentiality, and is impregnated with the sacred fire of the heart. Therefore, upon the path to the Hierarchy, upon the path of Great Service, upon the path of Communion, synthesis is the one luminous path of the heart. How can the manifested rays be radiated if the flame is not affirmed in the heart? It is precisely the quality of the magnet that is inherent in the heart. The highest creativeness is imbued with this great law. Hence, each consummation, each union, each great cosmic unification is achieved through the flame of the heart. By what means can the foundation of the great steps be laid? Verily, only through the heart. Thus the arcs of consciousness are fused by the flame of the heart.

Thus, we shall keep in memory the beauteous attraction of the magnet of the heart, which links all manifestations. Verily, the silver thread that links the Teacher with the disciple is the great magnet of the heart. The union between Teacher and disciple affirms the essence of all evolutions.

2. Many legends tell of the fulfilment of wishes, but they do not speak of the fundamental condition of issuelessness, which whets the desires to the point of immutability. Each tiny deviating path already dulls the arrow of immutability. But as one who is unaccustomed to the water can swim when in danger of being drawn to the bottom, so the solution of the fulfilment of a wish is found when all paths are cut off. People say a miracle has happened! But often it was only the intensification of the psychic energy. The heart, the sun of the organism, is the focus of psychic energy. Thus, in speaking of the heart we must have in mind the law of psychic energy. It is beautiful to sense the heart as the Sun of Suns of the universe. We must understand the Sun of the Highest Hierarch as our Banner. Beautiful is this Banner, like an invincible power if our eyes have assimilated its radiance, reflected in our heart.

3. Whether the heart be called the abode of the Elohim or the synthesis of syntheses, it still remains the focal point. Even those who recognise in the heart only its lower physiological functions,

even they have an attitude of care for the heart. How much more deeply, then, must he who knows about the magnet and silvery thread harken to the heart. Therefore the Teacher draws one away from everything narrowly physical, in order to remind about the spiritual world through each organ. It is a festival for Us each time a pure direction of thought is projected into the sphere of invisible existence. One must lead into the abode of the Elohim with complete perseverance, as though danger pursued the entering one. One can recognise the path of the chosen ones when the Invisible World has become real and accessible to them; then one can notice the growth of consciousness, and the very organs of the body become transformed, imbued by the link with Hierarchy.

4. The heart is a temple, but not an abode of idols. Thus We are not against the construction of a temple, but We object to fetishism and to bazaars. Likewise, when We speak of constructing a temple like a heart, We do not mean that it be of heart-shaped design, We speak of its inner significance. A temple cannot exist without realisation of the infinite chain; so, too, the heart contacts all the sensations of the Cosmos. The heart's anguish or joy inter-resounds with the far-off spheres. Why, then, is anguish sensed more often than joy? Of course, the constant cosmic perturbations agitate the heart that adheres to them. Therefore is the service of such a heart so great upon the scales of the world. Help the structure of the world! There is neither a day nor an hour when the world is not in danger! Two eyes alone cannot foresee these dangers, but only three, as upon the Banner of the Lords! One must comprehend the temple of the heart as an imminent sensation. Not without cause was the heart marked by the sign of the cross. Thus the sign of the cross eternally accompanied the temple of the heart.

5. New circumstances will indicate the path to the future. Truth is the same, but combinations vary, according to consciousness. How much of the beautiful is destroyed, owing to the ignoring of the temple – the heart! But let us irresistibly strive to a realisation of heartfelt warmth, and let us begin to feel ourselves as the bearers of the temple. Thus one can cross the threshold of the New World. How poor in spirit are those who believe that the New World is not for them! The bodies differ, but the spirit will not evade the New World.

6. Doubt is the destruction of quality. Doubt is the tomb of the heart. Doubt is the source of ugliness. Doubt must be mentioned in each talk, because where can we go without quality? What shall we understand without the heart? What shall we attain without beauty?

They will ask, Why first *Infinity*, then *Hierarchy*, and only then *Heart?* Why not the reverse? But first comes the direction, then the connection, and then the means. One must not spoil this sacred recourse by doubt. Let us regard the quality of the pulse of a man in doubt and also at the hour of devoted striving. If doubt can alter the pulse and the emanations, how physically deteriorating will be its action upon the nervous system! Psychic energy is simply devoured by doubt.

After doubt, let us recall treason itself, for who is closer to doubt than the traitor? But one can overcome that darkness only by adherence to Hierarchy, to the most inevitable, like the radiance of the sun. Truly, it burns, but lacking it there is darkness!

7. The heart is the focal point, but of all it is least egocentric. Not egoism dwells in the heart, but pan-humanity. Only reason enshrouds the heart with a cobweb of egocentricity. Mercy is measured not so much by so-called good actions, the cause of which can be too varied, but by the inmost kindliness; it kindles the light which shines in the darkness. Thus, the heart is verily an international organ. If we accept light as the symbol of the aura, then its parent will be the heart. How necessary it is to learn to feel one's heart not as one's own, but as the universal one. Only through this sensation can one liberate oneself from egoism, safeguarding the individuality of accumulations. It is difficult to contain individuality with universal containment, but not vainly is the magnet of the heart connected with the Chalice. One can understand how the heart radiates a special light, which is refracted in every way by the nerve substance. For the crystal of psychic energy can be variedly tinted.

8. The purification of the heart is difficult, when the web of egoism fattens it. The fat of egoism is a bestial heritage. The pure accumulations of individuality can explain that which reason cannot even conceive. It is especially difficult to inculcate someone with that which has never entered the circle of his imagination. The heart is considered the abode of imagination. How is it possible to move when the force of imagination is lacking? But whence will it come if there be no experimentation?

EILEEN CADDY

The Earth and All Humanity Made New

First Day

The first morning I went to the sanctuary I was not as early as I should have been. Some members of the community were there before me. I sat down and felt great peace and oneness.

Then most unexpectedly the top of the record player fell down with a crash. It was such a shock it seemed to shatter every nerve in my being. I burst into tears, shaking all over.

Two persons came and assured me that all was well. I knew it was, but I was not prepared for such shock treatment. After that a great peace descended upon me.

It seemed as if I had to have this shock to open up everything in me.

Second Day

The next morning I went in to the sanctuary really early, before anyone else had arrived. As I sat down I was told to sound the OM. It was something I had not done for a very long time, but I did what I was told and sounded it five times.

Then as I sat quietly, it was as if the top of my head opened up and light was being poured into my whole being. It could not be contained, so it flowed out of my fingertips and toes.

Third Day

This morning I again got to the sanctuary early, and again I was told to sound the OM.

Again the tremendous pure light and energy poured through the opening on the top of my head and through my whole being. But this time it was so great that it flowed through every atom of my being, out and out.

Then I seemed to be suffocating. It was as if there was something deep in my being trying to be released. I could not breathe and I started to get frightened.

These words came to me: '*Let go, and go with all that is taking place.*' This is not easy to do when you are struggling for breath; but I let go, and the thing within me came up and up, and a white dove flew out of my head and flew away.

I heard the words, '*I am free, free, free.*' I felt a wonderful sense of freedom.

Fourth Day

This morning I followed the same instructions about sounding the OM. It was made clear to me that the reason for this was to raise my vibrations. I had thought it was to raise the vibrations in the sanctuary.

Again the tremendous pure light and energy poured through and out of every atom of my whole being. Then my being seemed to undergo a strange transformation. For a second I was really afraid, but the words came to me, '*Be afraid of nothing. Go with all that is taking place.*'

My being seemed to become the Earth, and it was terribly battered and bruised. Then a terrible pain went through me. It was so bad I thought something awful was happeing to me. I remembered the words, '*I am with you always.*' So I just let go completely and allowed things to happen.

When the pain became so bad that I felt I could take no more, I felt it being very gently and lovingly pushed towards the sun; and the nearer it got to the sun the less it became, until it entered right into the sun and became nothing. Yet it became everything because it was one with *all*.

And I heard the words: '*The Earth and all humanity made new.*'

Fifth Day

On the last morning I went to the sanctuary early, and I was taken aback when I found a strange young man sitting in the chair just behind mine.

I knew I had to sound the OM, but did not know what to do about it. So I leant back and put my hand on the young man's knee and just told him I was going to sound the OM and for him not to be disturbed.

After I had done this I again experienced the tremendous pure light and energy pouring through my whole being and out of every atom. I felt as if my being was a transformer for the pure light and energy to flow through and out to those who were not ready to receive the pure light directly.

Then it was as if my skin was being peeled off me. It started from the opening at the top of my head and was slowly peeled off the whole of me, right off my toes, and was cast in front of me.

As I looked at it, it appeared to be like the skin a snake had shed, and it lay there shrivelling up into nothingness.

I knew then what it was to be a being of light, and I heard the words:

'*Now go forth, and be my light, my love, my wisdom.*'

The Key to Happiness is Within

The key to your happiness and contentment lies deep within
  each one of you,
Within your own hearts and minds.

The way you start each day is very important
You can start off on the right foot or the wrong.
You can wake up with a song of joy and gratitude in your
  hearts
For the new day,
For being alive,
For the very wonder of living
And of being in tune and harmony with the rhythm of all life.

You can expect the very best from the coming day
And therefore draw it to you;
Or you can start the day with a chip on your shoulder,
Really disgruntled and out of rhythm.
It all rests with you.
You cannot blame your state of mind on anyone else.

Because yesterday was not all it should have been does not
  matter:
Yesterday is finished and gone
You cannot do anything about it.
Today is a completely different matter;
It lies before you, untouched and unblemished
It is up to you to make it the most wonderful day.
It is up to you to choose what today is going to be
And then make it so.

How do you start off each day?
Remember it is no concern of anyone else.
This is something you and you alone have to choose to bring
  about.
This is where self-discipline comes in.
Try to start the day off with inner peace and contentment,
By taking time to be still
And allowing that peace to infill and enfold you.

Take time to get into tune.
And do not rush into the day unprepared and out of harmony.
If you do
It is easy to take that state of mind into the day,

Allowing it to affect the whole of the day and all those you
  contact.

You are responsible for what today will bring.
Knowing this gives you an even greater responsibility than
  those souls who are not aware of it
And therefore know no better.
From those to whom much is given, much is expected.

I pour down My blessings and My gifts upon each one of you.
You are all fully aware of this
And therefore you are open and ready to accept them or reject
  them.
It is simply up to you.

There are many, many souls who are not aware of this,
Who go through life completely blind
To all the wonderful things there are around and within them.
They are still asleep spiritually
And in that state miss much.

The way you live,
The way you are,
May help to awaken some slumbering soul,
So always give of your very best wherever you are
Or wherever you go
And so allow yourselves to be used to help your fellowman
Not by many words,
But by the way you live.

KEN CAREY

The Starseed Transmissions

The messages came first in non-verbal form, on waves, or
pulsations, that carried the concise symbolic content of what I term
'meta-conceptual information'. Automatically, it would seem, the
nearest approximating words or phrases from the English language
would be assigned to ride, as it were, the fluctuations of the non-
verbal communications. Often it was the case that the only human
conceptual system with approximating terminology was religious.
Hence, the occasional use of 'Christian' words and phrases. It is not

to be assumed that these always imply the usual assortment of meanings that are generally associated with them. Often the meta-conceptual reality that they are used to represent goes substantially beyond the meanings suggested by their contemporary usage.

The communications that are presented in this book seem to have been transmitted neurobiologically. As I communed with these spatial intelligences, our bio-gravitational fields seemed to merge, our awarenesses blend, and my nervous system seemed to become available to them as a channel for communication. During our interviews, I would perceive reality, not only through my own perceptual mechanism, but through theirs as well. The resulting synthesis provided for a relatively accurate approximation in human language of the awareness they brought.

In the course of my work with these creatures, I understood them to be focalisations of various essential perspectives. At times I considered these extra-terrestrial, at other times, angelic. Occasionally, I thought of the entities as informational cells within a Galactic organism of some sort. Towards the end of the transmissions, other, more mythical perspectives emerge, about which I will make no comment here. But by whatever term we choose to understand these entities their purpose in sending these messages has not been to teach us of themselves, but to teach us of our own nature and purpose upon this third planet from the star we call Sun.

In your natural state of being, you have no sense of identity distinct from the Creator, except when you are engaged in a relationship. On this level of being, identity comes into focus only in the context of a relationship with some other aspect of being that has become objectified, much as my identity as an angelic messenger comes into being through my relationship with you. When such a relationship is not taking place, that particular expression of you simply does not exist; you float effortlessly in the potential of God. You are not annihilated, but all definitions of you are, and you are released from their restraining influence, allowed to expand into a state of love and perfection.

By and by, if it should happen that you are needed for a particular function, you will still be there, for your form identity is a specific cell in a specific organ of a larger being. When the next energising impulse comes, it also brings your definition and instruction. You come into the necessary degree of focus for whatever is required.

Throughout the course of your existence, you continually oscillate, like the wave function that you essentially are, in and out of focus, in and out of definition, always moving back and forth, like the pendulum on a clock or the heart of an atom, out of the unity of being with God, into a finite expression of God's infinite potential, and then back into unity once more, back and forth, back and forth. This is the natural rhythm of your existence, just as it is mine. It is the song of God, the rhythm of Life itself.

Whenever the divine impulse calls upon your services and brings you into form, you encounter other beings of infinite variety, on errands and excursions in worlds of love and light that are impossible to describe. As this happens, you experience, for the duration of your contact, both an identity and a linear time world, but in the course of your encounter, you are still aware of your unity with the Creator. You do not lose the certainty of your oneness with God. You are aware of your form identity and of the motion of time, yet you oscillate, faster than the speed of light, back and forth between your pre-manifest state, and your species-role form.

This is nothing more or less than every atom of physical creation is doing all the time. Before the Fall, you had the ability to shift the centre of your awareness from deity to identity, from form to meta-form at will. You were free, as it were, to come and go as you pleased, free to emphasise whatever aspect of yourself suited the situation. It is thus that all creatures are made.

In a healthy state, you are functioning in two realities at once. Half of the time you are focussed on your form identity, and the other half on your identity with the Totality of What Is. In the fallen state of consciousness, you find yourself trapped with your awareness on one side only, while the actual substance of your being continues to function on both sides. This is what unconsciousness is all about. You still exist in that other reality, but you are asleep. In the reality you now think to be the only reality, you are fragmented; the human race seems to be composed of a multitude of beings. In the other reality, there is only you. We are here to wake you up. There is really only one of you who needs to hear this message.

It is important that you return to a consciousness of your true self. For though you still exist in both realities, unconsciousness of your identity with the Creator is cutting off the flow of Life-giving information to the part of you that exists in form. Your existence in identity with God is the reality from which all Life springs. Focussing your attention exclusively on form greatly restricts, and eventually curtails, the flow of Life currents.

As I search your symbol storage systems for a word with which to express something of the reality in which you exist as one with your Creator, I come across the American Indian word 'nagual'. It is a term which you understand to mean 'everything that cannot be named'. This is a good word for the region of being, the region of unity. I will use this word for a moment to emphasise a point.

In the pre-Fall state of awareness, you existed in the nagual, the all, the everything, the nothing, the primal void where all exists in a state of potential. This is the Creator that surrounds Creation like the sea surrounds a fish. Out of this nagual, you are called many times to dwell, for the space of a relationship, in its opposite, the 'tonal'. The tonal is everything that can be named. It is the imaginary world of God in which all apparent differences exist. It is the playground of What Is. The tonal draws all of its sustenance from the nagual. It cannot exist apart from the nagual. While the nagual is a dynamic, yet steady state of rest, the tonal, or manifest physical universe, is continuously flashing on and off. This oscillation occurs in all things manifest, from the smallest sub-atomic particle to the greatest galaxy.

All of us, angels, humans, anything that can be named, are only in form one half of the time. The other half of the time we exist in the Totality of Being. This Totality of Being that we have been calling the nagual, has also been called God the Father. It is the Life of God the Father that animates all Creation. It is this reality that all healthy creatures oscillate back and forth to and exist in half the time. In this reality, we do not exist in time or space, for we can name these; they are both features of the manifest universe. From this spaceless, timeless state we derive all energy, blessing and nourishment. This always holds true, even for you in the fallen condition. The difference is that in the fallen state you are not aware of this process and therefore unable to participate in it consciously.

By forfeiting your ability to oscillate in consciousness between the two realities in which you dwell, you are restricted to an awareness of just the tonal, just the material, conceptual world. You still receive your nourishment from the light of the nagual, but no longer directly, only through animals, plants and minerals. You are unconscious of being and conscious only of form.

How did you lose the ability to shift your awareness from deity to identity, from form to meta-form? How did you lose God-consciousness? How did you 'fall' into the illusion of separation?

I will tell you.

It was through a simple lack of faith.

It was through a loss of confidence in the absolute perfection of the universal design.

A COURSE IN MIRACLES
TIME AND REINCARNATION

The Function of Time

And now the reason why you are afraid of this course should be apparent. For this is a course on love, because it is about you. You have been told that your function in this world is healing, and your function in Heaven is creating. The ego teaches that your function on earth is destruction, and you have no function at all in Heaven. It would thus destroy you here and bury you here, leaving you no inheritance except the dust out of which it thinks you were made. As long as it is reasonably satisfied with you, as its reasoning goes, it offers you oblivion. When it becomes overtly savage, it offers you hell.

Yet neither oblivion nor hell is as unacceptable to you as Heaven. Your definition of Heaven *is* hell and oblivion, and the real Heaven is the greatest threat you think you could experience. For hell and oblivion are ideas that you made up, and you are bent on demonstrating their reality to establish yours. If their reality is questioned, you believe that yours is. For you believe that attack is your reality, and that your destruction is the final proof that you were right.

Under the circumstances, would it not be more desirable to have been wrong, even apart from the fact that you were wrong? While it could perhaps be argued that death suggests there *was* life, no one would claim that it proves there *is* life. Even the past life that death might indicate, could only have been futile if it must come to this, and needs this to prove that it was at all. You question Heaven, but you do not question this yet. You could heal and be healed if you did question it. And even though you know not Heaven, might it not be more desirable than death? You have been as selective in your questioning as in your perception. An open mind is more honest than this.

The ego has a strange notion of time, and it is with this notion that your questioning might well begin. The ego invests heavily in the past, and in the end believes that the past is the only aspect of time that is meaningful. Remember that its emphasis on guilt enables it to ensure its continuity by making the future like the past, and thus avoiding the present. By the notion of paying for the past in the future, the past becomes the determiner of the future, making them continuous without an intervening present. For the ego regards the present only as a brief transition to the future, in which it brings the past to the future by interpreting the present in past terms.

'Now' has no meaning to the ego. The present merely reminds it of past hurts, and it reacts to the present as if it *were* the past. The ego cannot tolerate release from the past, and although the past is over, the ego tries to preserve its image by responding as if it were present. It dictates your reactions to those you meet in the present from a past reference point, obscuring their present reality. In effect, if you follow the ego's dictates you will react to your brother as though he were someone else, and this will surely prevent you from recognising him as he is. And you will receive messages from him out of your own past because, by making it real in the present, you are forbidding yourself to let it go. You thus deny yourself the message of release that every brother offers you *now*.

The shadowy figures from the past are precisely what you must escape. They are not real, and have no hold over you unless you bring them with you. They carry the spots of pain in your mind, directing you to attack in the present in retaliation for a past that is no more. And this decision is one of future pain. Unless you learn that past pain is an illusion, you are choosing a future of illusions and losing the many opportunities you could find for release in the present. The ego would preserve your nightmares, and prevent you from awakening and understanding they are past. Would you recognise a holy encounter if you are merely perceiving it as a meeting with your own past? For you would be meeting no one, and the sharing of salvation, which makes the encounter holy, would be excluded from your sight. The Holy Spirit teaches that you always meet yourself, and the encounter is holy because you are. The ego teaches that you always encounter your past, and because your dreams were not holy, the future cannot be, and the present is without meaning.

It is evident that the Holy Spirit's perception of time is the exact look. God calls you and you do not hear, for you are preoccupied with your own voice. And the vision of Christ is not in your sight, for you look upon yourself alone.

Little child, would you offer this to your Father? For if you offer it to yourself, you *are* offering it to Him. And He will not return it, for it is unworthy of you because it is unworthy of Him. Yet He would release you from it and set you free. His sane Answer tells you what you have offered yourself is not true, but His offering to you has never changed. You who know not what you do can learn what insanity is, and look beyond it. It is given you to learn how to deny insanity, and come forth from your private world in peace. You will see all that you denied in your brothers because you denied it in yourself. For you will love them, and by drawing nigh unto them you will draw them to yourself, perceiving them as witnesses to the reality you share with God. I am with them as I am with you, and we will draw them from their private worlds, for as we are united so would we unite with them. The Father welcomes all of us in gladness, and gladness is what we should offer Him. For every Son of God is given you to whom God gave himself. And it is God Whom you must offer them, to recognise His gift to you.

Vision depends on light. You cannot see in darkness. Yet in darkness, in the private world of sleep, you see in dreams although your eyes are closed. And it is here that what you see you made. But let the darkness go and all you made you will no longer see, for sight of it depends upon denying vision. Yet from denying vision it does not follow you cannot see. But this is what denial does, for by it you accept insanity, believing you can make a private world and rule your own perception. Yet for this, light must be excluded. Dreams disappear when light has come and you can see.

Do not seek vision through your eyes, for you made your way of seeing that you might see in darkness, and in this you are deceived. Beyond this darkness, and yet still within you, is the vision of Christ, Who looks on all in light. Your 'vision' comes from fear, as His from love. And He sees for you, as your witness to the real world. He is the Holy Spirit's manifestation, looking always on the real world, and calling forth its witnesses and drawing them to you. He loves what He sees within you, and He would extend it. And He will not return unto the Father until He has extended your perception even unto Him. And there perception is no more, for He has returned you to the Father with Him.

You have but two emotions, and one you made and one was given you. Each is a way of seeing, and different worlds arise from their different sights. See through the vision that is given you, for through Christ's vision He beholds Himself. And seeing what He is, He knows His Father. Beyond your darkest dreams He sees God's guiltless Son within you, shining in perfect radiance that is undimmed by your dreams. And this *you* will see as you look with Him, for His vision is His gift of love to you, given Him of the Father for you.

The Holy Spirit is the Light in which Christ stands revealed. And all who would behold Him can see Him, for they have asked for light. Nor will they see Him alone, for He is no more alone than they are. Because they saw the Son, they have risen in Him to the Father. And all this will they understand, because they looked within and saw beyond the darkness the Christ in them, and recognised Him. In the sanity of His vision they looked upon themselves with love, seeing themselves as the Holy Spirit sees them. And with this vision of the truth in them came all the beauty of the world to shine upon them.

★ ★ ★

Is Reincarnation So?

In the ultimate sense, reincarnation is impossible. There is no past or future, and the idea of birth into a body has no meaning either once or many times. Reincarnation cannot, then, be true in any real sense. Our only question should be, 'Is the concept helpful?' And that depends, of course, on what it is used for. If it is used to strengthen the recognition of the eternal nature of life, it is helpful indeed. Is any other question about it really useful in lighting up the way? Like many other beliefs, it can be bitterly misused. At least, such misuse offers preoccupation and perhaps pride in the past. At worst, it induces inertia in the present. In between, many kinds of folly are possible.

Reincarnation would not, under any circumstances, be the problem to be dealt with *now*. If it were responsible for some of the difficulties the individual faces now, his task would still be only to escape from them now. If he is laying the groundwork for a future life, he can still work out his salvation only now. To some, there may be comfort in the concept, and if it heartens them its value is self-evident. It is certain, however, that the way to salvation can be found by those who believe in reincarnation and by those who do not. The idea cannot, therefore, be regarded as essential to the curriculum. There is always some risk in seeing the present in terms of the past. There is always some good in any thought which strengthens the idea that life and the body are not the same.

For our purposes, it would not be helpful to take any definite stand on reincarnation. A teacher of God should be as helpful to those who believe in it as to those who do not. If a definite stand were required of him, it would merely limit his usefulness, as well as his own decision-making. Our course is not concerned with any concept that is not acceptable to anyone, regardless of his formal beliefs. His ego will be enough for him to cope with, and it is not the part of wisdom to add sectarian controversies to his burdens. Nor would there be an advantage in his premature acceptance of the course merely because it advocates a long-held belief of his own.

It cannot be too strongly emphasised that this course aims at a complete reversal of thought. When this is finally accomplished, issues such as the validity of reincarnation become meaningless. Until then, they are likely to be merely controversial. The teacher of God is, therefore, wise to step away from all such questions, for he has much to teach and learn apart from them. He should both learn and teach that theoretical issues but waste time, draining it away from its appointed purpose. If there are aspects to any concept or belief that will be helpful, he will be told about it. He will also be told how to use it. What more need he know?

Does this mean that the teacher of God should not believe in reincarnation himself, or discuss it with others who do? The answer is, certainly not! If he does believe in reincarnation, it would be a mistake for him to renounce the belief unless his internal Teacher so advised. And this is most unlikely. He might be advised that he is misusing the belief in some way that is detrimental to his pupil's advance or his own. Reinterpretation would then be recommended, because it is necessary. All that must be recognised, however, is that birth was not the beginning, and death is not the end. Yet even this much is not required of the beginner. He need merely accept the idea that what he knows is not necessarily all there is to learn. His journey has begun.

The emphasis of this course always remains the same – it is at this moment that complete salvation is offered you, and it is at this moment that you can accept it. This is still your one responsibility. Atonement might be equated with total escape from the past and total lack of interest in the future. Heaven is here. There is nowhere else. Heaven is now. There is no other time. No teaching that does not lead to this is of concern to God's teachers. All beliefs will point to this if properly interpreted. In this sense, it can be said that their truth lies in their usefulness. All beliefs that lead to progress should be honoured. This is the sole criterion this course requires. No more than this is necessary.

JANE ROBERTS

The Dream World

Now, if you take a physical camera with you today and snap pictures as you go about your chores, walk, or talk with your friends, then you will have preserved scenes from the day's activities.

Your film, however, will only take pictures today, *of* today. No yesterday or tomorrow will suddenly appear in the snapshots of the present. The photographer in the dream world, though, will find an entirely different situation, for there consciousness can capture scenes from entirely different times as easily as the waking photographer can take pictures of different places. Unless you realise this, some of your 'dream albums' will make no sense to you.

In waking life you experience certain events as real, and generally these are the only ones that can be captured by an ordinary photographer. The dream world, however, presents a much larger category of events. Many events may later appear as physical ones, while others just as valid will not. The dream camera, therefore, will capture probable events also.

When you awaken with a dream photograph in mind, it may appear meaningless because it does not seem to correlate with the official order of activities you recognise. You may make one particular decision in physical and waking consciousness, and that decision may bring forth certain events. Using your dream camera, you can with practice discover the history of your own psyche, and find the many probable decisions experienced in dreams. These served as a basis from which you made your physical decision. There is some finesse required as you learn to interpret the individual pictures within your dream album. This should be easy to grasp, for if you tried to understand physical life having only a group of snapshots taken at different places and in different times, then it would be rather difficult to form a clear idea of the nature of the physical world.

The same applies to dream reality, for the dreams that you recall are indeed like quick pictures snapped under varying conditions. No one picture alone tells the entire story. You should write down your description of each dream picture, therefore, and keep a continuing record, for each one provides more knowledge about the nature of your own psyche and the unknown reality in which it has its existence.

When you take a physical photograph you have to know how your camera works. You must learn how to focus, how to emphasise those particular qualities you want to record, and how to cut out distracting influences. You know the difference between shadows, for example, and solid objects. Sometimes shadows themselves make fascinating photographic studies. You might utilise them in the background, but as a photographer you would not *confuse* the shadows with, say, the solid objects. No one would deny that shadows are real, however.

Now, using an analogy only, let me explain that your thoughts and feelings also give off shadows that we will here call hallucinations. They are quite valid. They have as strong a part to play in dream reality as shadows do in the physical world. They are beautiful in themselves. They add to the entire picture. A shadow of a tree cools the ground. It affects the environment. So hallucinations alter the environment, but in a different way at another level of reality. In the dream world hallucinations are like conscious shadows. They are not passive, nor is their shape dependent upon their origin. They have their own abilities.

Physically, an oak tree may cast a rich deep shadow upon the ground. It will move, faithfully mirroring the tiniest motion of the smallest leaf, but its freedom to move will be dictated by the motion of the oak. Not one oak leaf shadow will move unless its counterpart does.

Following our analogy, in the dream world the shadow of the oak tree, once cast, would then be free to pursue its own direction. Not only that, but there would be a creative give-and-take between it and the tree that gave it birth. Anyone fully accustomed to inner reality would have no difficulty in telling the dream oak tree from its frisky shadow, however, any more than a waking photographer would have trouble distinguishing the physical oak tree from its counterpart upon the grass.

When you, a dream tourist, wander about the inner landscape with your mental camera, however, it may take a while before you are able to tell the difference between dream events and *their* shadows or hallucinations. So you may take pictures of the shadows instead of the trees, and end up with a fine composition indeed – but one that would give you somewhat of a distorted version of inner reality. So you must learn how to aim and focus your dream camera.

In your daily world objects have shadows, and thoughts or feelings do not, so in your dream travels simply remember that *there* 'objects' do not possess shadows, but thoughts and feelings do.

Since these are far more lively than ordinary shadows, and are definitely more colourful, they may be more difficult to distinguish at first. You must remember that you are wandering through a mental or psychic landscape. You can stand before the shadow of a friend in the afternoon, in waking reality, and snap your fingers all you want to, but your friend's shadow will not move one whit. It will certainly not disappear because you tell it to. In the dream world, however, any hallucination will vanish immediately as soon as you recognise it as such, and tell it to go away. It was cast originally by your own thought or feeling, and when you *withdraw* that source, then its 'shadow' is automatically gone.

A stone's physical shadow will faithfully mirror its form. In those terms, little creativity is allowed it. Far greater leeway exists, however, as a thought or feeling in the dream world casts its greater shadow out upon the landscape of the mind.

Moods obviously exist when you are dreaming as well as when you are waking. Physically the day may be brilliant, but if you are in a blue mood you may automatically close yourself off from the day's natural light, not notice it – or even use that natural beauty as counterpoint that only makes you feel *more* disconsolate. Then you might look outward at the day through your mood and see its beauty as a meaningless or even cruel façade. Your mood, therefore, will alter your perception.

The same applies in the dream state; but there, the shadows of your thoughts may be projected outward into scenes of darkest desolation. In the physical world you have mass sense data about you. Each individual helps form that exterior environment. No matter how dark your mood on any given sunny day, your individual thoughts alone will not suddenly turn the blue skies into rainy ones. You alone do not have *that* kind of control over your fellows' environment. In the dream world, however, such thoughts will definitely form your environment.

Stormy dream landscapes are on the one hand hallucinations, cast upon the inner world by your thoughts or feelings. On the other hand, they are valid representations of your inner climate at the time of any given dream. Such scenes can be changed in the dream state itself if you recognise their origin. You might choose instead to learn from such hallucinations by allowing them to continue, while realising that they are indeed shadows cast by your own mind.

If you are honest with your thoughts and feelings, then you will express them in your waking life, and they will not cast disturbing shadows in your dreams.

You may be afraid that a beloved child or mate will die suddenly, yet you may never want to admit such a fear. The feeling itself may be generated because of your own doubts about *yourself*, however. You may be depending upon another such person too strongly, trying to live your own life secondhandedly through the life of another. Your own fear, admitted, would lead you to other feelings behind it, and to a greater understanding of yourself.

Unencountered in waking life, however, the fear might cast its dim shadow, so that you dream of your child's death, or of the death of another close to you. The dream experience would be cast into the dream landscape and encountered there. Period.

If you remembered such a dream, therefore, you might think that it was precognitive, and that the event would become physical. Instead, the whole portent of the dream event would be an educational one, bringing your fear into clear focus. In such cases you should think of the dire dream situation as a shadow, and look for its source within your mind.

Shadows can be pleasant and luxurious, and on a hot, sunny day you are certainly aware of their beneficial nature. So some dream hallucinations are beautiful, comforting, refreshing. They can bring great peace and be sought after for themselves. You may believe that God exists as a kindly father, or you might personify him as Christ or Buddha. In your dreams you might then encounter such personages. They are quite valid, but they are also hallucinations cast by your own thoughts and feelings. Dreams of Heaven and Hell alike fall into the same category, *in those terms*, as hallucinations.

Now. The physical shadow of a tree bears witness to the existence of a tree, even if you see only the shadow; so your hallucinations appearing in dreams also bear witness to their origin, and give testimony to a valid 'objective' dream object that is as 'solid' in *that* reality as the tree is in your world.

In physical reality there is a time lag that exists between the conception of an idea, say, and its materialisation. Beside that, other conditions operate that can slow down an idea's physical actualisation, or even impede it altogether. If not physically expressed, the thought will be actualised in another reality. An idea must have certain characteristics, for example, that agree with physical assumptions before it turns into a recognisable event. It must appear within your time context.

In the dream world, however, each feeling or idea can be immediately expressed and experienced. The physical world has buildings in it that you manufacture – that is, they do not spring up naturally from the ground itself. In the same way, your thoughts are 'manufactured products' in the dream world. They are a part of the environment and appear within its reality, though they change shape and form constantly, as physically manufactured objects do not.

The Earth has its own natural given data, however, and you must use this body of material to form all of your manufactured products. The dream world also possesses its own natural environment. You form your dreams from it, and use its natural products to manufacture dream images. Few view this natural inner environment, however . . . . When you look into a mirror you see your reflection, but it does not talk back to you. In the dream state you are looking into the mirror of the psyche, so to speak, and seeing the reflections of your own thoughts, fears, and desires.

Here, however, the 'reflections' do indeed speak, and take their own form. In a certain sense they are freewheeling, in that they have their own kind of reality. In the dream state your joys and fears talk back to you, perform, and act out the role in which you have cast them.

3

Healing

Richard Moss
Jane Roberts
Caroline Myss
Alice A. Bailey
Alan Young
Louise L. Hay
Shakti Gawain
Stephen Levine

Introduction

We are born, most of us, with these beautiful little bodies – but almost immediately things can go wrong with them. These illnesses and diseases can be brief and only uncomfortable. They can also be tragic, painful and fatal. Twentieth-century medicine has achieved miracles in relieving suffering and tending the physical body, but it misses understanding a whole dimension of this reality.

The physical body reflects the total inner state of a human being and her or his relationship with the world. All illness, therefore, reflects this relationship between the individual and her inner and outer environment. An individual's total state anchors in and manifests through the physical body. To cure or to attempt to cure illness, therefore, without also seeking to understand the total state is to miss the authentic happening and purpose. If we do not look for the lesson and the opportunity for release and transformation in our illnesses, then we are hardly conscious, barely aware. Years ago I lay in bed for several months with severe hepatitis-B wondering if I was going to live or die, frightened and then deeply reassured by a sequence of near-death, out of the body experiences; it then took me almost two years to recover. In the crisis of the illness and then the long recovery, I saw my neurotic urgency, my speeding ambitions, my materialistic fixations. The illness was a blessing.

In this section on healing, because of the shortage of space, it seemed appropriate not to try and cover the many forms of alternative healing that have been resurfacing over the last decades. Instead I have focussed on the spiritual and esoteric dynamic of healing.

This section opens with an account of a dramatic transformation described by the medical doctor, now a teaching mystic, Richard Moss. It is followed by a second contribution by Jane Roberts' Seth which introduces the whole notion of cellular awareness. Caroline Myss, today's most accurate intuitive diagnostician, describes how she understands illness and I have also included two of her general interpretations of specific maladies. There is then a second reading from Alice Bailey in which Djwhal Khul demonstrates his wide and expansive understanding; this is taken from *Esoteric Healing*, an indispensable text for all healers which also contains the most clarifying description of the death process currently available.

Alan Young follows with a description, in a style more devotional and spiritualistic, of the different techniques used by spiritual healers. This is echoed by extracts from Louise Hay and Shakti Gawain describing some of their own approaches. Louise Hay has been instrumental in popularising the use of affirmations and Shakti Gawain has been very influential in popularising the use of creative visualisation, both for healing others and for self-healing.

The section concludes with a beautiful passage from Stephen Levine which speaks of life and death.

RICHARD MOSS

An Invitation to Radical Change

It was the second day of the conference. For several hours Laura had been singing a childhood hymn, repeating it over and over. Suddenly the quality of her singing changed. She felt as though she were no longer singing. She *was* the song. She found herself lifted to her feet, her arms raised towards the sky, her head arched upwards. She said her hands did not end at her fingertips, but continued into the air and sky. The air and sky were alive, and she and they were the same. Her feet seemed to disappear into the earth. Earth, feet, body, arms, sky, song, singer – all were one living being. Laura did not consider what was happening, it just took her. She was the experience.

The next day her terminal liver cancer was gone. The grapefruit sized bowel metastasis that she had supported with her hand was gone. Three days later she realised that for the first time in thirty-eight years she hadn't taken her daily insulin injections. In the ensuing weeks, all the secondary complications of her diabetes and cancer – kidney failure, fluid in her lungs, tumour-ridden lymph nodes, partial blindness, loss of sensation in her hands and feet, addiction to pain medication – healed. Even a few recently broken toes were completely mended within days. She was radiant; a palpable presence poured from her body like a gentle flame and the whole understanding of her life was radically transformed.

Radical means 'root', the support or foundation, the fundamental, the basis or basic principle. Radical aliveness invites and challenges us to go to the root of aliveness, to the place from which our very sense of being emerges. It is a state that transcends any concept of ourselves. Laura spontaneously awakened to what might be called her fundamental nature, a condition in which her cancer and diabetes were not the final reality. For most of her life she had identified herself as diseased, and in recent years as a person dying of cancer. Suddenly she saw that this perception was a fiction. All her urgent efforts and her desire for health were outgrowths of that fiction. The woman who was dying was not who she really was. The woman who wanted to live was equally unreal. For a little while she experienced herself as pure Consciousness, and that realisation transformed her.

★ ★ ★

Laura did not simply access a higher energy by the release of a relative level of identity such as 'I can't sing, I'm afraid, I am too ordinary to experience a heightened state, I have to do it, I need to try harder,' or some such. These structures are powerful limiters of one's aliveness, and overcoming them forms the first hurdle in the singing. Most people pass through this and then begin to access a depth of creativity that is frequently astonishing. But here the fundamental energetic structure has been stretched to hold new aliveness, it has not been transcended. With Laura, it was precisely this self-transcendence that occurred. Her whole conscious identity released. She realised that everything she had known and lived and believed up to that moment was not real. Her personal identity was not real; her cancer was not real. There was a sense of witnessing; at no point did she become lost in the experience. But none of the structures of egoic mind carried the weight of reality while she was in this expanded state. She was Reality, Perfect Wholeness and Peace, but her old structures, which she could recall like phantoms, were not. At best they were veils, curtains of relative unconsciousness. It was the relative unconsciousness of her life that she had mistaken for the real. Immediately, she understood that nothing mattered as it had before. She was free in a way that she could never have dreamt possible.

Her group sensed that something astonishing was happening; the four of them had been there for hours, and now it was as though time stood still. The whole space had taken on a feeling of holiness.

They found themselves being profoundly nourished by the energy that poured from her. Wisdom guided them and no one interrupted Laura until the process subsided of itself.

Laura had awakened; she became and remains a person vibrating at a new note. Afterwards, she attempted to describe what had happened for the rest of the conference participants. She realised that she was an entirely new person, but didn't understand how or in what ways. It was as though she knew herself for the first time. She realised that she had ceased to be fully alive as early as age two when she started developing her sense of identity, the sense of being 'Laura'. She could look back and actually see how the development of the egoic self began to imprison her aliveness. It was then she began to die. Her report is on tape and as one listens to her voice, there is a powerful induction as though one were listening to a mystic. In fact, Laura was describing aspects of realisation fundamental to all mystical development, although in her outer life she had no such background. Her insight was awesome because it was spontaneous, out of the immediacy of her transformation. She did not speak from ideas or memory; her sharing was not intellectual, not some personalised transcription of what she had learned from others. As she spoke, her words were like an open door to her soul, to dimensions beyond her personal consciousness. This depth became available to her simultaneously with the realisation of oneness with existence.

JANE ROBERTS

Cellular Awareness

As most of you know, the atoms that compose your cells, as well as the cells themselves, constantly die and are replaced. The stuff of the internal organs changes and yet they always retain their form. Their identity is intact.

So is your own identity secure in the midst of all these births and deaths of which your conscious self is unaware. The memory of all of its experiences is retained. Each cell remembers its past though all of its parts have been and are being continually replaced.

As your cells have their own memories, so the conscious mind has a more overt kind of memory. Your conscious thoughts act as triggers, bringing both kinds of memory into activation. Within your physical being then each joyful, expanding, traumatic and tragic 'past' event lies indelibly written. In your terms this is your working material, the memory of your physical being since the time of its *conception* in corporeal form. There are [in your memory] the most complex organisations and associative frameworks, that exist both in the depths of your cellular structure and in the highest reaches of your conscious activity.

Earlier I compared your thoughts to viruses. Think of them now as living electromagnetic cells, differing from the physical cells in your body only in the nature of their materialisation. Your thoughts direct the overall functioning of your body's cells, even though you do not consciously know how those cells operate. That work *is* unconscious.

Each physical cell is in its way a miniature brain, with memory of all of its personal experiences and of its relationship with other cells, and with the body as a whole. In your terms this means that each cell operates with an innate picture of the body's entire history – past, present, and future.

Now this picture is ever-changing and mobile. An alteration in just one cell is instantly noted by the body consciousness (the combined consciousnesses of the cells), and the future effect perceived. This information is used together with all other data from the body, and a prediction made.

This body prediction is then assessed, and on more levels than it is possible for me to explain. Briefly, the picture is 'shown' in the invisible arena where flesh and spirit meet. This arena is not a place, of course, but an inner state of gestalt consciousness. The state is brought about through certain interactions that occur deep within the body. Magnetic structures are formed. They are created on a physical level through certain activations of the nerves in which the normal patterns are jumped, so to speak, and images are formed. The nerves and the cellular structures of their tips take pictures. These are all assembled and used to form the larger picture of the body's condition.

These are not images as you think of them but highly coded information, electromagnetically imprinted, that would not appear as images to the physical eye. In any case they cannot be perceived except by the body. But this procedure is so far superior to anything that you know that the body, therefore, actually takes precognitive pictures of its future condition – as if the body situation at the time were projected into the future.

This predictive picture is then set against two models. First it is checked against the body's ideal standard of health in its individual case – its own greatest fulfilment. Then it is checked against the image of the body sent to it by the conscious self. Correlations are made instantaneously. In an organisational framework that would certainly be envied by the most advanced technological concern, communications spring back and forth with great rapidity. The body makes whatever changes are necessary in order to bring the two images in line with the present corporeal condition.

There is a built-in equilibrium to some extent. The body is so responsive to conscious thought that it has its own innate system of self-preservation and its own guiding image of fulfilment.

Say that at the age of four you were severely injured. An accident took place at 3.20 in the afternoon. It was snowing. Your mother was roasting a turkey. Imagine that you burned a hand severely. Though all of the tissue in that hand has often been completely replaced by the time you are twenty-seven, for example, the identity within each of those present cells remembers that injury.

There were countless other events that happened to you on different afternoons at the same hour, both before and after that one. The cells within your hand contain within themselves memories your conscious mind would be dazzled to behold. Yet remember that the cells in your twenty-seven-year-old hand are in no physical way the same cells that experienced any of those events. In some underground of sensation, however, the buried evidences of stimuli and reaction experienced during those numberless 'past' afternoons still exist. Some of those memories will certainly be played back, to affect what you think of as your current experience at twenty-seven. Your conscious thoughts and habits regulate which of them will intermix into the maelstrom of the present.

You consciously give the signals for reaction. It is not the other way around. Past events do not intrude in this manner unless they are beckoned by the conscious expectations and thoughts that exist within your mind. Those unconscious memories will be activated according to your current beliefs. You will be replenished and renewed as your thoughts motivate joyful body sensations and physical events, or you will be depressed as you bring into your awareness unpleasant past body happenings.

At times of course both can be highly beneficial. A conscious realisation of danger, for example, will call up all information dealing with similar situations, so that the body can deal with it at once from the vast bank of its living memory. But constant unpleasant thoughts put the body into a state of turmoil that is 'unrealistic', and, in turn, force it to reactivate such old patterns.

The living flesh is quite aware of certain facts that escape you on a conscious level. It knows it dies and is reborn constantly, and yet retains itself. I use the terms 'dies' and 'is reborn' because you make sense of them, but the body does not. The body, while being always itself, comes and goes. It does not feel less or diminished when a cell dies, for it is also in the process of forming a new one.

For a moment, think of your body as one large cell in the moment of its being. You, the larger self, have many bodies, each turning into the other as one dies and is reborn; yet You maintain your identity and your memory even as the smallest cell in your present body does.

This is merely an analogy but it will explain your body's concept of itself; for as a whole it knows it 'dies', as now its portions do, but is also aware of its 'future' transformation. Within this framework it protects and maintains its own stability and survival.

At one level of your being there is a common ground where body consciousness merges with that higher consciousness from which your own identity springs. This is the ground of your being where soul and flesh meet, both in time and out of it.

CAROLINE MYSS

Redefining the Healing Process

What does it mean to heal? You might think the answer is obvious, but it is not.

Within the traditional medical model, healing means, quite simply, treating a disease until the disease is cured. Cured means successfully treated with drugs and/or surgery until the symptoms disappear.

The holistic model of health has introduced the study of the relationship among the mind, the body and the spirit. Recognising the influence of emotional, psychological and spiritual factors is redefining the nature of the healing process. Studies in this area strongly indicate that the healing process must be expanded to include giving much-needed attention to the inner life of the human being.

This shift in perspective is also broadening our understanding of what qualifies as legitimate illness. For example, alcoholism is now recognised as an illness, whereas previously it was thought to be a 'habit' or a lack of willpower. Likewise, depression and other sufferings of the mind and the spirit are gaining ground in terms of being accepted as forms of treatable illness.

Simultaneously, the holistic movement has approached the dying process with compassion and openness, thereby including the last stages of life as a vital part of an individual's healing journey. Within the traditional medical world, the dying process is viewed as the failure to heal, thereby implying that nothing of genuine value can occur within the human being once death is imminent. Yet what has become apparent to the many therapists who work with dying people is that the last stages of life provide opportunities for completion of a person's unfinished business. The experience of shedding troubled emotions and completing long-awaited conversations with family and friends brings to an appropriate conclusion all of the energies a person has set in motion during the course of a lifetime. This is a deeply healing process that allows the necessary moment of letting go to occur without residual guilt or angry emotions being retained by family members or friends. Though grief is present, it is not grief mixed with the crippling feelings that come from not having the final opportunity to say what is in your heart.

The impact of the holistic point of view, which includes the dying process as a healing journey, is redefining what it means to heal, and it illustrates time and again that treatment of the physical body alone is insufficient. Equally significant, the study of why and how we become ill is re-sensitising us to our own emotional nature. The study of why we break down is also the study of what we need to remain healthy. Many schools of psychotherapy, while they may differ in their particular approaches, nevertheless share one strong premise: that the human being is a deeply sensitive system of emotional, psychological and spiritual needs.

A chemical cure does not exist for emotional injuries. Nor can surgery remove painful memories of being abused as a child. The 'stuff' that disease is made of requires much more complex treatment than can be given through surgery or drugs alone. It requires, for example, the process of transforming inner grief into lessons that empower rather than destroy the individual.

There are several considerations to the healing journey that have been introduced through holistic thinking. Each one contributes valuable insights into what it means to heal and how an individual engages the full use of his or her inner resources to assist in that profound journey.

We are presenting the holistic concepts alongside the perceptions held by the traditional medical model in order to illustrate the natural transformation of thought that is taking place through the advent of the holistic paradigm.

Cure Versus Transformation

Consider that the word 'cure' implies that something external can be taken as treatment for something that is happening internally to the human body. In terms of infections and various viruses, this is accurate. But what happens to this system of treatment when emotional and psychological stress is introduced into the picture? Admittedly, there are drugs used for the treatment of depression, anxiety and stress, but do these drugs cure these illnesses or do they simply help the person to function until the symptoms abate? Drugs are effective in treating *reactions* to stress, but not the core of the stress itself.

The holistic model of treatment has brought to light the need to help a person heal the stresses of his or her life as an integral part of healing the body. In order to do this, a person must be willing and able to look at all of the pieces of his or her life, including emotional injuries (both given and received), unfulfilled emotional needs, disappointments in relationships, broken promises, unfulfilled ambitions, disappointments in oneself, and other patterns of unfinished business that form a person's inner grief.

In accepting the necessity of doing this quality of inner work, you are acknowledging the need to change or transform the areas of your life that are not conducive to regaining your health. As you do this, you alter the relationship you have with your disease. Rather than considering 'disease' as a condition that has spontaneously manifested in the midst of your life, you are able to think of it as a 'messenger'. The transformational process, then, becomes the experience of understanding the particular messages that the experience of illness brings into your life and the challenge to act on those messages in ways that are productive to your health. Inevitably, the messages will direct you towards re-evaluating who you think you are and what you realise you can live with versus a much more authentic appraisal of your real needs and considerations.

To put this description in the language of transformation, disease is unconscious change (or choice by default) manifesting in a person's body because the individual either (1) lacks the courage to look clearly at what is not working in his or her life; (2) does not believe that stress affects the body; or (3) lacks the skills of introspection and self-examination that allow the analysis, and thus the dissolution, of stress to take place through positive channels.

Transformation is the process of becoming conscious of the many levels on which we make our choices and learning to recognise what it is we create as a result of our choices. Choosing, therefore, becomes a conscious act rather than the unconscious activity of reacting to our fears and stresses. It is this step-by-step, self-study process that allows a person to realise that the choice to remain filled with anger, for example, is *exactly* the type of invisible, subtle choice that produces illness.

What is it that occurs within the process of transformation that makes it so healing? Self-analysis is certainly a part of the answer, but it is the goal of analysis that is healing and that goal is *completion* and *validation*.

Completion is the opportunity to understand and bring to a close – literally and figuratively – the open wounds of your life. Completion is the counterpart to creation: We want to see the energy we set in motion in our lives come full circle. We want to see our children grow up, we want to understand why some of our relationships failed, we want to see our businesses flourish, we want to see our creativity come into physical manifestation. And we want to see the seeds of our lives produce a harvest, even if we reap that harvest long after we first planted the seeds.

Wherever there is incompletion in our lives, there are strings attached, though these attachments may be unconscious. We remain tied through the invisible strings of our creative energy to all that we have set into motion, like hundreds of umbilical cords attached to our energy systems.

This is, perhaps, the dynamic that is responsible for causing us to recreate certain situations in our lives until we learn the lesson and can finally break the pattern by applying conscious choice. Consciously, or unconsciously, we are bound to what we create. Even if what we create is painful, the desire to see our creations through to completion is stronger than our capacity to walk away from them.

Once we become aware that we are repeating the same struggles, we can position ourselves to appreciate that *different choices produce different results*. Those who marry alcoholics will, more likely than not, continue to be involved with alcoholics until they look inside themselves to see what it is about their needs and beliefs that draws that type of imbalanced relationship into their lives. Perhaps it is a need to rescue someone, or perhaps it is the only way they have experienced being needed or loved. In either case, once awareness is brought to bear upon the pattern, the pattern can be released and a more fulfilling relationship can then be created.

Validation is the deeply healing process of sharing your pain with another, not so that the other person can make it go away, but because no one can bear the inner weight of suffering alone. Somehow, if only one other person is aware of the grief we carry, the burden becomes easier to bear because the suffering no longer seems meaningless and unacknowledged.

Suffering is an integral part of the human condition. The need to share one's suffering with another, to have a witness, so to speak, is deeply connected to the transformational journey and makes a necessary distinction between ego pain and the deeper sufferings of the soul.

Ego Pain Versus Soul Pain

Ego pain and soul pain both produce the experience of suffering. There is, however, a significant and noteworthy difference between these two dimensions of suffering. Ego pain is the result of fighting against changes that need to take place, not only in oneself but within one's physical environment as well. Soul pain comes from the process of undergoing the necessary changes that occur within one's life and require acceptance or release.

The challenge that each of us is confronted with during our periods of suffering is whether to allow pain to remain at the ego level or whether we can transform our ego pain into a process that strengthens our soul. While both ego and soul pain may seem to be somewhat indistinguishable in terms of how you feel, there is a qualitative difference in terms of how able you are to appreciate the purpose or necessary reason for the experience.

There is a quality of pain, for instance, that is very much associated with injuries to the ego. The needs of the ego are simply stated: attention, praise, admiration, acceptance, control, power, sex and money. The only variable is the degree to which a person needs this type of feedback and the extent to which a person will go to get this level of reinforcement.

Whenever this type of feedback is denied, or whenever one is on the receiving end of negative feedback, the ego hurts. The ego will go to great lengths to get its needs met, while at the same time denying any actual ego involvement. The need to impress others, the need for 'centre stage', the need to feel good about one's masculinity or femininity are all ego-based.

Certainly when we hunger for this feedback and it is not forthcoming, we hurt. And this hurt can lead to any level of negativity, either self-inflicted or directed towards others. Emotional rejection can lead to an emotional 'getting even'. Or it can lead to self-rejection and feelings of unworthiness. Ego pain can also lead to an embittered and self-pitying personality.

A person who is in the midst of an ego crisis is also in the midst of an opportunity to transform that ego pain into a process that leads to the deepening of personal awareness and insight. This is done by becoming open to the learning that is present in the situation. Just this one shift in perspective can begin the healing process and give the pain a direction in which to move rather than remain internalised for months, or even years. Choosing to view an ego crisis as a learning experience is choosing to involve one's soul in the healing process, thereby giving the crisis a purpose and meaning, one that cannot be realised if the pain remains at the ego level.

Soul pain is the processing of that which we cannot change, avoid or otherwise remove from our lives. While much about ego pain is optional (i.e. there are many ego choices we make that we *know* are not wise, but nonetheless we choose them), soul suffering is not optional. It has a purpose and a depth to it that is not present in ego pain.

Suffering that involves the soul teaches us about ourselves – our dark sides, our inner strengths and our capacity to rise beyond our previous limitations. This level of suffering is a 'shedding' process, a letting go of various parts of ourselves that interfere with the development of our inner selves.

The role that this level of suffering plays within the human experience relates directly to the higher, or spiritual, purpose of life itself. Consider these questions: Why does life continually present us with challenges? Are we meant to move towards the state of enlightenment? Why are 'learning' and 'suffering' such integral parts of the human experience? Indeed, what is the purpose of the experience of life?

These questions have been answered metaphysically, existentially and spiritually for centuries. Regardless of how an individual forms his or her personal conclusions about the purpose of life, the natural intelligence of Life itself flows in a cycle that continually produces challenging experiences that cause us to question our understanding of 'reality' and what part we, as individuals, serve within this vast expanse of life.

The conclusions each person draws in response to his or her critical crossroads are completely subjective. My experience has been that those individuals who reach for spiritual insight during these periods emerge more deeply conscious of the possibility that Life is a spiritual journey and that the contributions we make towards our own growth and that of others is of tremendous importance.

★ ★ ★

Energy Analysis of Stroke

A stroke causes a sudden loss of brain function. The question I focus on when doing a health evaluation is, 'What would cause an individual to shut off the activity of the brain?'

As in most illnesses, a warehouse of negative energy is amassed prior to the dysfunction physically manifesting. The specific patterns of stressful behaviour I have noted that contribute to the creation of a stroke relate to having a dominant and often obsessive need to control one's physical environment. This pattern develops in a person who finds it difficult, if not impossible, to trust the intention or activities of others. The marked lack of trust is a very significant factor in the creation of a stroke.

Because lack of trust is a major issue, certain fears become a compulsion. Specifically, the individual continually fears for his or her own financial and material security and well-being. Sometimes this is a conscious fear and sometimes it is unconscious. This fear has strong associations with feelings of vulnerability and the belief that the external world is unsafe. Consequently, it becomes crucial to be the person in charge of all decisions and all activity in one's work and living environment.

These patterns of fear and compulsive feelings of distrust cause a specific physical reaction in the body. As the energy of these negative stresses accumulates, it triggers charged emotional responses in the form of frustration, rage, anger and, of course, fear. The individual is challenged to remain 'in control' while these high-voltage currents of electrical energy are racing through the body, like the explosive energy of a geyser waiting to burst through the Earth. This energy can be temporarily released in small dosages through several conventional channels, such as emotional outbursts, re-establishing control in the business or home environment, alcohol or other means that bring temporary relief.

The reality is that what this type of temperament requires is behavioural modification that allows the individual to cope with daily stress effectively rather than internalising it and allowing emotional explosions (or implosions) to act as release mechanisms.

When a stroke does occur, it is an indication that the individual can no longer process the effects brought about by the particularly threatening or overwhelming stimuli from the outside world. The energy causes an eruption to occur and the brain shuts down. It is important to note that while the emotional stresses that create a stroke in people are remarkably similar, this similarity does not transfer to personality types. In other words, if one were to apply the description of stroke characteristics to human personalities, one would assume that only Type-A extroverts are stroke candidates. That is inaccurate. Internal stress of this nature is just as likely to be found in a mild-tempered individual as it is in a person with an explosive personality. It is easy to make false assumptions about these gentler individuals simply because they tend to internalise rather than externalise their stresses.

★ ★ ★

Energy Analysis of Osteoarthritis

All forms of arthritis are created in response to feelings of irritation, frustration and anger. In general, the causes generating these underlying, irritable feelings have to do with issues of control. These range from minor power confrontations that occur in daily life to major situations in which a person becomes obsessed with controlling another person or consumed in resentment over being controlled. How serious the condition is depends upon how intense and/or chronic the stressful emotions are inside of a person.

Osteoarthritis is rooted in irritation and frustration, like small deposits of 'energy grit' that get caught in the joints of the body. Interestingly, the specific joints that are affected are strong symbolic indications of the source of the stress. It is impossible, of course, to get through one's life, start to finish, without experiencing irritating encounters with other people. When these irritating experiences accumulate, however, the 'grit' in the joints builds to the point of pain and swelling.

ALICE A. BAILEY

Esoteric Healing

All initiates of the Ageless Wisdom are necessarily healers, though all may not heal the physical body. The reason for this is that all souls that have achieved any measure of true liberation are transmitters of spiritual energy. This automatically affects some aspect of the mechanism which is used by the souls they contact. When I employ the word 'mechanism' in these instructions I refer to different aspects of the instrument, the body or form nature, through which all souls seek manifestation. I refer, therefore, to:

1. *The dense physical body*, which is the sum total of all the organisms which compose it; these possess the varying functions which enable the soul to express itself on the physical or objective plane as part of a greater and more inclusive organism. The physical body is the response apparatus of the indwelling spiritual man and serves to put that spiritual entity *en rapport* with the response apparatus of the planetary Logos, the Life in which we live and move and have our being.

2. *The etheric body*, which has one main objective. This is to vitalise and energise the physical body and thus integrate it into the energy body of the Earth and of the solar system. It is a web of energy streams, of lines of force and of light. It constitutes part of the vast network of energies which underlies all forms whether great or small (microcosmic or macrocosmic). Along these lines of energy the cosmic forces flow, as the blood flows through the veins and arteries. This constant, individual – human, planetary and solar – circulation of life-forces through the etheric bodies of all forms is the basis of all manifested life, and the expression of the essential non-separateness of all life.

3. *The astral or desire body* (sometimes called the emotional body) is the effect of the interplay of desire and of sentient response upon the self at the centre, and the resultant effect – in that body – is experienced as emotion and as pain and pleasure and the other pairs of opposites. In these two bodies, the etheric and astral

bodies, ninety per cent of the causes of physical disease and troubles is to be found.

4. *The mental body*, or that much of the chitta or mind stuff which an individual human unit can use and impress, constitutes the fourth of the series of mechanisms at the disposal of the soul. At the same time let it not be forgotten that these four constitute one mechanism. Five per cent of all modern disease originates in this body or state of consciousness, and here I wish to enunciate the truth that the constant reiteration by certain schools of healers that the mind is the cause of all sickness is not as yet a fact. A million years hence, when the focus of human attention has shifted from the emotional nature to the mind, and when men are essentially mental as today they are essentially emotional, *then* the causes of disease must be sought in the mind realm. They are today to be found (except in a few rare cases) in lack of vitality or in too much stimulation, and in the realm of feeling, of desires (thwarted or over-indulged) and in the moods, suppressions, or expressions of the deep-seated longings, irritations, secret delights and the many hidden impulses which emanate from the desire life of the subject.

★　★　★

The basic law underlying all occult healing may be stated to be as follows:

Law I

All disease is the result of inhibited soul life, and that is true of all forms in all kingdoms. The art of the healer consists in releasing the soul, so that its life can flow through the aggregate of organisms which constitute any particular form.

It is interesting to note that the attempt of the scientist to release the energy of the atom is of the same general nature as the work of the esotericist when he endeavours to release the energy of the soul. In this release the nature of the true art of healing is hidden.

★　★　★

What is disease? I suggest the following:

1. All disease is disharmony and lack of alignment and control.
   (a) Disease is found in all the four kingdoms in nature.
   (b) Disease is purificatory in effect.
   (c) Definite methods of healing are peculiar to humanity, and mental in origin.

2. Disease is a fact in nature.
   (a) Antagonism to disease simply energises it.
   (b) Disease is not the result of wrong human thought.
3. Disease is a process of liberation and the enemy of that which is static.
4. The law of cause and effect governs disease as it governs all else in manifestation.

Healing is brought about in three ways:

1. Through the application of the methods of the many schools of medicine and surgery, and allied groups.
2. Through the use of psychology.
3. Through the activity of the soul.

The major causes of disease are three in number: they are psychological in nature; they are inherited through group contact; and they are karmic. . . .

The emotional causes of disease and the mental attitudes which produce physical discomfort are at this particular time those which are the most prevalent. When they are persisted in over a long period of time, and are carried over from life to life, they cause the more violent aspects of the conditions referred to above, and from them serious and destructive diseases can emerge, necessitating, for instance, the removal of the gall bladder or those operations incident to the appearance of chronic gastric ulcers. Other diseases grow from a constant pandering to the desire nature, though sexual diseases come under another category. It can be seen from the above how desirable it is that the true healer should combine in himself, not only a measure of esoteric knowledge, but – until he is an initiate – something of psychology, something of the work of a magnetic healer, and also be a trained medical man or surgeon.

Much of the healing now done is worse than useless, because the three above-mentioned conditions are lacking. Most doctors, especially those who are called general practitioners, are good psychologists and they have also a sound knowledge of symptoms and of anatomy and of curative measures which are usually lacking in the average metaphysical healer. But they are entirely ignorant of one great field of knowledge – that concerning the energies which meet and war within the human frame and of the potencies which can be set in motion if certain esoteric truths are admitted in place. Until they work with the etheric body and study the science of the centres, they can make little further progress. The esoteric healer knows much about the inner forces and energies and has some understanding of the basic causes of the exoteric diseases, but his ignorance of man's mechanism is deplorable, and he fails to realise two things:

> First, that disease is sometimes the working out into manifestation of undesirable subjective conditions. These, when externalised and brought to the surface of the human body, can then be known, dealt with and eliminated. It is well to remember also that sometimes this working out and eliminating may well bring about the death of that particular body. But the soul goes on. One short life counts for very little in the long cycle of the soul, and it is counted well worthwhile if a period of ill health (even if it eventuates in death) brings about the clearing away of wrong emotional and mental conditions.
>
> Second, disease is sometimes incident upon and part of the process of the withdrawal of the soul from its habitation. This we call death, and it can come quickly and unexpectedly when the soul withdraws with suddenness from its body. Or death can spread itself over a long period of time, and the soul may take several months or years for its slow and gradual emergence from the body, with the body dying by inches all the time.

There is not sufficient knowledge yet among healers to enable them to deal with wisdom in these matters. We might therefore conclude that:

> 1. Disease is a purificatory process, carried out in order to produce a purer expression, life aroma, influence and soul usefulness. When this is the case, a cure is possible.
> 2. Disease can be a gradual and slow process of dying and of thus releasing the soul. A cure then will not be possible, though palliative and ameliorative measures are needed and should most certainly be used. The length of the life can be prolonged, but a permanent and final cure is out of the question. This the average mental healer fails to realise. They make a horror out of death, whereas death is a beneficent friend.
> 3. Disease can be the sudden and final call to the body to relinquish the soul and set it free for other service.

In all these cases everything possible should be done from the standpoint of modern medical and surgical science and the allied sciences of which there are today so many. Much too can be done from the angle of mental and spiritual healing, aided by the science of psychology. Some day there must come cooperation in these various fields and a synthesising of their efforts.

ALAN YOUNG

Techniques Used by Spiritual Healers

Spiritual healers use various techniques which are mental aids for the healer and the one desiring to be healed. The methods themselves have no healing power; they are simply procedures which assist the healer in attuning to the Divine power, thus enabling the body to heal itself. In those cases where the healer's hands are used there is also a psychological assurance to the sick person that something is being done. This is particularly true when that person feels the healing energy that is coming through the healer's hands as warmth, tingling or pressure. This makes it easier for some people to believe that a healing will result. Jesus touched the sick person in a number of cases, probably for the same reason. Sometimes if there is a blockage to the flow of the energy within the subject's body the sense may be one of temporary pain.

Some of the techniques in use today are:

1. The healer prays to God for the sick person.
2. The healer endeavours to raise his consciousness to the Divine, and then mentally to merge his essence with the essence of the sick one, affirming the unity and perfection of all three. A healing is not requested or pictured but it frequently occurs.
3. The healer centres his thoughts and energy into the very centre of his being near his heart, and then mentally projects unconditional love-energy to the one in need, leaving the latter to use it in any way that his Higher Self chooses.
4. The healer visualises a ray of white light and love going from his heart centre to the person he has been asked to help. He pictures it like a laser beam which is not dissipated even when it is projected for thousands of miles. (*Note*: a real laser beam projected from the Earth to the moon spreads out less than two miles.)

The above methods are used in what is generally called non-contact Healing. Whether the one in need is thousands of miles away, or sitting in the same room, there is no attempt at any overt action by the healer. When the sick person is not even in the same room this method is also called Absent Healing. Many consider this to be the highest form of Spiritual Healing because no physical contact is involved, neither by hand, eye or voice, and frequently the one seeking help is unknown to the healer. Since there is no space or time in the spirit world, Absent Healing can be just as fast and effective as those methods involving the physical presence of both parties.

If the ability to channel healing power in this way is adequately developed it saves a great deal of time and thus enables the healer to help many more people. It also saves a lot of travel expense, and permits the healer to reach people who are too sick to travel, or too far away to make a visit economically feasible. Some Absent Healers find it helpful to hold a letter from, or a photograph of, the one in need in their hands at the time they channel the healing power to that person. The one disadvantage of Absent Healing is that it seems less likely to uncover the cause of the disease, and therefore the cure is not as likely to be permanent.

In contrast to all of this is Contact healing where both the healer and the sick person are present in the same place, and the healer's hands are involved in some way. Usually this is by the 'laying-on-of-hands' which is a very old method used by the Chinese, Egyptians and Greeks long before it was referred to in the New Testament as a method used by the Christians. It has been used by some priests, ministers and church elders ever since.

However, there are variations in the way that the hands are used. Three of the most common are:

1. The healer places his hands on the head or the shoulders of the sick person, or on the part of his body which is known to be diseased or in pain. The healer then prays for healing and mentally pictures the healing energy of God passing through his hands to the one in need.
2. The healer is sensitive to the energy emanating from different parts of the sick person's body, and from experience knows where the energy is abnormal, thus indicating a disease, a malfunction, or a blockage in that part of the body. The healer then places his hands over that particular area directing the healing power to that place.
3. The healer places his hands briefly over each part of the body while the sick person is lying down in a relaxed, receptive state. The sequence in which each part of the body is covered by the hands varies between healers. I believe there are three reasons for covering the whole body. The first is to ensure that healing energy is transferred to every one of the forty-nine energy centres of the physical body. These have been known for thousands of years to the Hindus who call them Chakras. This is a Sanskrit word meaning 'wheel', because to clairvoyants the centres look very much like a spinning wheel. Psychics who can see or feel the movement of energy have confirmed that there are vortexes of energy radiating from these same points. Much of this has also been scientifically supported by Kirlian photography.

The energy of life pours into these centres, giving life and health to the physical body. The energy also radiates outwards from each centre, contributing to the welfare of all within the body's environment. This two-way flow is necessary if stagnation and disease are to be avoided. Without the flow in both directions we would become like the Dead Sea in the Middle East, which has no outward flow, and has become so loaded with salt that nothing can live in it. When the healer passes his hands over the whole body, the life force energy which is channelled through him can then activate or recharge any of these energy centres which have become blocked or sluggish.

For an equally long time the Chinese have known about over 1,600 points in the body where the insertion of fine acupuncture needles will restore health by removing blockages in the flow of the energy of life which they call 'Chi'. Modern electronic instruments have detected these same points as having especially low skin resistance to electromagnetic energy. If the healer gradually covers the whole body with his hands he will automatically send energy to every acupuncture point. The energy of life being channelled through his hands, which energy is believed to be electromagnetic, will then activate any point that is blocked. This happens even if neither the healer nor the sick person knows which points are blocked.

The third reason for this procedure is that the one who is receiving the healing power can often feel it in the form of heat or tingling like an electric current in various parts of his body. Psychologically this is very reassuring that healing is actually taking place.

In all three of the above methods the healer may place his hands so that they are lightly touching the body, or he may keep them a few inches away, depending on his beliefs and what he feels is right for him.

Most agree that there is a coloured radiation of energy around the physical body. This is known as an aura, and it can be seen by some people. When a person is ill their aura will change from bright colours such as gold, blue, green, white, etc. to dull greys or browns. Some touch the physical body because they believe that the aura itself does not become diseased, but it merely mirrors the condition of the physical body. When the latter is healed the colours of the aura will become brighter and change from greys and browns to the other colours. Others do not touch because they believe that the aura does become diseased or malfunctioning, and that this in turn affects the physical body in the same way. Therefore, by holding the hands a few inches away from the body they will heal the aura. This will then result in a healing of the physical body.

Still others maintain that there is an Etheric body surrounding both the physical body and the aura. This is a complete body made of the ethers and it always retains its original state of perfection. They too will keep their hands a few inches away in order to channel the power through the etheric body to the physical, bringing the latter into alignment with the former.

Another difference that observers may notice is that some healers use both hands, whereas some use the left hand only and some the right, whichever seems best for them.

There is one other use of the hands for healing which is more direct. In the Philippines healers perform what they call 'psychic surgery'. This seems to involve the healer's hands separating the atoms of the flesh, or the cells of the body, without cutting them; then entering the body to remove diseased tissue; then immediately closing the separation without serious loss of blood or subsequent infection. This has become quite controversial. No doubt some fraudulent practitioners have entered the picture; however, those with uncontaminated reputations readily admit that the power to do this is not theirs and they give all the credit to God. The best of these healers also explain that the only reason they materialise blood and tissue is to satisfy the doubts of the sick people. Without this material evidence that 'surgery' has been performed many will not believe that a healing has occurred, even though it has. This disbelief can re-create the disease.

Further variations which may apply to any of the above techniques are:

1. The use of audible words such as prayers, affirmations or descriptions of what the healer believes is happening or what he psychically observes during the healing.
2. Background music. Some believe there is healing energy in the very vibrations of suitable music; others find that it adds to the relaxation and therefore to the receptivity of the patient.
3. Complete silence throughout the process.

The specific methods or techniques used are of minor importance compared to the faith that the healer has in the power and goodness of God, and that all things are possible. Actually, if one believes that God, or a Supreme Intelligence, or a Divine Energy, created human beings, including that marvellously complicated and organised vehicle for the soul known as the human body and the fantastic mind and spirit that inhabits that vehicle, then it is not so hard to believe that the same Supreme Intelligence can heal any disease or malfunction of that body or mind. Mentally visualising and affirming the perfection in which the whole person was created, *and now is*, contributes much towards effecting the healing.

It is on this point that spiritual healers diverge in their thinking, even though both approaches seem to be equally successful. Some hold the thought that all of God's creation, including every human being, is perfect and remains so; that disease is an illusion created by humanity (Joel Goldsmith called it Hypnotism), that simply does not exist in reality. They therefore concentrate on thoughts of God, the perfection of His creation, and the unity of God, the patient and themselves, with no attempt actually to heal the patient. If this higher consciousness is attained and the one in need is receptive, a healing will frequently follow.

Others hold that although God's creation is perfect and good, and His is the only power, the sick person has placed a mental block between himself and that realisation. This can be unblocked by the healer acting as a channel for the power of God, which can be directed by prayer to the problem that is carried in the consciousness of the one in need. With the blockage removed a healing will usually occur.

In either case the healer knows that the sick person is a child of God, and therefore loved by God with all the devotion of a father. He also remembers that the Kingdom of God, or a Divine Centre, is within the other, just as surely as it is within the healer, and that the ultimate authority over both is God.

Another ingredient that nearly all spiritual healers have in common is their desire that God's will be done, whatever that might be. Naturally the spiritual healer wants the sick person to be well, otherwise he would not be trying to serve humanity as a healer. However, if he is asking for specific results in accordance with his own will, then he may be healing for his own satisfaction or ego reinforcement. This would be contrary to Spiritual Law and probably make his efforts ineffectual. The desire to heal must always be secondary to the sincere wish or prayer that whatever transpires will be that which God sees as best for the other person's own soul evolution, even if it is the death of their physical body.

The healer must also have complete faith in the method that he is using. It is helpful but not essential that the sick person likewise believes in it. It *is* essential, however, that he be receptive to the healing energies, or at least to whatever is happening. If he is not, then it is highly unlikely that any healing will occur.

LOUISE L. HAY

Disease and Thought Patterns

I want to share with you one of the reasons I *know* that dis-ease can be reversed by simply reversing mental patterns.

A few years ago, I was diagnosed as having cancer of the vagina. With my background of being raped when I was five years old and being a battered child, it was no wonder I had manifested cancer in the vaginal area. Having already been a teacher of healing for several years, I was very aware that I was now being given a chance to practise on myself and prove what I had been teaching others.

Like anyone who has just been told they have cancer, I went into total panic. And yet I knew that mental healing worked. Being aware that cancer comes from a pattern of deep resentment that is held for a long time, until it literally eats away at the body, I knew I had a lot of mental work to do. I realised that if I had the operation to get rid of the cancer and did not clear the mental pattern that created it, then the doctors would just keep cutting Louise until there was no more Louise to cut. If I had the operation and cleared the mental pattern that was causing the cancer, then the cancer would not return. When cancer or any other illness returns, I do not believe it is because the doctor did not 'get it all out', but rather the patient has made no mental changes and so just recreates the same illness. I also knew if I could clear the mental pattern that created the condition called cancer, I would not need the doctor. So I bargained for time. The doctor grudgingly gave me three months, at the same time warning me that my life was endangered by the delay.

I immediately began to work with my own teacher to clear old patterns of resentment. Up to that time, I had not acknowledged that I harboured deep resentment. We are often so blind to our own patterns. A lot of forgiveness work was in order. The other thing I did was to go to a good nutritionist and completely detoxify my body. So between the mental and physical cleansing, in six months I was able to get the medical profession to agree with what I already knew; that I no longer had any form of cancer. I still keep the original lab report as a reminder of how negatively creative I could be.

Now when a client comes to me, no matter how dire their predicament seems to be, I *know* if they are *willing* to do the mental work of releasing and forgiving, almost anything can be healed. The word 'incurable', which is so frightening to so many people, really only means that the particular condition cannot be cured by 'outer' methods and that we must *go within* to effect the healing. The condition came from nothing and will go back to nothing.

Mental Equivalents: The Mental Thought Patterns That Form Our Experience

Both the good in our lives and the dis-ease are the results of mental thought patterns which form our experiences. We all have many thought patterns that produce good, positive experiences, and these we enjoy. It is the negative thought patterns that produce uncomfortable, unrewarding experiences with which we are concerned. It is our desire to change our dis-ease in life into perfect health.

We have learned that for every effect in our lives, there is a thought pattern that precedes and maintains it. Our consistent thinking patterns create our experiences. Therefore, by changing our thinking patterns, we can change our experiences.

What a joy it was when I first discovered the words *metaphysical causations*. This describes the power in the words and thoughts that create experiences. This new awareness brought me understanding of the connection between thoughts and the different parts of the body and physical problems. I learned how I had unknowingly created dis-ease in myself and this made a great difference in my life. Now I could stop blaming life and other people for what was wrong in my life and my body. I could now take full responsibility for my own health. Without either reproaching myself or feeling guilty, I began to see how to avoid creating thought patterns of dis-ease in the future.

For example, I could not understand why I repeatedly had problems with a stiff neck. Then I discovered that the neck represented being flexible on issues, being willing to see different sides of a question. I had been a very inflexible person, often refusing to listen to another side of a question out of fear. But, as I became more flexible in my thinking and able, with a loving understanding, to see another's viewpoint, my neck ceased to bother me. Now, if my neck becomes a bit stiff, I look to see where my thinking is stiff and rigid.

Replacing Old Patterns

In order to permanently eliminate a condition, we must first work to dissolve the mental cause. But most often, since we do not know what the cause is, we find it difficult to know where to begin. So, if you are saying, 'If I only knew what is causing this pain', I hope that this booklet will provide both a clue to find the causes and a helpful guide for building new thought patterns which will produce health in mind and body.

I have learned that for every condition in our lives, there is a *need for it*. Otherwise, we would not have it. The symptom is only an outer effect. We must go within to dissolve the mental cause. This is why willpower and discipline do not work. They are only battling the outer effect. It is like cutting down the weed instead of getting the root out. So before you begin the new thought pattern affirmations, work on the *willingness to release the need* for the cigarettes, or the headache, or the excess weight, or whatever. When the need is gone, the outer effect must die. No plant can live if the root is cut away.

The mental thought patterns that cause the most dis-ease in the body are *criticism, anger, resentment* and *guilt*. For instance, criticism indulged in long enough will often lead to dis-eases such as arthritis. Anger turns into things that boil and burn and infect the body. Resentment long held festers and eats away at the self and ultimately can lead to tumours and cancer. Guilt always seeks punishment and leads to pain. It is so much easier to release these negative thinking patterns from our minds when we are healthy than to try to dig them out when we are in a state of panic and under the threat of the surgeon's knife.

The following list of mental equivalents has been compiled from many years of study, my own work with clients, and my lectures and workshops. It is helpful as a quick reference guide to the probable mental patterns behind the dis-ease in your body. I offer these with love and a desire to share this simple method of helping to heal your body.

PROBLEM	PROBABLE CAUSE	NEW THOUGHT PATTERN
Abdominal Cramps	Fear, Stopping the process.	*I trust the process of life. I am safe.*
Abscess	Fermenting thoughts over hurts, slights and revenge.	*I allow my thoughts to be free. The past is over. I am at peace.*
Accidents	Inability to speak up for the self. Rebellion against authority. Belief in violence.	*I release the pattern in me that created this. I am at peace. I am worthwhile.*
Aches	Longing for love. Longing to be held.	*I love and approve of myself. I am loving and lovable.*
Acne	Not accepting the self. Dislike of the self.	*I am a Divine expression of life. I love and accept myself where I am right now.*
Addictions	Running from the self. Fear. Not knowing how to love the self.	*I now discover how wonderful I am. I choose to love and enjoy myself.*
Addison's Disease Also adrenal problems	Severe emotional malnutrition. Anger at the self.	*I lovingly take care of my body, my mind and my emotions.*
Adenoids	Family friction, arguments. Child feeling unwelcome, in the way.	*This child is wanted and welcomed and deeply loved.*
Adrenal Problems Also Addison's Disease, Cushing's Disease	Defeatism. No longer caring for the self. Anxiety.	*I love and approve of myself. It is safe for me to care for myself.*
Aging Problems	Social beliefs. Old thinking. Fear of being one's self. Rejection of the now.	*I love and accept myself at every age. Each moment in life is perfect.*

99

PROBLEM	PROBABLE CAUSE	NEW THOUGHT PATTERN
AIDS	Feeling defenceless and hopeless. Nobody cares. A strong belief in not being good enough. Denial of the self. Sexual guilt.	*I am part of the Universal design. I am important and I am loved by Life itself. I am powerful and capable. I love and appreciate all of myself.*
Alcoholism	'What's the use?' Feeling of futility, guilt, inadequacy. Self-rejection.	*I live in the now. Each moment is new. I choose to see my self-worth. I love and approve of myself.*

SHAKTI GAWAIN

Creative Visualisation

The scientific world is beginning to discover what metaphysical and spiritual teachers have known for centuries. Our physical Universe is not really composed of any 'matter' at all; its basic component is a kind of force or essence which we can call *energy*.

Things appear to be solid and separate from one another on the level at which our physical senses normally perceive them. On finer levels, however, atomic and sub-atomic levels, seemingly solid matter is seen to be smaller and smaller particles within particles, which eventually turn out to be just pure energy.

Physically, we are all energy, and everything within and around us is made up of energy. We are all part of one great energy field. Things which we perceive to be solid and separate are in reality just various forms of our essential energy which is common to all. We are all one, even in the literal, physical sense.

The energy is vibrating at different rates of speed, and thus has different qualities, from finer to denser. Thought is a relatively fine, light form of energy and therefore very quick and easy to change. Matter is relatively dense, compact energy, and therefore slower to move and change. Within matter there is great variation as well. Living flesh is relatively fine, changes quickly, and is easily affected by many things. A rock is a much denser form, slower to change and more difficult to affect. Yet even rock is eventually changed and affected by the fine, light energy of water, for example. All forms of energy are interrelated and can affect one another.

★　★　★

Using Creative Visualisation

The process of change does not occur on superficial levels, through mere 'positive thinking'. It involves exploring, discovering, and changing our deepest, most basic attitudes towards life. That is why learning to use creative visualisation can become a process of deep and meaningful growth. In the process we often discover ways in which we have been holding ourselves back, blocking ourselves from achieving satisfaction and fulfilment in life through our fears and negative concepts. Once seen clearly, these limiting attitudes can be dissolved through the creative visualisation process, leaving space for us to find and live our natural state of happiness, fulfilment, and love . . .

★   ★   ★

Healing Others

This meditation is to be done alone, *not* in the other person's presence. You may or may not wish to tell them that you are doing healing meditations for them, depending on how well they would accept that idea on a personality level.

Relax deeply and do whatever type of preparation you wish in order to enter a deep, quiet state of mind.

Think of yourself as a clear channel through which the healing energy of the Universe is pouring. This energy does not come from you personally, it comes from a higher source, and you serve to focus and direct it.

Now picture or think of the person as clearly as you can. Ask him if there is anything in particular he would like you to do for him in your meditation. If so, do it to the best of your ability, if it feels right to you.

If you feel the impulse to work on healing a particular part of his body, or a particular problem, do so. Just see all problems dissolved, everything being healed and functioning perfectly.

Then picture him surrounded in golden, healing light . . . looking radiantly healthy and happy. Speak to him directly (in your mind); remind him that he is actually a perfect, god-like being and that no illness or affliction need have any power over him. Tell him that you support him in being totally healthy and happy, and that you will continue to send him your loving support and energy.

When you feel complete, open your eyes and come back to the outer world feeling refreshed, renewed, healthy and invigorated.

From now on, in your meditations see the person as perfectly well. Don't give any more mental energy or power to the illness; just keep seeing him as completely healed.

Healing In Groups

Healings are very powerful when done in groups.

If the person to be healed is present in the room, have him lie down in the centre or sit in a chair (whichever is most comfortable) with everyone else seated in a circle around him.

Everyone should close their eyes, be quiet, and relax deeply, then begin to imagine sending healing energy to the person in the centre. Remember that it is the healing energy of the Universe which is being channelled through you. See the person surrounded in golden light, feeling well, and in perfect health.

If you wish, you can have everyone raise their hands with the palms facing out towards the person in the centre, and feel the energy flowing out to him through your hands.

It is especially powerful to have everyone chant 'OM' together for a few minutes while doing the healing, thus adding the healing vibration of sound to the process (to chant 'OM' you sing a long, deep resonant note with the syllable a-a-au-m-m, holding it as long as you can, and repeating it over and over).

If the person is not present in the room, just inform everyone of his name and the city where he is, and then proceed as if he were there. The power of healing energy is not affected at all by distance, and I have seen as many miraculous cures accomplished for people in distant cities as for those present in the room.

Healing Meditation for Pain

Here is a meditation technique you can do with a person who is experiencing a headache or any other specific pain.

Have the person lie down, close his eyes, and relax deeply. Have him focus on his breath for awhile, breathing deeply and slowly yet naturally. Have him count down from 10 to 1 slowly, feeling himself drift into a deeper, more relaxed state of being with each count.

When he is very deeply relaxed, have him picture or imagine a bright colour, any colour he wishes (have him take the first colour that comes to him). Ask him to picture it as a sphere of bright light about six inches in diameter. Now ask him to picture it gradually growing bigger and bigger, until eventually it fills his whole field of mental vision. When he has experienced this, ask him to picture it shrinking, growing smaller and smaller until it's back to its original size. Now have it grow smaller still, until it's only an inch or so in diameter, still shrinking, and finally disappearing completely.

Now go through the visualisation exercise again, and this time have the person imagine that the colour is his pain.

STEPHEN LEVINE

Healing into Life and Death

Most of the patients who came to us to prepare for death died within a year or two. While each approached the same work on themselves, some healed into death, while others, with advanced cancer or some other terminal prognosis, as they let go of the pains of the past, finishing their business with forgiveness and loving kindness, opening to death, returned to a state of considerable health. It was these 'healed ones' that originally drew our attention to the investigation of what healing might be. While some seemed completely cured, others in the process of seeing their life more clearly, though their body did not become completely well, stopped the progression of disease. Also it was noticed that many, in the course of using the healing meditations, though focussing on such as cancer, healed lesser, secondary ailments and discomforts, such as kidney stones, strep throats, constipation, minor infections, burns, broken bones, etc.

Though it was the healing of the body that originally drew our attention, it was the healings, yet deeper than the body, which continued to hold our interest. We saw several preparing for death by finishing business with themselves and all else, experiencing a sense of fulfilment that touched on levels of healing previously unimagined. We saw no less of a healing balance among those who moved peacefully through death than we did among those whose bodies re-established a certain degree of wellness. We saw so many, as they cleared their heart and resolved loose ends, discover a feeling of being 'more alive than ever', sometimes with considerable diminishing of pain and symptoms. Though their body did not reflect this extra 'wellness', something had healed so deeply into life that death was no longer a problem.

It became apparent that those whose bodies healed, as well as those who completed their life before they died, had the same process in common: an openness to their illness, a receptivity, a commitment to work directly with their illness. Each seemed to enter, in their own way, and as fully as possible, the feelings, fears, and hopes, the plans and doubts, the love and forgiveness that arises in the course of healing.

This attitude towards life, this willingness to allow healing in, to investigate the nature of disease as a means of investigating life seems a basis for healing. It approaches that which limits life. One such fellow whom we lovingly referred to as 'Loud Larry' had an incurable blood disease of extremely obscure origin for which there seemed no cure. Since its inception in his early teens, he had lost more and more of his physical vigour which he seemingly compensated for by louder and greater profusions of speech. By the time we met him in his late twenties one could hardly get a word in edgewise. In the midst of his second five-day conscious living/conscious dying retreat, Loud Larry fell in love. Soon thereafter he found that a different path opened up. It was a path of the heart. It was the first time Loud Larry cared for anything or anyone more than his degenerating body. When his heart reached out to his loved one, it touched his illness. As his heart and body converged during extended periods of forgiveness meditation, his body began to heal and his voice continued to soften. ('I no longer have to make more of myself than I am. I used to think the only way to survive was by making more of me. Now I find the less the better. There is so little to keep me from loving now.') The doctors asked him, 'How on earth did you heal?' He told them, 'I took the best medicine I could find. And I was the only physician who could prepare it. I took *me*, lock, stock and barrel.'

This work of opening to ourselves is taken a step at a time. It is begun with a heartful openness and investigative awareness which gently explores the physical/mental pains and holdings which become so noticeable around illness. It is an ongoing process of meeting our fear with forgiveness and a healing awareness, meeting our doubt with a new confidence which develops in each unknown step as the ground comes up to meet and support our progesss. And the next step follows naturally. It is the unfolding experience of the mind/body within an accepting awareness which choicelessly observes and examines mental states, feelings, emotions, and moods as they arise and dissolve in the vastness of being.

Just as pain uncovers deep holdings within us – ancient fears, subliminal imprints, long unnoticed desires for control – so the investigation of illness begins to heal these underlying tendencies. Thus we have seen that for many working with illness in the body means working with the discomforts of the mind – a healing of one's deepest clingings and fears – which led them to the discovery of joys unimagined and a spaciousness never dreamed of. Illness causes us to confront our most assiduous doubts about the nature of the Universe and the existence of God. It tears us open. It teaches us to keep our heart open in Hell.

Not all those we have known who have healed have participated in their injury or illness in the same way or at the same level. One enters oneself wherever an opening exists. Many investigated deeply the nature of their pain, releasing profound emotional energy stimulated by confusion and attending fears.

Some explored the nature of their spirit. Marty was such a person, who with years of meditative opening ended the progress of a genetic bone cancer. Letting his heart be torn open to the fears and immense questioning as to the nature of existence, his profound inquiry into 'who indeed it is that resides within this diseased body' led him deeper towards his healing. Marty's sister, sharing a similar genetic inheritance (which manifested in deformation of the bones and the constant possibility of further amputations) fought the disease and fought life itself. The struggle was just too much for her. She could no longer bear the rising pressure of unexamined fears, and became afraid of all that existed around the next corner. She now resides in a state mental institution.

Marty sought healing in the heart and discovered seeking an ongoing process within. His sister, however, seeking protection in the mind, was lost in confusion.

Each seeks their healing where it is to be found. Each approaches the heart to hear the subtle whisper of the appropriate. Each uncovers whatever blocks access to the heart, to the source of healing.

A friend very ill with an advanced cancer, visited a highly respected Zen Master, hoping for some answers to her questions about healing. After explaining her circumstances, she asked, 'Do I need to take on some spiritual path in order to be healed?' The Zen Master, smiling, leaned forward, pointing directly to her heart, and whispered, 'You are the path!'

Recognising that there was nowhere to go but in, that she was the path and had to tread herself wholeheartedly, her questions were answered.

Drawn by the sincerity and openness of this fine teacher, she began to attend meditation sittings each morning at the Zen Centre and to participate in as many weekend intensives as she felt appropriate. She meditated for some time, investigating the nature of what she called 'the visitor in the body and the egg that hatched it all'. Her six-month prognosis now, six years later, seems more an initiation than a tragedy. Looking back on the meditative practices she took on, motivated by a desire to heal the body, she recently remarked, 'You know, these techniques affected me in a way I never thought was possible. I saw that I could rebuild my body breath by breath, and open my mind, thought by thought.'

She began a wholehearted commitment to let go of the old, to start anew each moment, a path of wonderment and discovery.

She became, as she put it, 'a complete beginner'. She came naked to the truth. Trusting her 'new unknowing', she stepped child-like on to the wide, exciting path ahead. Willing to let go of old ways of thinking and hiding, she acknowledged 'complete ignorance of life' in the face of the great quandary of disease and possible death. It was her total entrance into the process that allowed her that fulfilling sense of completeness from the very first step. She said it took about three months, but gradually a sense of ease began to emerge. She said she didn't have to have all the answers in order to solve the problem. She saw that going wholeheartedly within the problem *was* the answer. She did not lug along old concepts but learned afresh each moment, 'a complete beginner', nothing absent, each moment anew. She trusted each step towards fullness, attuning to the subtle whispers of the heart, cultivating a healing awareness that received the moment in mercy, and allowed change instead of forcing it.

But just as the meditative work of the fellow with genetic bone cancer who spent so much time investigating the relationship of mind and body to the heart, is not for everyone, so our friend's way was a path she sensed was uniquely appropriate to her process. For many, the surrender, the willingness to investigate the nature of illness, comes in increments. A step at a time. The unfolding of insights and understandings deepens as one approaches the core of being.

In the beginning it may be an inner exploration of fifteen or twenty minutes every once in a while until, gradually, as the mind is drawn to the heart, yearning for spaciousness, a daily meditation practice develops. Sitting down quietly once or twice a day for a half hour to an hour, the healing extends from those quiet moments to permeate the whole day. And our healing becomes an ongoing practice of seeing the old in a brand-new way. Each moment of participating directly in the process, of seeing clearly the unfolding of mind/body in the spacious heart, each instance of insight, is a healing moment.

A healing moment is one in which the mind is not clinging to its passing show, not lost in the personal melodrama of its content, but tuned to the constant unfolding of the process in a moment of being fully alive, a moment of healing. Experiencing the vastness in which all floats for even a millisecond has the power to bring balance and harmony to the mind/body. Each moment of participating in the spaciousness of being deepens the context for healing. Each moment experienced directly releases the holding about our suffering. Insights accrue as wisdom. Mercy accrues as compassion. Healing accumulates from moment to moment when discomfort is met mindfully, openheartedly, in the present, where all that we seek is to be found.

Our old chiropractor friend Carl came to many of our conscious living/conscious dying workshops to, as he put it, 'sharpen my healing practice to serve others more fully'. Then Carl became ill. 'I found out how real it all was when the doctor told me it was cancer. There was no bullshitting, no time to waste. It was up to me to learn about healing from the inside out.' And this is just what he did. Allowing his body to be the laboratory for deeper investigations of healing, he experimented with various methods of healing. He worked with fever therapy, urine therapy, various herbs and nutritional techniques, as well as body and skeletal manipulations until it became evident that the tumour was continuing to grow. He was told by a number of physicians that his only hope was surgery, though even then the cancer might return. 'At first I was fighting it. I wasn't working with the idea of surgery at all. I was struggling against the disease, and then, when the operation came along, I really closed down. I had always been so wholistic, and here I was letting them intervene in a way I had suggested to many of my patients was not such a good idea. But I was convinced by the physicians that it was a state-of-the-art surgery and that I had nothing to worry about. But the operation was not successful and the tumour did not go away. When I found out, I became really depressed, but then something broke through. I didn't know how to get 'this cure' I was looking for, but I knew I wasn't going deeply enough for my healing. So I went to this very powerful spiritual teacher whom I had heard so many good things about. I was all worn out and confused and just asked her straight out how to rid my body of cancer. And you know what she told me? 'Just love yourself.' It knocked me off my feet. I was shocked. I just didn't know what to say. She had hit the nail right on the head, and the nail was driven right through my heart. I thought she was going to give me a mantra or a visualisation or something, some way to change the illness, but instead she insisted I change myself. Those were the most difficult words I have ever heard, but it was the healing that I came for. When I started to send love to myself, I discovered how much I had blocked, and it really frightened me. I saw that only by examining and letting go of that fear of loving would I ever get healthy again.'

It has been nearly two and a half years now since Carl was told to 'tidy up any legal loose ends'. The other day he told me, 'The better I like myself, the better I feel. When I look into the eyes of my fourteen-month-old son now, I realise that he was conceived at almost precisely the time they said I was going to die. Things change when you let them.' As Carl walked the path of healing, spending an hour or two a day in silent contemplation, sharing with a trusted counsellor and looking deeply into the mirror of his wife's heart, he was able to use his own heart as a compass towards the sometimes clouded shores of life. He discovered deeper and deeper levels of wholeness. Now he speaks of healing not as somewhere we are going, but as an ever-present process, unfolding moment to moment. The other day he said that completing our birth was the first stage of healing. He said that if we did not allow ourselves to be born, to become fully aware, to attend to our life, then we would never be able to fully live or fully die.

Human Potential

M. Scott Peck
C.G. Jung
Abraham H. Maslow
Roberto Assagioli
Marion Woodman
Gabriel Roth
Leonard Orr and Sondra Ray
Roger J. Woolger

Introduction

The analogy is often drawn that just as it would be naïve and ignorant to think that the actual box of a television set is the source of its programmes, so it is equally naïve to think that the brain is the source of all human consciousness. A television set receives its communications – invisible but real! The physical brain is only the anchor for consciousness – also invisible but real.

Two core concepts, then, of the human potential movement are: first, the brain is the vehicle and not the source of consciousness; second, there are wide areas of consciousness into which we can expand our awareness and thereby achieve our true potential. This, of course, is the very substance of true meditation: an attitude of detachment towards the brain and the personality, and a quiet opening awareness to everything else. But to flow into expanding our awareness is not easy. The challenge is that we have blockages, neuroses, injuries, memories and *karma* (the Sanskrit word for the results of our past actions) which lock us in, hold us back and deny our expansion into our full selves.

The human potential aspect of the New Age movement is concerned with healing and releasing our blocks, and achieving our full expansive potential. It is particularly interesting because its tools range from the methods of orthodox psychotherapy through to the esoteric techniques of the wisdom traditions. A significant feature of New Age culture is indeed the intertwining of the psychotherapeutic and spiritual approaches. Because of the shortage of space, I have focussed in this section on the more psychological end of the spectrum, but we need to remember that all wisdom traditions contain techniques which heal, alter and expand consciousness. The extract in this section on rebirthing, for example, is an interesting example of the modern usage of yoga breathing methods adapted for deep psychological transformation.

I have a particular interest in this whole area as my father was a psychiatrist – *ah ha! that explains everything!* – and I have my own orthodox background of three years' psychoanalysis and a doctorate in psychology. But I have also used many of the new therapies and can personally testify to their deep and graceful effectiveness.

This section opens with a portion from Scott Peck's influential book on relationships, *The Road Less Travelled*. This portion is about love, falling in love and the illusion of romantic love; it demonstrates the quality of wisdom that can emerge from the marriage of the psychological and spiritual approaches.

Then comes an extract from Jung which expands the notion of consciousness to include archetypes, the shadow and the anima. This is followed by a piece from Abraham Maslow which describes peak-experiences as a natural psychological phenomenon. Maslow also put forward the crucial notion that there exists a hierarchy of human needs and that we cannot progress in one until the one before it has been fulfilled. For example, we cannot achieve psychological security about our identity unless we are first fed and housed; equally, we cannot fulfil ourselves unless we first have a secure psychological identity; and so on. What both Jung and Maslow also put forward was the idea that it is the natural process of every human to *realise* her or himself, to completely fulfil her potential as an integrated individual.

Roberto Assagioli then provided a clear theoretical bridge out of psychoanalytic theory into the spiritual or transpersonal realm, and I include here some pages which very clearly articulate his basic premise about what he called psychosynthesis.

The links between body and psyche are then movingly described by Marion Woodman, the Canadian therapist. Then follows a passage with very interesting insights about the role of our fathers, from the dancer and 'urban shaman', Gabrielle Roth.

The section concludes with a wonderful passage on rebirthing followed by an extract from the most credible of all the recent books on reincarnation, Roger Woolger's *Other Lives, Other Selves*.

M. SCOTT PECK

Love

Discipline, it has been suggested, is the means of human spiritual evolution. This section will examine what lies behind discipline – what provides the motive, the energy for discipline. This force I believe to be love. I am very conscious of the fact that in attempting to examine love we will be beginning to toy with mystery. In a very real sense we will be attempting to examine the unexaminable and to know the unknowable. Love is too large, too deep ever to be truly understood or measured or limited within the framework of words. I would not write this if I did not believe the attempt to have value, but no matter how valuable I begin with the certain knowledge that the attempt will be in some ways inadequate.

One result of the mysterious nature of love is that no one has ever, to my knowledge, arrived at a truly satisfactory definition of love. In an effort to explain it, therefore, love has been divided into various categories: eros, philia, agape; perfect love and imperfect love, and so on. I am presuming, however, to give a single definition of love, again with the awareness that it is likely to be in some way or ways inadequate. I define love thus: the will to extend one's self for the purpose of nurturing one's own or another's spiritual growth. . . .

Falling in 'Love'

Of all the misconceptions about love the most powerful and pervasive is the belief that 'falling in love' is love or at least one of the manifestations of love. It is a potent misconception, because falling in love is subjectively experienced in a very powerful fashion as an experience of love. When a person falls in love what he or she certainly feels is 'I love him' or 'I love her'. But two problems are immediately apparent. The first is that the experience of falling in love is specifically a sex-linked erotic experience. We do not fall in love with our children even though we may love them very deeply. We do not fall in love with our friends of the same sex – unless we are homosexually oriented – even though we may care for them greatly. We fall in love only when we are consciously or unconsciously sexually motivated. The second problem is that the experience of falling in love is invariably temporary. No matter whom we fall in love with, we sooner or later fall out of love if the relationship continues long enough. This is not to say that we invariably cease loving the person with whom we fell in love. But it is to say that the feeling of ecstatic lovingness that characterises the experience of falling in love always passes. The honeymoon always ends. The bloom of romance always fades.

* * *

Falling in love is not an act of will. It is not a conscious choice. No matter how open to or eager for it we may be, the experience may still elude us. Contrarily, the experience may capture us at times when we are definitely not seeking it, when it is inconvenient and undesirable. We are as likely to fall in love with someone with whom we are obviously ill matched as with someone more suitable. Indeed, we may not even like or admire the object of our passion, yet, try as we might, we may not be able to fall in love with a person whom we deeply respect and with whom a deep relationship would be in all ways desirable. This is not to say that the experience of falling in love is immune to discipline. Psychiatrists, for instance, frequently fall in love with their patients, just as patients fall in love with them, yet out of duty to the patient and their role they are usually able to abort the collapse of their ego boundaries and give up the patient as a romantic object. The struggle and suffering of the discipline involved may be enormous. But discipline and will can only control the experience; they cannot create it. We can choose how to respond to the experience of falling in love, but we cannot choose the experience itself.

Falling in love is not an extension of one's limits or boundaries; it is a partial and temporary collapse of them. The extension of one's limits requires effort; falling in love is effortless. Lazy and undisciplined individuals are as likely to fall in love as energetic and dedicated ones. Once the precious moment of falling in love has passed and the boundaries have snapped back into place, the individual may be disillusioned, but is usually none the larger for the experience. When limits are extended or stretched, however, they tend to stay stretched. Real love is a permanently self-enlarging experience. Falling in love is not.

Falling in love has little to do with purposively nurturing one's spiritual development. If we have any purpose in mind when we fall in love it is to terminate our own loneliness and perhaps insure this result through marriage. Certainly we are not thinking of spiritual development. Indeed, after we have fallen in love and before we have fallen out of love again we feel that we have arrived, that the heights have been attained, that there is both no need and no possibility of going higher. We do not feel ourselves to be in any need of development; we are totally content to be where we are. Our spirit is at peace. Nor do we perceive our beloved as being in need of spiritual development. To the contrary, we perceive him or her as

112

perfect, as having been perfected. If we see any faults in our beloved, we perceive them as insignificant – little quirks or darling eccentricities that only add colour and charm.

If falling in love is not love, then what is it other than a temporary and partial collapse of ego boundaries? I do not know. But the sexual specificity of the phenomenon leads me to suspect that is a genetically determined instinctual component of mating behaviour. In other words, the temporary collapse of ego boundaries that constitutes falling in love is a stereotypic response of human beings to a configuration of internal sexual drives and external sexual stimuli, which serves to increase the probability of sexual pairing and bonding so as to enhance the survival of the species. Or to put it in another, rather crass way, falling in love is a trick that our genes pull on our otherwise perceptive mind to hoodwink or trap us into marriage. Frequently the trick goes awry one way or another, as when the sexual drives and stimuli are homosexual or when other forces – parental interference, mental illness, conflicting responsibilities or mature self-discipline – supervene to prevent the bonding. On the other hand, without this trick, this illusory and inevitably temporary (it would not be practical were it not temporary) regression to infantile merging and omnipotence, many of us who are happily or unhappily married today would have retreated in wholehearted terror from the realism of the marriage vows.

The Myth of Romantic Love

To serve as effectively as it does to trap us into marriage, the experience of falling in love probably must have as one of its characteristics the illusion that the experience will last forever. This illusion is fostered in our culture by the commonly held myth of romantic love, which has its origins in our favourite childhood fairy tales, wherein the prince and princess, once united, live happily forever after. The myth of romantic love tells us, in effect, that for every young man in the world there is a young woman who was 'meant for him', and vice versa. Moreover, the myth implies that there is only one man meant for a woman and only one woman for a man and this has been predetermined 'in the stars'. When we meet the person for whom we are intended, recognition comes through the fact that we fall in love. We have met the person for whom all the heavens intended us, and since the match is perfect, we will then be able to satisfy all of each other's needs forever and ever, and therefore live happily forever after in perfect union and harmony. Should it come to pass, however, that we do not satisfy or meet all of each other's needs and friction arises and we fall out of love, then it is clear that a dreadful mistake was made, we misread the stars, we did not hook up with our one and only perfect match, what we thought was love was not real or 'true' love, and nothing can be done about the situation except to live unhappily ever after or get divorced.

While I generally find that great myths are great precisely because they represent and embody great universal truths, the myth of romantic love is a dreadful lie. Perhaps it is a necessary lie in that it ensures the survival of the species by its encouragement and seeming validation of the falling-in-love experience that traps us into marriage. But as a psychiatrist I weep in my heart almost daily for the ghastly confusion and suffering that this myth fosters. Millions of people waste vast amounts of energy desperately and futilely attempting to make the reality of their lives conform to the unreality of the myth.

C.G. JUNG

Archetypes, Shadows and the Anima

A more or less superficial layer of the unconscious is undoubtedly personal. I call it the *personal unconscious*. But this personal unconscious rests upon a deeper layer, which does not derive from personal experience and is not a personal acquisition but is inborn. This deeper layer I call the *collective unconscious*. I have chosen the term 'collective' because this part of the unconscious is not individual but universal; in contrast to the personal psyche, it has contents and modes of behaviour that are more or less the same everywhere and in all individuals. It is, in other words, identical in all men and thus constitutes a common psychic substrate of a supra-personal nature which is present in every one of us.

Psychic existence can be recognised only by the presence of contents that are *capable of consciousness*. We can therefore speak of an unconscious only in so far as we are able to demonstrate its contents. The contents of the personal unconscious are chiefly the *feeling-toned complexes*, as they are called; they constitute the personal and private side of psychic life. The contents of the collective unconscious, on the other hand, are known as *archetypes*. . . .

For our purposes this term is apposite and helpful, because it tells us that so far as the collective unconscious contents are concerned we are dealing with archaic or – I would say – primordial types, that is, with universal images that have existed since the remotest times. The term '*representations collective*', used by Lévy-Bruhl to denote the symbolic figures in the primitive view of the world, could easily be applied to unconscious contents as well, since it means practically the same thing. Primitive tribal lore is concerned with archetypes that have been modified in a special way. They are no longer contents of the unconscious, but have already been changed into conscious formulae taught according to tradition, generally in the form of esoteric teaching. This last is a typical means of expression for the transmission of collective contents originally derived from the unconscious.

★ ★ ★

Why is psychology the youngest of the empirical sciences? Why have we not long since discovered the unconscious and raised up its treasure-house of eternal images? Simply because we had a religious formula for everything psychic – and one that is far more beautiful and comprehensive than immediate experience. Though the Christian view of the world has paled for many people, the symbolic treasure-rooms of the East are still full of marvels that can nourish for a long time to come the passion for show and new clothes. What is more, these images – be they Christian or Buddhist or what you will – are lovely, mysterious, richly intuitive.

★ ★ ★

The unconscious is commonly regarded as a sort of incapsulated fragment of our most personal and intimate life – something like what the Bible calls the 'heart' and considers the source of all evil thoughts. In the chambers of the heart dwell the wicked blood-spirits, swift anger and sensual weakness. This is how the unconscious looks when seen from the conscious side. But consciousness appears to be essentially an affair of the cerebrum, which sees everything separately and in isolation, and therefore sees the unconscious in this way too, regarding it outright as *my* unconscious. Hence it is generally believed that anyone who descends into the unconscious gets into a suffocating atmosphere of egocentric subjectivity, and in this blind alley is exposed to the attack of all the ferocious beasts which the caverns of the psychic underworld are supposed to harbour.

True, whoever looks into the mirror of the water will see first of all his own face. Whoever goes to himself risks a confrontation with himself. The mirror does not flatter, it faithfully shows whatever looks into it; namely, the face we never show to the world because we cover it with the *persona*, the mask of the actor. But the mirror lies behind the mask and shows the true face.

This confrontation is the first test of courage on the inner way, a

115

test sufficient to frighten off most people, for the meeting with ourselves belongs to the more unpleasant things that can be avoided so long as we can project everything negative into the environment. But if we are able to see our own shadow and can bear knowing about it, then a small part of the problem has already been solved: we have at least brought up the personal unconscious. The shadow is a living part of the personality and therefore wants to live with it in some form. It cannot be argued out of existence or rationalised into harmlessness. This problem is exceedingly difficult, because it not only challenges the whole man, but reminds him at the same time of his helplessness and ineffectuality. Strong natures – or should one rather call them weak? – do not like to be reminded of this, but prefer to think of themselves as heroes who are beyond good and evil, and to cut the Gordian knot instead of untying it. Nevertheless, the account has to be settled sooner or later. In the end one has to admit that there are problems which one simply cannot solve on one's own resources. Such an admission has the advantage of being honest, truthful, and in accord with reality, and this prepares the ground for a compensatory reaction from the collective unconscious: you are now more inclined to give heed to a helpful idea or intuition, or to notice thoughts which had not been allowed to voice themselves before. Perhaps you will pay attention to the dreams that visit you at such moments, or will reflect on certain inner and outer occurrences that take place just at this time. If you have an attitude of this kind, then the helpful powers slumbering in the deeper strata of man's nature can come awake and intervene, for helplessness and weakness are the eternal experience and the eternal problem of mankind. To this problem there is also an eternal answer, otherwise it would have been all up with humanity long ago. When you have done everything that could possibly be done, the only thing that remains is what you could still do if only you knew it. But how much do we know of ourselves? Precious little, to judge by experience. Hence there is still a great deal of room left for the unconscious. Prayer, as we know, calls for a very similar attitude and therefore has much the same effect.

The necessary and needful reaction from the collective unconscious expresses itself in archetypally formed ideas. The meeting with oneself is, at first, the meeting with one's own shadow. The shadow is a tight passage, a narrow door, whose painful constriction no one is spared who goes down to the deep well. But one must learn to know oneself in order to know who one is. For what comes after the door is, surprisingly enough, a boundless expanse full of unprecedented uncertainty, with apparently no inside and no outside, no above and no below, no here and no there, no mine and no thine, no good and no bad. It is the world of water, where all life floats in suspension; where the realm of the sympathetic system, the soul of everything living, begins; where I am indivisibly this *and* that; where I experience the other in myself and the other-than-myself experiences me.

No, the collective unconscious is anything but an incapsulated personal system; it is sheer objectivity, as wide as the world and open to all the world. There I am the object of every subject, in complete reversal of my ordinary consciousness, where I am always the subject that has an object. There I am utterly one with the world, so much a part of it that I forget all too easily who I really am. 'Lost in oneself' is a good way of describing this state. But this self is the world, if only a consciousness could see it. That is why we must know who we are.

* * *

With her cunning play of illusions the soul lures into life the inertness of matter that does not want to live. She makes us believe incredible things, that life may be lived. She is full of snares and traps, in order that Man should fall, should reach the earth, entangle himself there, and stay caught, so that life should be lived; as Eve in the garden of Eden could not rest content until she had convinced Adam of the goodness of the forbidden apple. Were it not for the leaping and twinkling of the soul, Man would rot away in his greatest passion, idleness. A certain kind of reasonableness is its advocate, and a certain kind of morality adds its blessing. But to have soul is the whole venture of life, for soul is a life-giving daemon who plays his elfin game above and below human existence, for which reason – in the realm of dogma – he is threatened and propitiated with superhuman punishments and blessings that go far beyond the possible deserts of human beings. Heaven and hell are the fates meted out to the soul and not to civilised man, who in his nakedness and timidity would have no idea of what to do with himself in a heavenly Jerusalem.

The anima is not the soul in the dogmatic sense, not an *anima rationalis*, which is a philosophical conception, but a natural archetype that satisfactorily sums up all the statements of the unconscious, of the primitive mind, of the history of language and religion. It is a 'factor' in the proper sense of the word. Man cannot make it; on the contrary, it is always the *a priori* element in his moods, reactions, impulses, and whatever else is spontaneous in psychic life. It is something that lives of itself, that makes us live; it is a life behind consciousness that cannot be completely integrated with it, but from which, on the contrary, consciousness arises. For, in the last analysis, psychic life is for the greater part an unconscious life that surrounds consciousness on all sides – a notion that is sufficiently obvious when one considers how much unconscious preparation is needed, for instance, to register a sense-impression.

Although it seems as if the whole of our unconscious psychic life could be ascribed to the anima, she is yet only one archetype among many. Therefore, she is not characteristic of the unconscious in its entirety. She is only one of its aspects. This is shown by the very fact of her femininity. What is not-I, not masculine, is most probably feminine, and because the not-I is felt as not belonging to me and therefore as outside me, the anima-image is usually projected upon women. Either sex is inhabited by the opposite sex up to a point, for biologically speaking, it is simply the greater number of masculine genes that tips the scales in favour of masculinity. The smaller number of feminine genes seems to form a feminine character, which usually remains unconscious because of its subordinate position.

With the archetype of the anima we enter the realm of the gods, or rather, the realm that metaphysics has reserved for itself. Everything the anima touches becomes numinous – unconditional, dangerous, taboo, magical. She is the serpent in the paradise of the harmless man with good resolutions and still better intentions. She affords the most convincing reasons for not prying into the unconscious, an occupation that would break down our moral inhibitions and unleash forces that would be better left unconscious and undisturbed.

ABRAHAM H. MASLOW

Peak-experiences

The very beginning, the intrinsic core, the essence, the universal nucleus of every known high religion (unless Confucianism is also called a religion) has been the private, lonely, personal illumination, revelation, or ecstasy of some acutely sensitive prophet or seer. The high religions call themselves revealed religions and each of them tends to rest its validity, its function, and its right to exist on the codification and the communication of this original mystic experience or revelation from the lonely prophet to the mass of human beings in general.

But it has recently begun to appear that these 'revelations' or mystical illuminations can be subsumed under the head of the 'peak-experiences' or 'ecstasies' or 'transcendent' experiences which are now being eagerly investigated by many psychologists. That is to say, it is very likely, indeed almost certain, that these older reports, phrased in terms of supernatural revelation, were, in fact, perfectly natural, human peak-experiences of the kind that can easily be examined today, which, however, were phrased in terms of whatever conceptual, cultural, and linguistic framework the particular seer had available in his time.

★　★　★

Practically everything that happens in the peak-experiences, naturalistic though they are, could be listed under the headings of religious happenings, or indeed have been in the past considered to be only religious experiences.

1. For instance, it is quite characteristic in peak-experiences that the whole Universe is perceived as an integrated and unified whole. This is not as simple a happening as one might imagine from the bare words themselves. To have a clear perception (rather than a purely abstract and verbal philosophical acceptance) that the Universe is all of a piece and that one has his place in it – one is a part of it, one belongs in it – can be so profound and shaking an experience that it can change the person's character and his *Weltanschauung* forever after. In my own experience I have two subjects who, because of such an experience, were totally, immediately, and permanently cured of (in one case) chronic anxiety neurosis and (in the other case) of strong obsessional thoughts of suicide.

This, of course, is a basic meaning of religious faith for many people. People who might otherwise lose their 'faith' will hang on to because it gives a meaningfulness to the Universe, a unity, a single philosophical explanation which makes it all hang together. Many orthodoxly religious people would be so frightened by giving up the notion that the Universe has integration, unity, and, therefore, meaningfulness (which is given to it by the fact that it was all created by God or ruled by God or *is* God) that the only alternative for them would be to see the Universe as a totally unintegrated chaos.

2. In the cognition that comes in peak-experiences, characteristically the percept is exclusively and fully attended to. That is, there is tremendous concentration of a kind which does not normally occur. There is the truest and most total kind of visual perceiving or listening or feeling. Part of what this involves is a peculiar change which can best be described as non-evaluating, non-comparing, or non-judging cognition. That is to say, figure and ground are less sharply differentiated. Important and unimportant are also less sharply differentiated, i.e. there is a tendency for things to become equally important rather than to be ranged in a hierarchy from very

important to quite unimportant. For instance, the mother examining in loving ecstasy her new-born infant may be enthralled by every single part of him, one part as much as another one, one little toenail as much as another little toenail, and be struck into a kind of religious awe in this way. This same kind of total, non-comparing acceptance of everything, as if everything were equally important, holds also for the perception of people. Thus it comes about that in peak-experience cognition a person is most easily seen *per se*, in himself, by himself, uniquely and idiosyncratically as if he were the sole member of his class. Of course, this is a very common aspect not only of religious experience but of most theologies as well, i.e. the person is unique, the person is sacred, one person in principle is worth as much as any other person, everyone is a child of God, etc.

3. The cognition of being (B-cognition) that occurs in peak-experiences tends to perceive external objects, the world, and individual people as more detached from human concerns. Normally we perceive everything as relevant to human concerns and more particularly to our own private selfish concerns. In the peak-experiences, we become more detached, more objective, and more able to perceive the world as if it were independent not only of the perceiver but even of human beings in general. The perceiver can more readily look upon nature as if it were there in itself and for itself, not simply as if it were a human playground put there for human purposes. He can more easily refrain from projecting human purposes upon it. In a word, he can see it in its own Being (as an end in itself) rather than as something to be used or something to be afraid of or something to wish for or to be reacted to in some other personal, human, self-centred way. That is to say, B-cognition, because it makes human irrelevance more possible, enables us thereby to see more truly the nature of the object in itself. This is a little like talking about God-like perception, superhuman perception. The peak-experience seems to lift us to greater than normal heights so that we can see and perceive in a higher than usual way. We become larger, greater, stronger, bigger, taller people and tend to perceive accordingly.

4. To say this in a different way, perception in the peak-experiences can be relatively ego-transcending, self-forgetful, egoless, unselfish. It can come closer to being unmotivated, impersonal, desireless, detached, not needing or wishing. Which is to say, that it becomes more object-centred than ego-centred. The perceptual experience can be more organised around the object itself as a centring point rather than being based upon the selfish ego. This means in turn that objects and people are more readily perceived as having independent reality of their own.

5. The peak-experience is felt as a self-validating, self-justifying moment which carries its own intrinsic value with it. It is felt to be a highly valuable – even uniquely valuable – experience, so great an experience sometimes that even to attempt to justify it takes away from its dignity and worth. As a matter of fact, so many people find this so great and high an experience that it justifies not only itself but even living itself. Peak-experiences can make life worthwhile by their occasional occurrence. They give meaning to life itself. They prove it to be worthwhile. To say this in a negative way, I would guess that peak-experiences help to prevent suicide.

6. Recognising these experiences as end-experiences rather than as means-experiences makes another point. For one thing, it proves to the experiencer that there are ends in the world, that there are things or objects or experiences to yearn for which are worthwhile in themselves. This in itself is a refutation of the proposition that life and living is meaningless. In other words, peak-experiences are one part of the operational definition of the statement that 'life is worthwhile' or 'life is meaningful'.

7. In the peak-experience there is a very characteristic disorientation in time and space, or even the lack of consciousness of time and space. Phrased positively, this is like experiencing universality and eternity. Certainly we have here, in a very operational sense, a real and scientific meaning of 'under the aspect of eternity'. This kind of timelessness and spacelessness contrasts very sharply with normal experience. The person in the peak-experiences may feel a day passing as if it were minutes or also a minute so intensely lived that it might feel like a day or a year or an eternity even. He may also lose his consciousness of being located in a particular place.

8. The world seen in the peak-experiences is seen only as beautiful, good, desirable, worthwhile, etc. and is never experienced as evil or undesirable. The world is accepted. People will say that then they understand it. Most important of all for comparison with religious thinking is that somehow they become reconciled to evil. Evil itself is accepted and understood and seen in its proper place in the whole, as belonging there, as unavoidable, as necessary, and, therefore, as proper. Of course, the way in which I (and Laski also) gathered peak-experiences was by asking for reports of ecstasies and raptures, of the most blissful and perfect moments of life. Then, of course, life *would* look beautiful. And then all the foregoing might seem like discovering something that had been put in *a priori*. But observe that what I am talking about is the perception of evil, of pain, of disease, of death. In the peak-experiences, not only is the world seen as acceptable and beautiful, but, and this is what I am stressing, the

bad things about life are accepted more totally than they are at other times. It is as if the peak-experience reconciled people to the presence of evil in the world.

9. Of course, this is another way of becoming 'god-like'. The gods who can contemplate and encompass the whole of being and who, therefore, understand it must see it as good, just, inevitable, and must see 'evil' as a product of limited or selfish vision and understanding. If we could be god-like in this sense, then we, too, out of universal understanding would never blame or condemn or be disappointed or shocked. Our only possible emotions would be pity, charity, kindliness, perhaps sadness or amusement. But this is precisely the way in which self-actualising people do at times react to the world, and in which all of us react in our peak-experiences.

10. Perhaps my most important finding was the discovery of what I am calling B-values or the intrinsic values of Being. When I asked the question, 'How does the world look different in peak-experiences?' the hundreds of answers that I got could be boiled down to a quintessential list of characteristics which, though they overlap very much with one another can still be considered as separate for the sake of research. What is important for us in this context is that this list of the described characteristics of the world as it is perceived in our most perspicuous moments is about the same as what people through the ages have called eternal verities, or the spiritual values, or the highest values, or the religious values. What this says is that facts and values are not totally different from each other; under certain circumstances, they fuse. Most religions have either explicitly or by implication affirmed some relationship or even an overlapping or fusion between facts and values. For instance, people not only existed but they were also sacred. The world was not only merely existent but it was also sacred.

11. B-cognition in the peak-experience is much more passive and receptive, much more humble, than normal perception is. It is much more ready to listen and much more able to hear.

12. In the peak-experience, such emotions as wonder, awe, reverence, humility, surrender, and even worship before the greatness of the experience are often reported. This may go so far as to involve thoughts of death in a peculiar way. Peak-experiences can be so wonderful that they can parallel the experience of dying, that is of an eager and happy dying. It is a kind of reconciliation and acceptance of death. Scientists have never considered as a scientific problem the question of the 'good death'; but here in these experiences we discover a parallel to what has been considered to be the religious attitude towards death, i.e. humility or dignity before

it, willingness to accept it, possibly even a happiness with it.

13. In peak-experiences, the dichotomies, polarities, and conflicts of life tend to be transcended or resolved. That is to say, there tends to be a moving towards the perception of unity and integration in the world. The person himself tends to move towards fusion, integration, and unity and away from splitting, conflicts, and oppositions.

14. In the peak-experiences, there tends to be a loss, even though transient, of fear, anxiety, inhibition, of defence and control, of perplexity, confusion, conflict, of delay and restraint. The profound fear of disintegration, of insanity, of death, all tend to disappear for the moment. Perhaps this amounts to saying that fear disappears.

15. Peak-experiences sometimes have immediate effects or after-effects upon the person. Sometimes their after-effects are so profound and so great as to remind us of the profound religious conversions which forever after changed the person. Lesser effects could be called therapeutic. These can range from very great to minimal or even to no effects at all. This is an easy concept for religious people to accept, accustomed as they are to thinking in terms of conversions, of great illuminations, of great moments of insight, etc.

16. I have likened the peak-experience in a metaphor to a visit to a personally defined heaven from which the person then returns to Earth. This is like giving a naturalistic meaning to the concept of heaven. Of course, it is quite different from the conception of heaven as a place somewhere into which one physically steps after life on this Earth is over. The conception of heaven that emerges from the peak-experiences is one which exists all the time all around us, always available to step into for a little while at least.

17. In peak-experiences, there is a tendency to move more closely to a perfect identity, or uniqueness, or to the idiosyncracy of the person or to his real self, to have become more a real person.

18. The person feels himself more than at other times to be responsible, active, the creative centre of his own activities and of his own perceptions, more self-determined, more a free agent, with more 'free will' than at other times.

19. But it has also been discovered that precisely those persons who have the clearest and strongest identity are exactly the ones who are most able to transcend the ego or the self and to become selfless, who are at least relatively selfless and relatively egoless.

20. The peak-experiencer becomes more loving and more accepting, and so he becomes more spontaneous and honest and innocent.

21. He becomes less an object, less a thing, less a thing of the world

living under the laws of the physical world, and he becomes more a psyche, more a person, more subject to the psychological laws, especially the laws of what people have called the 'higher life'.

22. Because he becomes more unmotivated, that is to say, closer to non-striving, non-needing, non-wishing, he asks less for himself in such moments. He is less selfish. (We must remember that the gods have been considered generally to have no needs or wants, no deficiencies, no lacks, and to be gratified in all things. In this sense, the unmotivated human being becomes more god-like.)

23. People during and after peak-experiences characteristically feel lucky, fortunate, graced. A common reaction is 'I don't deserve this.' A common consequence is a feeling of gratitude, in religious persons, to their God, in others, to fate or to Nature or to just good fortune. It is interesting in the present context that this can go over into worship, giving thanks, adoring, giving praise, oblation, and other reactions which fit very easily into orthodox religious frameworks. In that context we are accustomed to this sort of thing – that is, to the feeling of gratitude or all-embracing love for everybody and for everything, leading to an impulse to do something good for the world, an eagerness to repay, even a sense of obligation and dedication.

24. The dichotomy or polarity between humility and pride tends to be resolved in the peak-experiences and also in self-actualising persons. Such people resolve the dichotomy between pride and humility by fusing them into a single complex superordinate unity, that is by being proud (in a certain sense) and also humble (in a certain sense). Pride (fused with humility) is not hubris nor is it paranoia; humility (fused with pride) is not masochism.

25. What has been called the 'unitive consciousness' is often given in peak-experiences, i.e. a sense of the sacred glimpsed *in* and *through* the particular instance of the momentary, the secular, the worldly.

ROBERTO ASSAGIOLI

Psychosynthesis

Let us examine *whether* and *how* it is possible to solve this central problem of human life, to heal this fundamental infirmity of Man. Let us see how he may free himself from this enslavement and achieve a harmonious inner integration, true Self-realisation, and right relationships with others.

The task is certainly neither easy nor simple, but that it can be accomplished has been demonstrated by the success of those who have used adequate and appropriate means.

The stages for the attainment of this goal may be tabulated as follows:

1. Thorough knowledge of one's personality.
2. Control of its various elements.
3. Realisation of one's true Self – the discovery or creation of a unifying centre.
4. Psychosynthesis: the formation or reconstruction of the personality around the new centre.

Let us examine each of these stages.

1. Thorough Knowledge of One's Personality

We have recognised that in order really to know ourselves it is not enough to make an inventory of the elements that form our conscious being. An extensive exploration of the vast regions of our unconscious must also be undertaken. We have first to penetrate courageously into the pit of our lower unconscious in order to discover the dark forces that ensnare and menace us – the 'phantasms', the ancestral or childish images that obsess or silently dominate us, the fears that paralyse us, the conflicts that waste our energies. It is possible to do this by the use of the methods of psychoanalysis.

This search can be undertaken by oneself but it is accomplished more easily with the help of another. In any case the methods must be employed in a genuinely scientific manner, with the greatest objectivity and impartiality; without preconceived theories and without allowing ourselves to be deterred or led astray by the covert or violent resistance of our fears, our desires, our emotional attachments.

Psychoanalysis generally stops here; but this limitation is not justified. The regions of the middle and higher unconscious should likewise be explored. In that way we shall discover in ourselves hitherto unknown abilities, our true vocations, our higher potentialities which seek to express themselves, but which we often repel and repress through lack of understanding, through prejudice or fear. We shall also discover the immense reserve of undifferentiated psychic energy latent in every one of us; that is, the plastic part of our unconscious which lies at our disposal, empowering us with an unlimited capacity to learn and to create.

2. Control of the Various Elements of the Personality

After having discovered all these elements, we have to take possession of them and acquire control over them. The most effective method by which we can achieve this is that of disidentification. This is based on a fundamental psychological principle which may be formulated as follows:

> *We are dominated by everything with which our self becomes identified. We can dominate and control everything from which we disidentify ourselves.*

In this principle lies the secret of our enslavement or of our liberty. Every time we 'identify' ourselves with a weakness, a fault, a fear or any personal emotion or drive, we limit and paralyse ourselves. Every time we admit 'I am discouraged' or 'I am irritated', we become more and more dominated by depression or anger. We have accepted those limitations; we have ourselves put on our chains. If, instead, in the same situation we say, 'A wave of discouragement is *trying* to submerge me' or 'An impulse of anger is *attempting* to overpower me,' the situation is very different. Then there are two forces confronting each other; on one side our vigilant self and on the other the discouragement or the anger. And the vigilant self does not submit to that invasion; it can objectively and critically survey those impulses of discouragement or anger; it can look for their origin, foresee their deleterious effects, and realise their unfoundedness. This is often sufficient to withstand an attack of such forces and win the battle.

But even when these forces within ourselves are temporarily stronger, when the conscious personality is at first overwhelmed by their violence, the vigilant self is never really conquered. It can retire to an inner fortress and there prepare for and await the favourable moment in which to counter-attack. It may lose some of the battles, but if it does not give up its arms and surrender, the ultimate issue is not compromised, and it will achieve victory in the end.

Then, besides repelling one by one the attacks that come from the unconscious, we can apply a more fundamental and decisive method: we can tackle the deep-seated causes of these attacks and cut away the roots of the difficulty. This procedure may be divided into two phases:

1. *The disintegration of the harmful images or complexes.*
2. *The control and utilisation of the energies thus set free.*

Psychoanalysis has demonstrated that the power of these images and complexes lies chiefly in the fact that we are unconscious of them, that we do not recognise them as such. When they are unmasked, understood, and resolved into their elements, they often cease to obsess us; in any case we are then much better able to defend ourselves against them. In order to dissolve them we should use the methods of *objectification*, of *critical analysis* and of *discrimination*. That is to say, we must employ cold, impersonal observation as if they were mere natural phenomena, occurring outside ourselves. We should create a 'psychological distance' between ourselves and them, keeping these images or complexes at arm's length, so to speak, and then quietly consider their origin, their nature and – their stupidity! This does not mean the suppression or repression of the energies inherent in those manifestations but their control and redirection into constructive channels.

It is well known that too much criticism and analysis are apt to paralyse and even kill our emotions and feelings. This critical faculty, which we often employ indiscriminately and harmfully against our higher feelings and creative potentialities, should instead be used to free ourselves from undesirable impulses and tendencies. But such analysis and criticism are not always sufficient. There are certain strong trends, certain vital elements which, however much we may disparage and condemn them, obstinately persist. This is true especially concerning sexual and aggressive drives. These, when detached from the complexes or diverted from their previous channels, create in us a state of agitation and unrest and may find new but equally undesirable outlets.

These forces, therefore, must not be left to run wild, but should be disposed of in harmless ways or, better still, used for constructive purposes: creative activities of various kinds; the re-building of our personality, contributing to our psychosynthesis. But in order to be able to do this we must start from the centre, we must have established and made efficient *the unifying and controlling Principle of our life.*

3. Realisation of One's True Self –
The Discovery or Creation of a Unifying Centre

On the basis of what we have said about the nature and power of the Self, it is not difficult to point out *theoretically* how to reach this aim. What has to be achieved is to expand the personal consciousness into that of the Self; to reach up, following the thread or ray to the star; to unite the lower with the higher Self. But this, which is so easily expressed in words, is in reality a tremendous undertaking. It constitutes a magnificent endeavour, but certainly a long and arduous one, and not everybody is ready for it. But between the starting point in the lowlands of our ordinary consciousness and the shining peak of Self-realisation there are intermediate phases, plateaus at various altitudes on which a man may rest or even make his abode, if his lack of strength precludes or his will does not choose a further ascent.

In favourable cases the ascent takes place to some extent spontaneously through a process of natural inner growth, fostered by the manifold experiences of life; but often the process is very slow. In all cases, however, it can be considerably accelerated by our deliberate conscious action and by the use of appropriate active techniques.

The intermediate stages imply new identifications. The men and women who cannot reach their true Self in its pure essence can create a picture and an ideal of perfected personality adequate to their calibre, their stage of development and their psychological type, and therefore can make this ideal practicable in actual life. . . .

4. Psychosynthesis: the Formation or Reconstruction of the Personality Around the New Centre

When the unifying centre has been found or created, we are in a position to build around it a new personality – coherent, organised, and unified.

This is the actual *psychosynthesis*, which also has several stages. The first essential is to decide the plan of action, to formulate the 'inner program'. We must visualise the purpose to be achieved – that is, the new personality to be developed – and have a clear realisation of the various tasks it entails.

Some people have a distinct vision of their aim from the outset. They are capable of forming a clear picture of themselves as they can and intend to become. This picture should be realistic and 'authentic', that is, in line with the natural development of the given individual and therefore capable – at least in some measure – of realisation, and should not be a neurotic, unreal 'idealised image' in the sense of Karen Horney. A genuine 'ideal model' has a dynamic creative power; it facilitates the task by eliminating uncertainties and mistakes; it concentrates the energies and utilises the great suggestive and creative power of images.

Other individuals of a more plastic psychological constitution, who live spontaneously, following indications and intuitions rather than definite plans, find it difficult to formulate such a programme, to build according to a pattern; they may even positively dislike such a method. Their tendency is to let themselves be led by the Spirit within or by the will of God, leaving Him to choose what they should become. They feel that they can best reach the goal by eliminating, as much as possible, the obstacles and resistances inherent in their personality; by widening the channel of communication with the higher Self through aspiration and devotion and then letting the creative power of the Spirit act, trusting and obeying it. Some take a similar attitude but express it in a different way; they speak of tuning in with the cosmic order, with the universal harmony, of letting Life act in and through them (the Wu-Wei of Taoists).

Both methods are effective, and each is appropriate to the corresponding type. But it is well to know, to appreciate and to use both to some extent in order to avoid the limitations and the exaggerations of each by correcting and enriching the one with elements taken from the other. . . .

The 'ideal models' or images that one can create are many, but they can be divided into two principal groups. The first is formed of images representing harmonious development, an all-round personal or spiritual perfection. This kind of ideal is aimed at chiefly by introverts. The second group represents specialised efficiency. The purpose here is the utmost development of an ability or quality corresponding to the particular line of self-expression and the social role or roles which the individual has chosen. This is the ideal of the artist, the teacher, the advocate of a good cause, etc. Such models are generally preferred by extroverts.

Once the choice of the ideal form has been made, *practical psychosynthesis, the actual construction of the new personality, begins.* This work may be divided into three principal parts:

1. *Utilization* of the available energies. These are (a) the forces released by the analysis and disintegration of the unconscious complexes; (b) the tendencies latent, and until now neglected, which exist on the various psychological levels. Such utilisation demands the transmutation of many of these unconscious forces. Their inherent plasticity and mutability makes this possible. In fact, such transmutation is a process that is continually taking place within us. Just as heat is changed into motion and electric energy, and *vice versa*, our emotions and impulses are transformed into physical actions or into imaginative and intellectual activities. Conversely, ideas stir up emotions or are transformed into plans and hence into actions. . . .

2. *Development* of the aspects of the personality which are either deficient or inadequate for the purpose we desire to attain. This development can be carried out in two ways: by means of evocation, autosuggestion, creative affirmation; or by the methodical training of the undeveloped functions (such as memory, imagination, will) – a training analogous to that used in physical culture or in developing technical skills such as singing or playing an instrument.

3. *Coordination and subordination* of the various psychological energies and functions, the creation of a firm organisation of the personality. This ordering presents interesting and suggestive analogies with that of a modern state, with the various groupings of the citizens into communities, social classes, professions and trades, and the different grades of town, district and state officials.

Such is, in brief outline, the process by which psychosynthesis is accomplished. But it should be made clear that all the various stages and methods mentioned above are closely interrelated and need not be followed in a strict succession of distinct periods or phases. A living human being is not a building, for which the foundations must be laid, then the walls erected and, finally, the roof added. The carrying out of the vast inner programme of psychosynthesis may be started from various points and angles at the same time, and the different methods and activities can be wisely alternated through shorter or longer cycles, according to circumstances and inner conditions.

All this may at first appear rather formidable, but there is no reason for doubt or discouragement. The help of a competent therapist or teacher obviously makes the task much easier; on the other hand, one may also reach a satisfactory result by one's own unaided efforts and through one's own trials and errors. Having absorbed the preliminary instruction on the psychological principles and laws involved, and having learned the various psychosynthetic techniques to be followed, the rest is a question of practice, experience, intelligence, and intuition, which increase according to the need and to the steadfastness of the endeavour. In this way the new regenerated personality is formed, and a new and higher life begins, the *true life*, for which the preceding one can be considered as a mere preparation, almost a gestation.

MARION WOODMAN

Reclaiming the Body

Body awareness has become an important focus in my analytic practice because of my experience with both women and men who, despite earnest commitment to their dreams and to their own growth, are still unable to trust the process. Their souls are dislocated in bodies so wounded that the ego's willingness in itself is simply not enough.

Failure in travailing life's junctures is not necessarily the failure of the ego to adopt a new attitude towards the Self by sacrificing the old. Many of my analysands have what I believe to be appropriate ego attitudes; their bodies, however, have at some point been traumatised. While their egos can be approached through confrontation, challenge or humour, their bodies cannot respond. The more quickly the ego moves ahead, the more terrorised the body becomes. The task then is to find some means of going back to the point of wounding to reconnect with the abandoned child. The body, like the child, tells the truth, and tells it through movement or lack of movement.

A trained observer can discern whether the soul has taken up residence in the body, or whether the body image is so intolerable that the flesh is barely inhabited. The body can be so retarded that it cannot even imagine itself as an adult. If, as James Hillman says, 'the image by which the flesh lives is the ultimate ruling necessity', then some means must be found to create an adequate image – physically as well as psychically. Body awareness, as I understand it, has nothing to do with the technology of the body. It is not fitness or longevity that is at stake, although these may be by-products. What is at stake is the integration of body, soul and spirit.

So long as we are in this world, the psyche is enacted through the medium of the body. William Blake described the body as 'that portion of Soul discerned by the five Senses'. The soul is, of course, much more than the bodily 'portion' of itself. It is not limited to manifesting in the physical body; it manifests also in that infinite body which constitutes the 'body' of the imagination, a body that includes the entire visionary world of the arts – music, sculpture, painting, poetry, dance, architecture. Each of these visionary or imaginary worlds may be thought of as larger human bodies, or a single giant human body. That it may act in another world, of which the arts are an expression, is one of the oldest speculations about the immortality of the soul, and art as an expression of it.

The soul, then, manifests in a multiplicity of forms. While it is on Earth, it must have a body image as its home, as its primary medium of expression. The soul will not naturally reject its body image any more than the mother's breast will naturally reject her baby. The body mirrors the soul. Where rejection occurs, something has gone seriously wrong. But no matter what went wrong, the soul will do everything in its power to correct it. . . .

The woman who has been a 'Daddy's girl', for example, has seldom if ever experienced her 'dark' side, her rage and jealousy, lust and ecstasy. Alienated from her body, she does not know the magnificent energy that is blocked from consciousness, so blocked that it rarely manifests in dreams. She can spend the analytic hour in a euphoria of golden dream images, then awkwardly pull herself together and sadly resume the unbearable burden of her own body. Her dreams often mirror this self-alienation: she may appear as an animated object – a golfball, a cloud, a sausage with a head; sometimes a head moves two inches above a severed neck; sometimes a tight rope or scarf blocks communication between head and heart; sometimes her father's rotting head putrifies her abdomen.

While such images clearly demonstrate the enormity of the shadow problem, as analyst I cannot simply say, 'There, you see, there is the severance from your own feelings. There's where your evil witch is separating you from yourself.' That approach could only fall on deaf ears because a soul that has chosen to cut itself off from a 'filthy' world is not going to recognise a self-murderer in its midst, nor will it acknowledge such demeaning human passions as greed, lust, power, and 'the thousand natural shocks that flesh is heir to'.

Body work can release the witch. She dare not be confronted directly through facing the eating disorder with forced feeding or deprivation, but she can be beheaded through skilful manoeuvres with shield and sword, as Perseus dealt with Medusa, while bringing the body to consciousness. Body work accelerates the process and creates a strong container for the ego.

Analysis attempts to uncover the complexes in which repressed energy is held. If the analysand has a relative harmonious body/ psyche relationship, the shadow material is obvious in the dreams. In many people, however, body and psyche were split apart at a very early age. In cases where a person was unwanted, or unwelcome because of gender, the body/psyche split began *in utero* or at birth, as if the soul had chosen not to enter the body, but instead remained in exile from it. The energy is centred in or above the head, and the person has to make a concentrated effort to stay out of a fantasy world in order to deal with the simplest details of everyday reality. Denied a bodily home, such people are possessed by a longing for some home that is not of this Earth. Their early dreams in analysis are usually very positive, full of numinous visions of golden cities, golden birds and specific places where they are assured of security and love. It is as if the Self knows their hold on the everyday world is tenuous and gives these magnificent dreams as anchor points to which they can return when suicidal despair manifests, as it inevitably does in the later stages of analysis.

★ ★ ★

Months may pass in the analytic process before the conflict appears in dreams. Body work, which must be handled with considerable patience and love, reaches out to that lost infant whose little body –

132

strong, tender, sure – was never allowed to develop. The body is suspicious and terrified, and only gradually can it learn to trust its own instincts and discipline them into a firm steady base for the maturing psyche. Unless the body knows it is loved, that its responses are acceptable, the psyche does not have the basis of certainty in the instincts that it requires; sooner or later in the analysis the person will become stuck because the ego is afraid to trust; at the point of surrender the ego becomes paralysed. Unless the body knows that there are inner loving arms strong enough to contain it, however fierce or broken it may be, it will hang on to its own rigidity in an effort to survive. That rigidity is echoed in the rigidity of the persona and the ego.

A woman whose mother did not love her own femininity, and who therefore rejected the female body of her daughter, almost inevitably goes through a period of lesbian dreams or lesbian acting-out because her body requires the acceptance of a woman. Usually this is only temporary and the woman's energy gradually turns towards men. If the lesbian phase has been carefully integrated, ensuring that the feminine ego is firmly located in the female body, then the woman who has never been able to surrender to orgasm experiences a new world of sexuality. Energy blocks that were knotted into her pelvis and thighs from early childhood and puberty are released and energy flows naturally into ecstasy. Once that release is achieved, a woman who formerly looked for cuddling and holding in a man's embrace no longer attempts to turn her lover into a mother. Her man is free to experience his own masculinity in the giving and receiving of the sexual relationship.

Body work must be approached with the same respect and attentiveness that one gives to dreams. The body has a wisdom of its own. However slowly and circuitously that wisdom manifests, once it is experienced it is a foundation, a basis of knowing that gives confidence and total support to the ego. To reach its wisdom requires absolute concentration; dropping the mind into the body, breathing into whatever is ready to be released, and allowing the process of expression until the negative, dammed energy is out, making room for the positive energy, genuine Light, to flood in. After body work, the dreams bring to consciousness the complexes that have been threatened or released. Ancient toilets that have been overflowing, broken or plugged begin to flush; animals that have been dead, disabled, frenzied or starving begin to be healed; automobiles with faulty starters, flat tyres and smashed-in rear trunks are repaired; houses with defective wiring, where short circuits amass too much energy in one socket with no current in another, are recircuited. Often new windows replace little old garret slits, or big secret rooms are discovered in the old house.

If the individual is ready, and if the experience has been one of trust, a powerfully numinous dream of the Great Mother as nourishing, loving protector is often given. Rarely does she show her face, but her love infiltrates the body with a soft, luminous Light, an experience so powerful that the woman returns to that moment again and again when the Gethsemane days of the analysis seem unendurable. Repeatedly, analysands say, 'I don't know what happened. I am not a religious person, but I know Somebody loves me.' . . . .

As the body becomes more conscious, its messages become clearer and more trustworthy. Many intuitives who have trusted their intuition all their lives realise through body work that their bodies are just as intuitive as their psyches. One woman, for example, was with a male friend one night when suddenly her body began to shake. Formerly she would have ignored it; now she recognised its dread. The next day her friend phoned to tell her he wished to end the relationship. Her body had *known*. The body is the medium through which the soul enacts itself. No matter how blocked the medium is, unless it is completely destroyed the body will still register the soul's activity.

GABRIELLE ROTH

Your Father, Your Lesson

Whether you are wounded or blessed (or most likely some of both) in the first cycle of life, you then move into childhood and need to meet your father as your sacred teacher. He is mother turned inside out, the authority to her permission, the line through her circle, the worldly wise 'no' to her cosmic 'yes'. Through your mother your self-image grows; through your father it becomes defined. In/out, wait for it/go for it, surrender/control, allow/demand, feminine/masculine. Between mother and father you learn to dance the tango of life.

Your mother taught you how to be in your body. Your father teaches you how to express your heart as he initiates you into the world of relationships with others. He teaches the art of how best to relate to another person, because he is the first person outside of yourself that you have to relate to, that is, build a relationship with.

You came out of your mother's body; that relationship is real and immediate. It is a psychic 'given'. You and your mother are inescapably one. Father is outside you. He is your first friend and your task (and his teaching) is to connect to him. In the creation of this relationship, you build the foundation for all your future one-to-one relationships; you learn to relate to the world of people through your father. In your later life, you relate to people as your father related to you and you to him. It is from father that we either do or do not receive the ability to instinctively know the answer to the question, 'What does this other person truly need from me?' It is from father that we first learn the art of give and take, of giving and receiving, the high commerce of friendship. It is the father's role to pass on the paternal instinct, the instinctive ability to relate appropriately to others, teaching loyalty, companionship, sharing, and fairness.

Your father teaches you to draw the line, to feel your own sense of authority, to balance your self-nurturing feeling of boundless permission. 'The Child is father to the Man,' as Wordworth puts it. In this whole process you learn to become, to a greater or lesser degree, your own father, your own friend.

Your relationship to your father determines whether you can be yourself and express your heart, or whether you must achieve, perform, charm, seduce, compete, please, demand, negate or destroy to feel recognised. These patterns are created early. In all our one-to-one relationships we tend to do whatever we had to do to get daddy's attention and approval when we were a child. As Robert Frost put it, 'You don't have to deserve your mother's love. You have to deserve your father's. He's more particular.'

All friends are fathers in disguise. If your father was there for you, giving you what you needed in the moment, responding from his heart to your heart, cheering you on and reining you in, affirming and consoling, cautioning and encouraging, then the world wears a welcoming face and you'll know how to be a friend. If he was present for you, you will instinctively know how to be present for others. I remember watching my father taking care of his dying brother. My uncle had a brain tumour, and every day a new piece of his body didn't work. He got to the point where only his face moved, and there was my dad telling him stories, massaging his feet, lighting his damn cigarettes, giving him what he needed. I realised that this was the quality of attention I had become accustomed to.

To whatever degree your father didn't or doesn't know how to relate to you, he can't know how to relate to others. The distant, absent father is distant and absent in other relationships as well. He tends to relate on the surface and perform, hide his feelings, think and plan, judge and compare. He must analyse his relationships because they're not instinctive to him. He has to *decide* how and what to feel, making lists of people's good and bad qualities so he can determine whether to be in relationship to them. He doesn't dare to be spontaneous, because he can't trust himself to respond appropriately. So he develops pre-planned and market-tested ways of being with others. Fathers who are wounded are suffering. And they create children who are wounded.

People with a limited paternal instinct develop coping patterns. They become performers, flatterers, deliberators. They hide behind their work or their kids. They worry a lot about titles, credentials, status, wealth, prestige, about who's in and who's out, because they don't trust themselves to be able to respond to another person and be responded to just for who each is. They use money to win control, love, influence. They adopt some pose, some strategy that allows them to get by without really entering into relationships and commitments heart and soul, here and now. I know a kid whose father sent him elaborate presents on his birthday but never showed up himself. When he grew up he gave his dad all kinds of presents – a condominium in Florida, a baby grand piano, a trip to Paris – but he never showed up either. The person without an instinct for relating is, in any encounter with another person or in a social or collaborative situation, ill at ease, in pain, in deceit, and quietly desperate. It's no wonder they act so inappropriately so often.

Children with father wounds are everywhere – surely many of us. They're easy to spot. Without the heart in their day-to-day living, without the colour of feelings, life is drab. They can go to all the right parties in all the right clothes and still never have a good time. Pervading their lives is a lack of *élan*, a theme of melancholy – regret, despair even – that underlies their apparently successful life stories. The spark is missing.

Since many more children now grow up without fathers or with part-time fathers only, whether because of divorce or because many men devote so much of their time to work and other activities rather than to fathering, the number of adult children of absentee fathers is astronomical and growing higher daily. Of course, single mothers and full-time mothers, as well as other parental figures, can and do supply some of the fathering role, and some women have strong paternal instincts to pass on. As we know, some fathers have strong maternal instincts and offer what mothers deficient in nurturing instincts can't offer. But prior to all our social arrangements and penchant for creating structures to fit our worldly goals, there is an elemental and natural power to men playing the paternal role and women playing the maternal role.

The ideal is to have a biological mother who teaches us how to be in a body and trust ourselves, and a biological father who teaches us how to express our hearts. Just having parents doesn't guarantee success. Natural parents can fail their natural children – and adoptive, single, or foster parents can raise their children with instincts intact, as can parents who themselves have been wounded but through awareness and devotion have made the quantum leap into conscious parenting. My dad was one of these.

I've worked a lot with people with father wounds. I had a physician study with me who related to everyone as doctor to patient. It was as if he couldn't take off his white coat even for his lovers. He's not alone. Think of the talk-show host who can't talk to someone unless there's a microphone between them. Actors who never seem to leave the stage. Executives who run their families like they run their business. Trial lawyers who map out strategies for all their relationships as if they are going to trial. Awareness of this 'act' is the beginning of healing this wound.

* * *

This father wound, like the mother wound, has reached epidemic proportions. It is everywhere, breeding, loneliness, alienation, distrust, deceit. We lie to each other about what we think and feel and do, and don't remember how to tell the truth. And we desperately need to speak and to hear the truth. We readily see right through others' efforts to hide their pain, shame, disregard. We forget that they also see right through us. They see the fear, anger, sorrow – the real energy we struggle to mask. We pretend to care about each other, but end up sharing the worst of ourselves, the stuff that doesn't work. We're as predictable as daily headlines, as spirited as muzak.

Father wounds take a great toll on our intimate relationships. If we don't know how to talk to each other or to be together without talking, if we don't know how to give and receive, how can we make love? How can we move one another? How can we be touching? How can we be real? We all expect to have wonderful intimate relationships, but how can we be real lovers if we don't know how to be true friends?

Can you remember your last real heart-to-heart conversation, where you really hooked into each other, following every move, every gesture, every wave of emotion, riding the waves together, connected? When did you last partake of such holy communion?

Communion heals the father wound. Communion with friends, lovers, parents, strangers, even enemies. But mostly with friends. Through hard trial and error and working with thousands of people, I've discovered that the heart needs to open up as fully as possible. It is a waste of time to pretend that we can't be hurt. If we're going to be fully alive, we have to be ready to get hurt and even to hurt others. Otherwise, we're dead. Or immobilised in protective armour.

In vulnerability one practises the art of friendship, the art of the heart. It is an essential spiritual practice.

If you don't do it instinctively, you must do it consciously. Stop and focus on your relationships and let them each teach you what you need to know. The more you give to them, the more you will get back. The more attention you pay, the more natural relating will feel, until the impulse to take special care of your relationships becomes internalised and instinctive.

It's interesting to make a list of your friends, then sit and contemplate what each has to teach you. Meditate on each name and ask yourself, 'What does this person really need from me?'; 'What do I really need from him or her?' Keep asking until answers come.'

Who nourishes you? How? Why? Who drains you? How? Why? Who do you avoid? How? Why? Who do you reach out to? How? Why?

Bring your relationships into the moment, including the one with your father. Erase the past, stay out of the future with all its expectations. Let yourself be surprised. Practice 'loving the one you're with'. Everyone you know is dying for some real attention, someone who really hears what they're saying, sees their vision, cheers them on into the heights and depths of being real.

We need relationships that are alive, vital, changing, moving – relationships that move through all the rhythms. Sometimes they flow, sometimes they pulse, sometimes they erupt, sometimes they lilt along, and sometimes they're very still. It is particularly important to have a moving relationship with one's father, as this relationship is the key to all other friendships.

Here are some exercises to help you discover and befriend your father. With courage and creative reflection often we can forge anew a very special bond of friendship, regardless of time or distance. Or we can at least learn concretely the truth of our childhood and determine what aspects of fathering we need in order to complete our childhood cycle.

1. An easy way to begin learning about our childhood cycle is with the mirror opposite of the father/child relationship you may have missed out on. Make friends with a young child, age five, six, or seven. Children at this age are usually spontaneous, warm and enthusiastic. They live here and now. They will be emotionally direct, demand flexibility and patience, and reward your attention with a joy in being that can't be measured.

2. Write down your memories of your father before you were five, and what you've been told about him. What was he like? Where was he? Recall his varied guises, smells, habits; the way he talked, sang, cried (or didn't).

3. Sit back, relax, and feel yourself moving backwards in time like a movie in reverse. Stop when you get to five years old. Imagine your five-year-old self in a familiar room with your father. How do you feel? Do you make contact? What kind? Are you touching, talking, laughing, cowering, uncomfortable, insecure? Fast forward to about ten years old and see yourself in the same room: how do you relate to your father; how does he relate to you?

4. Write a dialogue between your father and yourself at age ten. If you can't, that will tell you something.

5. Who is he? Capture him in an image, a metaphor, a quintessential photo, a characteristic statement, a telling story.

6. In your journal, visualise your relationship to your father in an 'energy drawing' that clearly conveys the undercurrent as well as the surface waves that flow between you and your father.

7. Write a capsule account of your father's life story, tracing the movement of his life from infancy through childhood and adolescence to adulthood, middle age, and final years. Did he or is he likely to die satisfied, fulfilled, serene?

8. How would your mother tell his story? How would he?

9. How would you speak to your father if you were his friend, not his child? What would you say as his best friend? Somebody has to break the wall of silence: pick up the phone; get on the plane; talk real things out heart to heart. He's probably as lonely as you are. Are you afraid of your father? Afraid for him? Are you angry with him? How does he bring you joy? What's the most compassionate thing you could do for him? Let it all out now. The healing will be wonderful for you both.

10. Since your father was your first friend, you probably treat your friends the way he treated you. Write portraits of three different friends, and your relationship to each. Read them over and over, looking for repetitive patterns, positive as well as negative. Do you run each relationship or do you get pushed around? Do you play hard to get? Are you flirtatious, overbearing, timid? How do you relate? Do you relate at all, or do you perform, plan, seduce, etc.?

Maybe it's instinctive for you to move heart to heart and easy for you to know what another needs; maybe you come from your heart most of the time. If so, you have your father to thank. If not, forgive him: this is also his pain. You do have something in common.

Life is raw material that cries out to be transformed into art – survival art rooted in truth, carved into poems, into songs, into albums, into communications straight from the heart. You can turn your relationship to your father into art. Think about it, write about it, embrace your childhood, your heart.

Meditating on your father can also be rewarding: sit back, take a deep breath, settle into a comfortable position.

Father meditation: Imagine your father sitting opposite you: how does he hold himself, how does he look, what is the basic impression he makes on you – weariness, anger, impatience, ebullience, calm?

Think of three things you love about him, three qualities you find endearing. Think of three things that put you off, alienate you. Reflect on how all these qualities are in you as well, on how much alive you are, how intimately connected.

Look your dad in the eye. Let your feelings about him surface, and imagine saying them to him. Empty your heart of all the things you might have choked back for years, telling him everything you feel till there's nothing left. Imagine what he would say in response and let him say his piece. Then breathe calm into the empty space that is left.

Imagine, too, making physical contact with your father, touching him, holding his hand, hugging him, rocking him. Let the blocked affection for him flow and receive his in return.

Then let him go back to his place. Look him in the eye again and search your heart for the courage to thank and forgive him, to forgive and thank yourself. Forgive him for his weaknesses and failings; thank him for making you who you are and being there for you when he was.

When I have meditated on my dad, I've appreciated his generosity, his loyalty, his serenity. I've acknowledged his stubborn pride, his prejudices, his timidity – all part of me. I've swooped him up in my arms, held him close and rocked him like a baby, wiped the tears from his face and pressed his ear to my heart.

Everyone has a father. Some active and reporting for duty, some missing in action. Some out of step with the beat of their own hearts. Some too busy to relate to the most important charges in their lives. If we haven't found our father outside, we have to find him within, and to reconnect with our father if and when we can. It's a sacred task, a vital undertaking.

As we heal ourselves, we release our parents in some beautiful way to heal themselves. I've seen this pattern repeat itself in many lives. It has inspired and given me hope. We can effect change by changing. And what a gift to be able to heal your parents just by healing yourself. We have the power to give them back the freedom to be who they really are – wounded, human, vulnerable, not giants in a fairytale or society's police force. But real people – your people.

As we become our own parents, become whole, it lifts a psychic burden off our parents' shoulders; they no longer need worry about what they did and didn't do for you, and are free to become themselves.

LEONARD ORR and SONDRA RAY

Rebirthing

At the moment of birth, you formed impressions about the world which you have carried all your life; these impressions control you from a subconscious level. Many of them are negative:

Life is a struggle.
The Universe is a hostile place.
The Universe is against me.
I can't get what I need.
People hurt me.
There must be something wrong with me.
Life is painful.
Love is dangerous.
I am not wanted.
I can't get enough love.

Your impressions are negative because your parents and others who cared for you didn't know what you needed when you were born, and gave you a lot of things you didn't need: lights that were too bright for your sensitive eyes, sounds that were too harsh for your ears, and touches of hands and fabrics too rough for your delicate skin. Some of you, despite the fact that your spines had been curled up for several months, were jerked upside down by your heels and beaten, which produced excruciating pain. Breathing became associated with pain and your breathing has been too shallow ever since.

But the physical pain is nothing compared to the psychic pain of birth. Nature provided that as a newborn you could receive oxygen through the umbilical cord while learning to breathe in the atmosphere (which was a totally new experience after having been in water), but the custom has been to cut the cord immediately, throwing you into a panic where you felt you were surely going to die right at birth.

Another significant psychic pain occurred when you were snatched away from your mother and stuck in a little box in the nursery. Most people never recover from this mishandling of the separation of mother and child. For nine months you knew nothing but the inside of your mother's womb. It was warm and comfortable until it got too small for you. What you needed was to be shown that the world outside is a far more interesting place, with a lot more possibilities than the womb, and that it could be just as comfortable, safe, and pleasurable as the place you had been. However, since your leaving that place was so traumatic, you have probably spent your entire life trying to get back there, never noticing or experiencing the full extent of the possibilities out here.

*   *   *

In California, Leonard Orr developed a way of helping a person of any age to get in touch with his birth trauma and remove it from consciousness. The process he created is very simple and yet extremely powerful. In the beginning, all rebirths were done in a hot tub. The rebirthee entered the tub with a snorkel and noseplug and floated face down while the rebirther and the assistant gently held him in place. The water proved a powerful stimulus in triggering the experience of being in the womb and being forced out of it. In fact, as the process evolved, it became clear that going in the water for the first rebirth was so powerful that it was too scary for some people. To avoid overwhelming them, Leonard devised the dry rebirth, which is primarily used today. He had noticed that it is the breathing and relaxing in the presence of a rebirther that is crucial to the success of the rebirth, and not the water, as he'd thought originally. The process works best when a person is dry-rebirthed until he has a breathing release, and then moves into wet rebirths.

*   *   *

The Breathing Release

Rebirthing is merging the inner and outer breath to experience the fullness of divine energy in the physical body. Re-experiencing birth is only necessary as long as it is inhibiting the breathing mechanism; so we have stuck with the term rebirthing and applied it to physical birth because the basic inhibition on the breathing mechanism was implanted on the individual consciousness during the first breath. It is also called rebirthing because in each session the divine infant is born again in human flesh.

The breathing release is the most important aspect of rebirthing. It is a critical release of all your resistance to life. The breathing release happens when you feel safe enough to re-live the moment of your first breath. It is physiologically, psychologically, and spiritually reliving the moment when you started to breathe for the first time. The breath mechanism is freed and transformed so that, from that moment on, a person knows when his breathing is inhibited and is able to correct it.

*   *   *

Major Points of the Energy Release

1. Relaxation causes inner and outer breath to merge and the breath opens.
2. When the breath opens, the merging of the inhale with the exhale brings about the experience of Infinite Being on the physical level.
3. This breathing cycle cleanses the mind and body; there isn't necessarily any tingling or vibrating with this cleansing process.
4. If there is resistance or fear, then the body will tingle and vibrate. The vibration is not the energy but resistance to the energy. However, vibration is the cleansing process and should be welcomed. Resistance is negative thought previously impressed on the mind and body. At the completion of a breathing cycle resistance is dissolved and the person is breathing faster and there is no tingling. Understanding this is helpful for people being rebirthed the first time, otherwise they will have no way of knowing that rapid breathing eliminates the tingling. The assumption that most have is that rapid breathing *causes* the tingling.
5. The truth is that rapid breathing is dissolving and pumping out of tension and negative thought from the body and vibrating is incidental to the cleansing process.
6. After the cleansing, Divine Energy is coming in with every breath. There is no sensation, but the increase in vitality and health is evident in the body and one experiences bliss in the mind.
7. The energy release is actually dissolving resistance to Divine Energy.

The energy release in the body is so dramatic that many people are afraid of the vibrating sensations and try to stop them. Since the energy is your own life-force, you should not try to stop it. When you try to stop your own energy moving in your own body, it causes tightness, cramping, or temporary paralysis. Consider what your mind might go through at this point: the body is reconnected to the pleasure it felt when it was in the womb. The last time you experienced that much pleasure it led to your birth and the resulting trauma. Therefore, you believe that something terrible will happen again. This is where the pleasure precedes pain philosophy started; that is, the bliss and pleasure of the womb led to the pain of the birth trauma. So the pleasure being experienced through the vibrations creates a fear of the 'inevitable' (which never happens). In experiencing a pleasure for the first time, we concern our minds with how we will eventually have to pay for the enjoyment, to the detriment of the pleasure. Therefore, you might try to suppress the vibrations to reject the sensation of your own life-force.

★   ★   ★

The First Rebirth

I lie down in a small New York bedroom and take off my shirt. This is so he can watch my breathing, Dave tells me, as if to reassure me. He asks me if I have any considerations or questions, which I don't. After all, as a New Age journalist, sixties veteran, and practising Buddhist, I've been through more than a few trips and I figure I can handle this one.

As I start breathing through my mouth, which is open wider than usual, according to rebirthing practice, I feel a tingling, not unpleasant, above my knees. Suddenly it's hard to breathe. My chest feels like an iron band around my lungs. Dave pushes my jaw down, gently. It feels tight, and I tell him so, but the words come out so strangled that I have to repeat them more than once. I can see that, he says. My feet tingle, tiny pins and needles, and then turn solid as wood. It's uncanny how fast it is all happening, and just from this simple way of breathing: *pulling* the inhale and then just releasing the exhale. My hands, too, turn to wood. I am sweating now, thinking, this stuff is powerful – and therefore dangerous. I try crossing my hands over my chest, looking for a position that will ease the pain. There is none. Keep breathing, says David. There seems to be no space between the cells of my body. The feeling is not just numb and wooden now, but there is contraction, a paralysis pressing in, an implosion. Desperately, I try to relax and escape the pain. I can't.

I can't stand it, I try to say. My open jaws are clenched so tight Dave can't understand the words. The muscles of my hands are frozen into claws, and there is something prehistoric, fossil-like, about my posture. I move my hands, throbbing with pain, over my head, this way, that way, but it doesn't help. The truth is I *can't* relax. Beneath my sweating skin, stretched taut as a drum, the muscles are contracting by themselves.

I know it feels like you have to relax, says Dave, but the only way to do it is to stay with the breathing. As far as I'm concerned he's out of his mind, but I try to follow his advice, since he got me into this. What had started out as another interesting experiment, another more or less valuable experience to add to my storehouse of spiritual-psychological tales, has turned into more pain than I bargained for. It hurts like hell.

'Do you usually try to push, to plough through things?' asks Dave.

'No,' I say in a voice that hardly seems my own. 'I usually try to ignore them.'

'Well,' David answers, 'you can't ignore *this*.'

I have no argument with this. There is obviously no way to avoid your own birth, or, by extension, anything else that's yours by birthright. I stay with the breathing and with the pain.

Every now and then Dave touches me lightly, above the knee, on my ankle, my chest, and reminds me not to push the air out. Somehow, without my noticing it, the blocks of my hands and feet start tingling, bubbles of feeling arise, and then fade, dissolve, and disappear. Without planning it I sneak a deep relaxed out-breath, a simple and profound sigh, which opens the door of my chest. 'Ah, that was a good one,' says Dave. He sounds pleased, as if it were his breath too.

My eyes are half open. The soft afternoon light washes pleasurably in. Waves of intense pleasure roll through my body, waves of light, of feeling, of movement. I have as little to do with them as the ocean with its waves: they just rise and fall, rise and fall. Ah, pleasure – the other side of pain, I think. Dave feels it too. It illuminates the narrow little bedroom. The light is rosy through the drawn shade. The oceanic streamings flow, reach a peak, ebb, and slowly subside.

There is still a little tingling, and a few hard knots in my body. I want it to be over, now that it's already happened. 'Take your time,' says Dave. It's true, I see, that I am always in a hurry, speedy. I rest. More pleasure-waves, and a light bubbly euphoria. Dave leaves, and I notice a sweet odour in the room, a little too sweet and heavy, familiar and yet unplaceable. I get up, piss, then walk out into the larger room where people are scattered around, sprawled casually on the rug as if they were lying on a beach, after the group rebirth. I see Leonard talking to someone, and a flash, a spark of acknowledgement, jumps from his eyes to mine. I thank him and go out to the terrace, where I swing in a hammock, easily and peacefully, back and forth, and there is nowhere else to go.

Later, after an hour or two of feeling light and good, I come down, as we say. I feel hot and irritable and tired, which is not surprising since I'd had about three hours' sleep the night before. I argue with Sara, who had had *her* first rebirth screaming and crying in the room next to mine, about whether to go dancing downtown. She wants to go to the Ocean Club. I decide to let her go on alone while I stay home to quietly absorb the rebirthing experience. Dancing, she says, is her way of absorbing a new experience. Yet we both want to be together – it is that kind of argument.

When I go out on Christopher Street, a summer night crowd stands around a man playing a very, very mellow sax for all he is worth. I wonder what I am so uptight about. And what are all these people doing out late Sunday night? Then I remember it is Saturday night, not Sunday, and the next morning is not a Monday morning. For some reason this gives me a great sense of relief. I go back down to the subway to go dancing.

ROGER J. WOOLGER

Past Lives

I found myself almost grunting out the story of a very crude peasant-turned-mercenary soldier of that same period. This rough-and-ready character I seemed to have assumed was originally from the south of Naples and ended up in the papal army raised by the King of France to exterminate the heresy in the South. As this highly unsavoury individual, I found myself in the thick of some of the most hideous massacres, in which the inhabitants of whole French cities were hacked to pieces and burnt in huge pyres in the name of the Church.

Images from that first remembrance haunted me for years, and it took three more two-hour regressions to complete a story I was, and still am, loathe to look at. Yet, amazingly, it started to explain to me disturbing fragments of torture and killing that had come in dreams, meditation, and unbidden fantasy over the years, images that no amount of psychotherapy had ever really touched. Also, the way the story ended seemed to explain a phobia, a fear of fire, I have had all my life. After one of the sieges, the mercenary I seem to have been, deserted and joined the heretics, eventually only to be caught and burned at the stake himself.

As I reflected on the story more and more, other pieces of my personal history in this life started to fall into place. Since adolescence I had developed a very cynical attitude to almost all orthodox religion, especially Christianity. I found it hard to see any Church as anything but authoritarian and dogmatic, denying people the freedom of personal enquiry and experiment. But even more adamant had been my early rejection of all forms of militarism and a strong inclination toward pacifism. I even refused to join the Boy Scouts for reasons I could scarcely articulate as a teenager. Could it be that from early on I had unconsciously been reminded of parts of that soldier's brutal experience?

The most painful recognition of how that soldier still lived in me was remembering one fight I had got into at school at around twelve years of age. In a classroom one day I had become so wild with rage at a boy I considered a hypocrite that four other boys had to drag me off of him. I had been ready to kill. I vowed never to lose my temper again; a part of me recognised how easily I could kill.

Why did such a painful 'past life' memory come to me and not something more edifying, glamorous, or reassuring?

Part of the answer lies in the experience of self-examination I had learned from my training as a Jungian analyst while in Zurich and from my years of meditation. Jung insisted that all would-be analysts undergo analysis themselves, so that they would not project their less acceptable qualities on to future patients. 'Physician, heal thyself' remains the first maxim of all psychoanalysis, Freudian or Jungian. Jung once put it even more radically: 'We do not become enlightened by imagining figures of light, but by making the darkness conscious.'

In my own personal analysis in England and Zurich, I had begun to own many pieces of my less sociable, violent, angry, brutal self, the opposite, or *shadow*, of my nice, amenable, sociable self or *persona*. So I had already had glimpses of my brutal mercenary in dreams over the years, but never until this 'memory' were the glimpses so vivid or disturbing. I was reminded, too, that the work of analysis and self-analysis, in whatever form, is a life's work and that just getting a certificate or a Ph.D. from a prestigious school or institute is by no means a guarantee of psychological maturity. To this day I continue to struggle with that soldier and his unfinished guilt. As a shadow, he is to me, as Jung again put it so wisely, 'a moral problem that challenges the whole personality'.

I was later to learn that most people, when they first have past life regressions, rarely get such violent or horrible memories. As a rule, the unconscious mind – which I now believe to carry past life memories, as well as forgotten childhood events and archetypes – will, in its wisdom, only send us past life memories that we are ready to deal with and are able to integrate into our conscious personality structure. Those who have little experience of therapy or meditation more often start gently. The first past life memories that come tend to be more benign. Beginners not subject to pressure or neurosis are usually shown other selves from the past, that can be more easily assimilated and dealt with. This is as it should be.

In the workshops my wife Jennifer and I give, we often remind our students of the oriental image of *the guardian of the threshold*, a frightening monster depicted at the gates of a temple or bordering a sacred *mandala*, or meditation picture. These guardians are images of our own fear and are there to prevent us entering realms of the psyche we are not ready for. Whether we are aware of them or not, each of us has our own inner guardians of the threshold to prevent us from going too deep, too fast. There is a subtle inner economy of psychic and spiritual unfolding in which every individual proceeds at his or her own pace, governed by these inner guardians and guides. These inner figures become very clear when we learn to understand our dreams.

I tell my story of my first past life encounter as both a warning to the unwary and a stimulus for those who are ready to explore. Any psychological work that goes into the deeper layers of the unconscious mind is likely to bring up powerful emotions, disturbing memories, and fantasy material. Such often overwhelming psychic contents may seem to the uninitiated and even to experts to belong to the realms of classical madness. Past life exploration can be like taking the lid off Pandora's Box; it can unleash potent forces over which we may have little control. For this reason, it is my firm belief that *guiding regressions and research into past lives should only be undertaken by those fully trained in psychotherapy.* This is not a parlour game, simple as the procedures many seem when first witnessed.

At the same time, there is powerful learning to be had from this extraordinary process. It is no exaggeration to say that there are among my clients those whose whole life orientation has been changed by only one or two past life sessions. The opportunity to confront one's true self, naked and unadorned, to see the essence of one's 'stuckness' in even a single story, is unparallelled in any other psychological discipline that I know.

For example, a very successful businessman consulted me once and described himself as a Type A personality, one of those who is driven in everything he does. This man felt constantly inadequate, that he was not strong or assertive enough, and described how, despite more success than most men ever achieve, he punished himself by overwork. In addition, he had a history of physical accidents in which he had broken his ankles, hip, shoulder, and wrist at one time or another. One accident to his shoulder seemed to bring out inexplicable feelings of injustice in which he found himself thinking, 'Why me?'

When directed into a past life connected in some way with this, his body became tense, he clenched his fists and jaw, and uttered the following words:

It's no use. I can't do anything. I'm not strong enough. I won't let go. I won't let go. I can't hold on any more. I don't want to die. I'm falling . . .

What he was reliving were the last agonising moments of a soldier on the edge of a cliff, unable to muster the strength to climb to the top. Another sadistic soldier was taunting him with the words, 'You're weak. You're no good. If you were really strong, you'd make it.' When he failed, the soldier hit him on the head with a rifle butt and he fell to his death, shattered on the rocks below.

In the last agonising moments before letting go, he has the following thoughts:

It's a test . . . I've failed. I wasn't strong enough. I was weak and helpless. I'm ashamed. I could have done better. I didn't deserve to die. I'll never do that again. I'll never give up again. Anything but failure. I'm gonna hold on.

The death, as he relived it, was over in an instant, and after the titanic struggle his body suddenly became limp. A flood of insight came as he saw that his whole life had been a constant repetition of the soldier's dying thoughts: 'I'll never give up again. Anything but failure. I'm gonna hold on.' It was obvious to him that these thoughts had been governing his life metaphorically, and that he could now choose to change them, and was no longer doomed to relive an old story that was no longer his.

Unfinished Dramas of the Soul

From nearly a decade of taking clients and colleagues through past life experiences and continuing my own personal explorations, I have come to regard this technique as one of the most concentrated and powerful tools available to psychotherapy short of psychedelic drugs.

Not every client goes directly to dramas like that relived by this businessman – he had an extensive background in other therapies – but almost everyone I have worked with can easily identify two major ways in which past lives seem to be influencing current behaviour. The first is a recognition that these characters from previous eras are recognisable as *other selves*, that we dimly know have always been there in the background of our consciousness. Often in the rap part of our session, I will say: 'Do you know that character?' And be he or she rebellious slave, depressed scullery maid, arrogant overlord, obsequious courtier, or likable charlatan, my client will inevitably reply with a sigh or an embarrassed smile, 'Oh yes, I know *him* (or *her*)!

The second feature that stands out almost universally is an inescapable feeling that this character's past life *story* is somehow being re-enacted in this life and that it still remains unfinished:

A woman client still cannot have children because of guilt about abandoning an infant during a famine.

A man remembers being sexually humiliated as a young servant by older women to whom he is indentured and withdraws into the company of men, a pattern today repeated in homosexual relations.

A woman who has successfully had three children in her current life suffers from severe premenstrual cramps which lead her into a past life memory of her painful death in childbirth in a tribal life.

Each other life that comes to us, however, brief or fragmentary, is a piece of another self. The personality is not single, it is multiple – not in the psychiatric sense of multiple personality, but in that there are many levels to the self like many skins to an onion. We peel off these selves as we look into our past lives or as we look into our own dreams.

★ ★ ★

To give the reader some idea of the remarkable range of human problems that have responded to past life regression in my psychotherapy practice, here is a list of some of the more common psychological issues I have treated. Many of these will be elaborated in later chapters.

Insecurity and fear of abandonment. Often related to past life memories of literal abandonment as a child, separation during a crisis or a war, being orphaned, sold into slavery, being left out to die in times of famine, etc.

Depression and low energy. Past life memories of loss of a loved one or parent, unfinished grieving, suicide memories, despair as a result of war, massacre, deportation, etc.

Phobias and irrational fears. Every kind of trauma in a past life: death by fire, water, suffocation, animals, knives, insects, natural disasters, etc.

Sadomasochistic behaviour problems. Usually related to a past life memory of torture, often with loss of consciousness, usually with sexual overtones; the pain and rage seem to perpetuate hatred and a desire to revenge oneself in the same way.

Guilt and martyr complexes. Commonly stem from past life memories of having directly killed loved ones or from feeling responsible for the deaths of others (e.g. in a fire): human sacrifice of one's child, having ordered the deaths of others unnecessarily, etc. The entrenched thought is most often, 'It's all my fault. I deserve this.'

Material insecurity and eating disorders. Often the re-running of past life memories of starvation, economic collapse, or inescapable poverty; manifests as anorexia, bulimia, or obesity.

Accidents, violence, physical brutality. Repetition of old battlefield memories from warrior lives; unfulfilled quests for power, love of adventure cut off; common in adolescence, the time historically when many soldiers met their deaths.

Family struggles. Usually there are old past life scores to settle with parents, children, or siblings: betrayal, abuse of power, inheritance injustices, rivalry, etc.; includes most Freudian Oedipal dynamics.

Sexual difficulties and abuse. Frequently problems of frigidity, impotence, and genital infections have past life stories of rape, abuse, or torture behind them. Many incest and child abuse stories turn out to be re-runs of old patterns where emotional release was blocked.

Marital difficulties. These often derive from past lives with the same mate in a different power, class, or sexual constellation: e.g. as mistress, slave, prostitute, concubine, where the sex roles were reversed.

Chronic physical ailments. Past life reliving of death or traumatic injuries to the head, the limbs, the back, etc. Therapy often relieves chronic pain in these areas; headaches may relate to intolerable mental choices in other lives; throat ailments to verbal denunciations or unspoken thoughts; ulcers to memories of terror, neckaches to hanging or strangling.

From this list, which is far from exhaustive, it is clear the one person may have several themes and related past life stories that will need to be worked through in the course of therapy.

5

Gaia

Fritjof Capra
David Bohm
Rupert Sheldrake
James Lovelock
Elisabet Sahtouris
John Michell
William Bloom and Marko Pogacnik
Tom Graves
Dorothy Maclean

Introduction

As children, like the shamans and magicians of tribal societies, we give all objects personalities and life. Growing up, however, we become 'sensible' and objects become just objects with no dynamic or meaning other than how they are of use to us. If we observe the living essence of things around us, we are described as, at best, poetic and lyrical and, at worst, childish and escapist; we are certainly not realists; we are not serious. We have evolved a culture interested only in the obvious, the tangible and the usable.

The green movement has woken us to the disastrous ecological results of giving no respect to the life of our environment generally. The New Age movement, drawing on the new physics and biology, goes further than this and presents us with an understanding of the inner life of the matter that makes up our earth and cosmos.

In this section we start with the relatively scientifically respectable and move across towards the more mystical. We begin with four scientists who have been instrumental in shifting our understanding of matter. The first contributor is Fritjof Capra whose *The Tao of Physics* has been the key text for introducing people to the mystical concepts of sub-atomic physics. Then there is David Bohm who introduced the powerful thought that the Universe is enfolded multi-dimensionally in on itself. Like a hologram in which any single part contains a picture of the whole, so the Universe, although manifest in an infinite number of forms, is nevertheless contained holographically in any particle. Rupert Sheldrake, the biologist, then suggests that there are invisible force fields which contain archetypal patterns of the forms and structures of living organisms. This is followed by a second biologist, James Lovelock, who suggests that, because of the self-regulatory system of Earth's atmosphere and temperature, it is reasonable to perceive the planet as a living organism, *Gaia*.

All of the above may be revolutionary stuff for scientists, but students of the wisdom traditions claim to have known all that for millennia. They see these radical scientific theorists gradually bridging the mainstream worldview into the ageless spiritual understanding. This is either sense or arrogance depending on your perspective.

Elisabet Sahtouris then presents a cosmic picture of Gaia's nature and, although a scientist, the lyricism of her prose brings her more easily into the spiritual camp.

We then begin truly to approach the wisdom traditions with an extract from John Michell in which he describes the Chinese art of locating all objects in relation to Earth energies. This is followed by some writing of my own, in partnership with the Yugoslav sculptor and mystic Marko Pogacnik, describing the basics of ley lines, the energy network which covers the Earth in the same way that acupuncture meridiens cover the human body. Tom Graves, the dowsing expert, continues with a description of how this awareness can be used for healing landscape.

Finally there is a contribution from Dorothy Maclean in which she describes her work with the fairy and angelic realms. Whether you find these final ideas preposterous or not, some sections of the New Age movement give great respect to this parallel life-stream and would even say that Jung's archetypes and Rupert Sheldrake's morphogenetic fields are, in fact, the domain of angelic awareness.

FRITJOF CAPRA

The Tao of Physics

The classical, mechanistic world view was based on the notion of solid, indestructible particles moving in the void. Modern physics has brought about a radical revision of this picture. It has led not only to a completely new notion of 'particles', but has also transformed the classical concept of the void in a profound way. This transformation took place in the so-called field theories. It began with Einstein's idea of associating the gravitational field with the geometry of space, and became even more pronounced when quantum theory and relativity theory were combined to describe the force fields of sub-atomic particles. In these 'quantum field theories', the distinction between particles and the space surrounding them loses its original sharpness and the void is recognised as a dynamic quantity of paramount importance.

★ ★ ★

Matter and empty space – the full and the void – were the two fundamentally distinct concepts on which the atomism of Democritus and of Newton was based. In general relativity, these two concepts can no longer be separated. Wherever there is a massive body, there will also be a gravitational field, and this field will manifest itself as the curvature of the space surrounding that body. We must not think, however, that the field fills the space and 'curves' it. The two cannot be distinguished; the field *is* the curved space! In general relativity, the gravitational field and the structure, or geometry, of space are identical. They are represented in Einstein's field equations by one and the same mathematical quantity. In Einstein's theory, then, matter cannot be separated from its field of gravity, and the field of gravity cannot be separated from the curved space. Matter and space are thus seen to be inseparable and interdependent parts of a single whole.

Material objects not only determine the structure of the surrounding space but are, in turn, influenced by their environment in an essential way.

★ ★ ★

The unity and interrelation between a material object and its environment, which is manifest on the macroscopic scale in the general theory of relativity, appears in an even more striking form at the sub-atomic level. Here, the ideas of classical field theory are combined with those of quantum theory to describe the interactions between sub-atomic particles. Such a combination has not yet been possible for the gravitational interaction because of the complicated mathematical form of Einstein's theory of gravity; but the other classical field theory, electrodynamics, has been merged with quantum theory into a theory called 'quantum electrodynamics' which describes all electromagnetic interactions between sub-atomic particles. This theory incorporates both quantum theory and relativity theory. It was the first 'quantum-relativistic' model of modern physics and is still the most successful.

The striking new feature of quantum electrodynamics arises from the combination of two concepts; that of the electromagnetic field, and that of photons as the particle manifestations of electromagnetic waves. Since photons are also electromagnetic waves, and since these waves are vibrating fields, the photons must be manifestations of electromagnetic fields. Hence the concept of a 'quantum field', that is, of a field which can take the form of quanta, or particles. This is indeed an entirely new concept which has been extended to describe all sub-atomic particles and their interactions, each type of particle corresponding to a different field. In these 'quantum field theories', the classical contrast between the solid particles and the space surrounding them is completely overcome. The quantum field is seen as the fundamental physical entity; a continuous medium which is present everywhere in space. Particles are merely local condensations of the field; concentrations of energy which come and go, thereby losing their individual character and dissolving into the underlying field. In the words of Albert Einstein:

> We may therefore regard matter as being constituted by the regions of space in which the field is extremely intense . . . There is no place in this new kind of physics both for the field and matter, for the field is the only reality.

The conception of physical things and phenomena as transient manifestations of an underlying fundamental entity is not only a basic element of quantum field theory, but also a basic element of the Eastern world view. Like Einstein, the Eastern mystics consider this underlying entity as the only reality: all its phenomenal manifestations are seen as transitory and illusory. This reality of the Eastern mystic cannot be identified with the quantum field of the physicist because it is seen as the essence of *all* phenomena in this world and, consequently, is beyond all concepts and ideas. The quantum field, on the other hand, is a well-defined concept which only accounts for some of the physical phenomena. Nevertheless, the intuition behind the physicist's interpretation of the sub-atomic world, in terms of the quantum field, is closely parallelled by that of the Eastern mystic who interprets his or her experience of the world in terms of an ultimate underlying reality. Subsequent to the emergence of the field concept, physicists have attempted to unify the various fields into a single fundamental field which would incorporate all physical phenomena. Einstein, in particular, spent the last years of his life searching for such a unified field. The *Brahman* of the Hindus, like the *Dharmakaya* of the Buddhists and the *Tao* of the Taoists, can be seen, perhaps, as the ultimate unified field from which spring not only the phenomena studied in physics, but all other phenomena as well.

In the Eastern view, the reality underlying all phenomena is beyond all forms and defies all description and specification. It is therefore often said to be formless, empty or void. But this emptiness is not to be taken for mere nothingness. It is, on the contrary, the essence of all forms and the source of all life. Thus the *Upanishads* say,

> *Brahman* is life. *Brahman* is joy. *Brahman* is the Void . . .
> Joy, verily, that is the same as the Void.
> The Void, verily, that is the same as joy.

Buddhists express the same idea when they call the ultimate reality *Sunyata* – 'Emptiness', or 'the Void' – and affirm that it is a living Void which gives birth to all forms in the phenomenal world. The Taoists ascribe a similar infinite and endless creativity to the *Tao* and, again, call it empty. 'The *Tao* of Heaven is empty and formless' says the *Kuan-tzu*, and Lao Tzu uses several metaphors to illustrate this emptiness. He often compares the *Tao* to a hollow valley, or to a vessel which is forever empty and thus has the potential of containing an infinity of things.

In spite of using terms like empty and void, the Eastern sages make it clear that they do not mean ordinary emptiness when they talk about *Brahman*, *Sunyata* or *Tao*, but, on the contrary, a Void which has an infinite creative potential. Thus, the Void of the Eastern mystics can easily be compared to the quantum field of sub-atomic physics. Like the quantum field, it gives birth to an infinite variety of forms which it sustains and, eventually, reabsorbs. As the *Upanishads* say,

> Tranquil, let one worship it
> As that from which he came forth,
> As that into which he will be dissolved,
> As that in which he breathes.

The phenomenal manifestations of the mystical Void, like the sub-atomic particles, are not static and permanent, but dynamic and transitory, coming into being and vanishing in one ceaseless dance of movement and energy. Like the sub-atomic world of the physicist, the phenomenal world of the Eastern mystic is a world of *samsara* – of continuous birth and death. Being transient manifestations of the Void, the things in this world do not have any fundamental identity. This is especially emphasised in Buddhist philosophy which denies the existence of any material substance and also holds that the idea of a constant 'self' undergoing successive experiences is an illusion. Buddhists have frequently compared this illusion of a material substance and an individual self to the phenomenon of a water wave, in which the up-and-down movement of the water particles makes us believe that a 'piece' of water moves over the surface. It is interesting to note that physicists have used the same analogy in the context of field theory to point out the illusion of a material substance by a moving particle.

DAVID BOHM

Implicate Order

What is being suggested here is that the consideration of the difference between lens and hologram can play a significant part in the perception of a new order that is relevant for physical law. As Galileo noted the distinction between a viscous medium and a vacuum and saw that physical law should refer primarily to the order of motion of an object in a vacuum, so we might now note the distinction between a lens and a hologram and consider the possibility that physical law should refer primarily to an order of undivided wholeness of the content of a description similar to that indicated by the hologram rather than to an order of analysis of such content into separate parts indicated by a lens.

However, when Aristotle's ideas on movement were dropped, Galileo and those who followed him had to consider the question of how the new order of motion was to be described in adequate details. The answer came in the form of Cartesian coordinates extended to the language of the calculus (differential equations, etc.). But this kind of description is of course appropriate only in a context in which analysis into distinct and autonomous parts is relevant, and will therefore in turn have to be dropped. What, then, will be the new kind of description appropriate to the present context?

As happened with Cartesian coordinates and the calculus, such a question cannot be answered immediately in terms of definite prescriptions as to what to do. Rather, one has to observe the new situation very broadly and tentatively and to 'feel out' what may be the relevant new features. From this, there will arise a discernment of the new order, which will articulate and unfold in a natural way (and not as a result of efforts to make it fit well-defined and preconceived notions as to what this order should be able to achieve).

We can begin such an inquiry by noting that in some subtle sense, which does not appear in ordinary vision, the interference pattern in the whole plate can distinguish different orders and measures in the whole illuminated structure. For example, the illuminated structure may contain all sorts of shapes and sizes of geometric forms, as well as topological relationships, such as inside and outside, and intersection and separation. All of these lead to different interference patterns and it is this difference that is somehow to be described in detail.

The differences indicated above are, however, not only in the plate. Indeed, the latter is of secondary significance, in the sense that its main function is to make a relatively permanent 'written record' of the interference pattern of the light that is present in each region of space. More generally, however, in each such region, the movement of the light implicitly contains a vast range of distinctions of order and measure, appropriate to a whole illuminated structure. Indeed, in principle, this structure extends over the whole Universe and over the whole past, with implications for the whole future. Consider, for example, how on looking at the night sky, we are able to discern structures covering immense stretches of space and time, which are in some sense contained in the movements of light in the tiny space encompassed by the eye (and also how instruments, such as optical and radio telescopes, can discern more and more of this totality, contained in each region of space).

There is the germ of a new notion of order here. This order is not to be understood solely in terms of a regular arrangement of *objects* (e.g. in rows) or as a regular arrangement of *events* (e.g. in a series). Rather, a *total order* is contained, in some *implicit* sense, in each region of space and time.

Now, the word 'implicit' is based on the verb 'to implicate'. This means 'to fold inward' (as multiplication means 'folding many times'). So we may be led to explore the notion that in some sense each region contains a total structure 'enfolded' within it.

It will be useful in such an exploration to consider some further examples of enfolded or *implicate* order. Thus, in a television broadcast, the visual image is translated into a time order, which is 'carried' by the radio wave. Points that are near each other in the visual image are not necessarily 'near' in the order of the radio signal. Thus, the radio wave carries the visual image in an implicate order. The function of the receiver is then to *explicate* this order, i.e. to 'unfold' it in the form of a new visual image.

A more striking example of implicate order can be demonstrated in the laboratory, with a transparent container full of a very viscous fluid, such as treacle, and equipped with a mechanical rotator that can 'stir' the fluid very slowly but very thoroughly. If an insoluble droplet of ink is placed in the fluid and the stirring device is set in motion, the ink drop is gradually transformed into a thread that extends over the whole fluid. The latter now appears to be distributed more or less at 'random' so that it is seen as some shade of grey. But if the mechanical stirring device is now turned in the opposite direction, the transformation is reversed, and the droplet of dye suddenly appears, reconstituted.

When the dye was distributed in what appeared to be a random way, it nevertheless had *some kind* of order which is different, for example, from that arising from another droplet originally placed in a different position. But this order is *enfolded* or *implicated* in the 'grey mass' that is visible in the fluid. Indeed, one could thus 'enfold' a whole picture. Different pictures would look indistinguishable and yet have different implicate orders, which differences would be revealed when they were explicated, as the stirring device was turned in a reverse direction.

What happens here is evidently similar in certain crucial ways to what happens with the hologram. To be sure, there are differences. Thus, in a fine enough analysis, one could see that the *parts* of the ink droplet remain in a one-to-one correspondence as they are stirred up and the fluid moves continuously. On the other hand, in the functioning of the hologram there is no such one-to-one correspond- ence. So in the hologram (as also in experiments in a 'quantum' context), there is no way ultimately to reduce the implicate order to a finer and more complex type of explicate order.

All this calls attention to the relevance of a new distinction between implicate and explicate order. Generally speaking, the laws of physics have thus far referred mainly to the explicate order. Indeed, it may be said that the principle function of Cartesian coordinates is just to give a clear and precise description of explicate order. Now, we are proposing that in the formulation of the laws of physics, primary relevance is to be given to the implicate order, while the explicate order is to have a secondary kind of significance (e.g. as happened with Aristotle's notion of movement, after the develop- ment of classical physics). Thus, it may be expected that a description in terms of Cartesian coordinates can no longer be given a primary emphasis, and that a new kind of description will indeed have to be developed for discussing the laws of physics.

RUPERT SHELDRAKE
Morphogenetic Fields

The hypothesis of *formative causation* proposes that morphogenetic fields play a causal role in the development and maintenance of the forms of systems at all levels of complexity. In this context, the word 'form' is taken to include not only the shape of the outer surface or boundary of a system, but also its internal structure. This suggested causation of form by morphogenetic fields is called formative causation in order to distinguish it from the energetic type of causation with which physics already deals so thoroughly. For although morphogenetic fields can only bring about their effects in conjunction with energetic processes, they are not in themselves energetic.

The idea of non-energetic formative causation is easier to grasp with the help of an architectural analogy. In order to construct a house, bricks and other building materials are necessary; so are the builders who put the materials into place; and so is the architectural plan which determines the form of the house. The same builders doing the same total amount of work using the same quantity of building materials could produce a house of different form on the basis of a different plan. Thus the plan can be regarded as a *cause* of the specific form of the house, although of course it is not the only cause: it could never be realised without the building materials and the activity of the builders. Similarly, a specific morphogenetic field is a cause of the specific form taken up by a system, although it cannot act without suitable 'building blocks' and without the energy necessary to move them into place.

This analogy is not intended to suggest that the causative role of morphogenetic fields depends on conscious design, but only to emphasise that not all causation need be energetic, even though all processes of change involve energy. The plan of a house is not in itself a type of energy. Even when it is drawn on paper, or finally realised in the form of the house, it does not weigh anything or have any energy of its own. If the paper is burnt or the house is demolished, there is no measurable change in the total amount of mass and energy; the plan simply vanishes. Likewise, according to the hypothesis of formative causation, morphogenetic fields are not in themselves energetic; but nevertheless they play a causal role in determining the forms of the systems with which they are associated. For if a system were associated with a different morphogenetic field, it would develop differently. This hypothesis is empirically testable in cases where the morphogenetic fields acting on systems can be altered.

Morphogenetic fields can be regarded as analogous to the known fields of physics in that they are capable of ordering physical changes, even though they themselves cannot be observed directly. Gravitational and electromagnetic fields are spatial structures which are invisible, intangible, inaudible, tasteless and odourless; they are detectable only through their respective gravitational and electro-magnetic effects. In order to account for the fact that physical systems influence each other at a distance without any apparent material connection between them, these hypothetical fields are endowed with the property of traversing empty space, or even actually constituting it. In one sense, they are non-material; but in another sense they are aspects of matter because they can only be known through their effects on material systems. In effect, the scientific definition of matter has simply been widened to take them into account. Similarly, morphogenetic fields are spatial structures detectable only through their morphogenetic effects on material systems; they too can be regarded as aspects of matter if the definition of matter is widened still further to include them.

Although only the morphogenesis of biological and complex chemical systems has been discussed, the hypothesis of formative causation will be assumed to apply to biological and physical systems at all levels of complexity. Since each kind of system has its own characteristic form, each must have a specific kind of morphogenetic field: thus there must be one kind of morphogenetic field for protons; another for nitrogen atoms; another for water molecules; another for sodium chloride crystals; another for the muscle cells of earthworms; another for the kidneys of sheep; another for elephants; another for beech trees; and so on.

★   ★   ★

Atoms are in turn the morphogenetic germs of molecules, and small molecules the germs of larger molecules. Chemical reactions involve either the aggregation of atoms and molecules into larger molecules – for example in the formation of polymers – or the fragmentation of molecules into smaller ones, or into atoms and ions, which may then aggregate with others, for example in combustion: under the influence of external energy, molecules fragment into atoms and ions which then combine with those of oxygen to form small, simple molecules like H_2O and CO_2. These chemical changes involve the actualisation of virtual forms associated with the atoms or molecules which act as morphogenetic germs.

The idea that molecules have virtual forms before they are actualised is illustrated particularly clearly by the familiar fact that entirely new compounds can first be 'designed' on the basis of empirically determined principles of chemical combination and then actually synthesised by organic chemists. These laboratory syntheses are carried out step by step; in each step a particular molecular form serves as the morphogenetic germ for the next virtual form to be synthesised, ending up with the form of the entirely new molecule.

If it seems rather artificial to think of chemical reactions as morphogenetic processes, it should be remembered that much of the effect of catalysts, both inorganic and organic, depends on their morphology. For example, enzymes, the specific catalysts of the numerous reactions of biochemistry, provide surfaces, grooves, notches or basins into which the reacting molecules fit with a specificity which is often compared to that of a lock and key. The catalytic effect of enzymes depends to a large extent on the way in which they hold reactant molecules in the appropriate relative positions for reaction to occur. (In free solution the chance collisions of the molecules occur in all possible orientations, most of which are inappropriate.)

The details of chemical morphogeneses are vague, partly because of their great rapidity, partly because the intermediate forms may be highly unstable, and also because the ultimate changes consist of probabilistic quantum jumps of electrons between the orbitals which constitute the chemical bonds. The virtual form of the molecule-to-be is outlined in the morphogenetic field associated with the atomic or molecular morphogenetic germ; when the other atom or molecule approaches in an appropriate orientation, the form of the product molecule is actualised by means of quantum jumps of electrons into orbitals which previously existed only as virtual forms; at the same time energy is released, usually as thermal motion. The role of the morphogenetic field in this process is, as it were, energetically passive, but morphologically active; it creates virtual structures which are then actualised as lower-level morphic units 'slot' or 'snap' into them, releasing energy as they do so.

Any given type of atom or molecule can take part in many different types of chemical reaction, and it is therefore the potential germ of many different morphogenetic fields. These could be thought of as possibilities 'hovering' around it. However, it may not take on its role as the germ of a particular morphogenetic field until an appropriate reagent atom or molecule approaches it, perhaps owing to specific electromagnetic or other effects of the latter upon it.

The morphogenesis of crystals differs from that of atoms and molecules in that a particular pattern of atomic or molecular arrangement is repeated indefinitely. The morphogenetic germ is provided by this pattern itself. It is well known that the addition of 'seeds' or 'nuclei' of the appropriate type of crystal greatly accelerates the crystallisation of super-cooled liquids or super-saturated solutions. In the absence of these seeds or nuclei, morphogenetic germs of the crystal come into being only when the atoms or molecules take up their appropriate relative positions by chance, owing to thermal agitation. Once the germ is present, the virtual forms of repetitions of the lattice structure given by the morphogenetic field extend outwards from the surfaces of the growing crystal. Appropriate free atoms or molecules which approach these surfaces are captured and 'slot' into position; again thermal energy is released as they do so.

* * *

But then what determines the particular form of the morphogenetic field? One possible answer is that morphogenetic fields are eternal. They are simply given, and are not explicable in terms of anything else. Thus even before this planet appeared, there already existed in a latent state the morphogenetic fields of all the chemicals, crystals, animals and plants that have ever occurred on the earth, or that will ever come into being in the future.

This answer is essentially Platonic, or even Aristotelian in so far as Aristotle believed in the eternal fixity of specific forms. It differs from the conventional physical theory in that these forms would not be predictable in terms of energetic causation; but it agrees with it in taking for granted that behind all empirical phenomena lie pre-existing principles of order.

The other possible answer is radically different. Chemical and biological forms are repeated not because they are determined by changeless laws or eternal Forms, but because of a *causal influence from previous similar forms*. This influence would require an action across space *and time* unlike any known type of physical action.

JAMES LOVELOCK

Gaia

Back home in the quiet countryside of Wiltshire, after my visits to the Jet Propulsion Laboratories, I had time to do more thinking and reading about the real character of life and how one might recognise it anywhere and in any guise. I expected to discover somewhere in the scientific literature a comprehensive definition of life as a physical process, on which one could base the design of life-detection experiments, but I was surprised to find how little had been written about the nature of life itself. The present interest in ecology and the application of systems analysis to biology had barely begun and there was still in those days the dusty academic air of the classroom about the life sciences. Data galore had been accumulated on every conceivable aspect of living species, from their outermost to their innermost parts, but in the whole vast encyclopaedia of facts the crux of the matter, life itself, was almost totally ignored. At best, the literature read like a collection of expert reports, as if a group of scientists from another world had taken a television receiver home with them and had reported on it. The chemist said it was made of wood, glass, and metal. The physicist said it radiated heat and light. The engineer said the supporting wheels were too small and in the wrong place for it to run smoothly on a flat surface. But nobody said what it was.

★　★　★

The design of a universal life-detection experiment based on entropy reduction seemed at this time to be a somewhat unpromising exercise. However, assuming that life on any planet would be bound to use the fluid media – oceans, atmosphere, or both – as conveyor-belts for raw materials and waste products, it occurred to me that some of the activity associated with concentrated entropy reduction within a living system might spill over into the conveyor-belt regions and alter their composition. The atmosphere of a life-bearing planet would thus become recognisably different from that of a dead planet.

Mars has no oceans. If life had established itself there, it would have had to make use of the atmosphere or stagnate. Mars, therefore, seemed a suitable planet for a life-detection exercise based on chemical analysis of the atmosphere. Moreover, this could be carried out regardless of the choice of landing site. Most life-detection experiments are effective only within a suitable target area. Even on Earth, local search techniques would be unlikely to yield much positive evidence of life if the landfall occurred on the Antarctic ice sheet or the Sahara desert or in the middle of a salt lake.

While I was thinking on these lines, Dian Hitchcock visited the Jet Propulsion Laboratories. Her task was to compare and evaluate the logic and information-potential of the many suggestions for detecting life on Mars. The notion of life detection by atmospheric analysis appealed to her, and we began developing the idea together. Using our own planet as a model, we examined the extent to which simple knowledge of the chemical composition of the Earth's atmosphere, when coupled with such readily accessible information as the degree of solar radiation and the presence of oceans as well as land masses on the Earth's surface, could provide evidence for life.

Our results convinced us that the only feasible explanation of the Earth's highly improbable atmosphere was that it was being manipulated on a day-to-day basis from the surface, and that the manipulator was life itself. The significant decrease in entropy – or, as a chemist would put it, the persistent state of disequilibrium among the atmospheric gases – was on its own clear proof of life's activity. Take, for example, the simultaneous presence of methane and oxygen in our atmosphere. In sunlight, these two gases react chemically to give carbon dioxide and water vapour. The rate of this reaction is such that to sustain the amount of methane always present in the air, at least 1,000 million tons of this gas must be introduced into the atmosphere yearly. In addition, there must be some means of replacing the oxygen used up in oxidizing methane and this requires a production of at least twice as much oxygen as methane. The quantities of both of these gases required to keep the Earth's extraordinary atmospheric mixture constant was improbable on an abiological basis by at least 100 orders of magnitude.

Here, in one comparatively simple test, was convincing evidence for life on Earth, evidence, moreover, which could be picked up by an infra-red telescope sited as far away as Mars. The same argument applies to other atmospheric gases, especially to the ensemble of reactive gases constituting the atmosphere as a whole. The presence of nitrous oxide and of ammonia is as anomalous as that of methane in our oxidising atmosphere. Even nitrogen in gaseous form is out of place, for with the Earth's abundant and neutral oceans, we should expect to find this element in the chemically stable form of the nitrate ion dissolved in the sea.

Our findings and conclusions were, of course, very much out of step with conventional geochemical wisdom in the mid-sixties. . . . Working in a new intellectual environment, I was able to forget Mars and to concentrate on the Earth and the nature of its atmosphere. The result of this more single-minded approach was the development of the hypothesis that the entire range of living matter on Earth, from whales to viruses, and from oaks to algae, could be regarded as constituting a single living entity, capable of manipulating the Earth's atmosphere to suit its overall needs and endowed with faculties and powers far beyond those of its constituent parts.

It is a long way from a plausible life-detection experiment to the hypothesis that the Earth's atmosphere is actively maintained and regulated by life on the surface, that is, by the biosphere. Much of this book deals with more recent evidence in support of this view. In 1967 the reasons for making the hypothetical stride were briefly these:

Life first appeared on the Earth about 3,500 million years ago. From that time until now, the presence of fossils shows that the Earth's climate has changed very little. Yet the output of heat from the sun, the surface properties of the Earth, and the composition of the atmosphere have almost certainly varied greatly over the same period.

The chemical composition of the atmosphere bears no relation to the expectations of steady-state chemical equilibrium. The presence of methane, nitrous oxide, and even nitrogen in our present oxidising atmosphere represents violation of the rules of chemistry to be measured in tens of orders of magnitude. Disequilibria on this scale suggest that the atmosphere is not merely a biological product, but more probably a biological construction: not living, but like a cat's fur, a bird's feathers, or the paper of a wasp's nest, an extension of a living system designed to maintain a chosen environment. Thus the atmospheric concentration of gases such as oxygen and ammonia is found to be kept at an optimum value from which even small departures could have disastrous consequences for life.

The climate and the chemical properties of the Earth now and throughout its history seem always to have been optimal for life. For this to have happened by chance is as unlikely as to survive unscathed a drive blindfold through rush-hour traffic.

By now a planet-sized entity, albeit hypothetical, had been born, with properties which could not be predicted from the sum of its parts. It needed a name. Fortunately the author William Golding was a fellow-villager. Without hesitation he recommended that this creature be called Gaia, after the Greek Earth goddess also known as Ge, from which root the sciences of geography and geology derive their names. In spite of my ignorance of the classics, the suitability of this choice was obvious. It was a real four-lettered word and would thus forestall the creation of barbarous acronyms, such as Biocybernetic Universal System Tendency/Homoeostasis. I felt also that in the days of Ancient Greece the concept itself was probably a familiar aspect of life, even if not formally expressed. Scientists are usually condemned to lead urban lives, but I find that country people still living close to the Earth often seem puzzled that anyone should need to make a formal proposition of anything as obvious as the Gaia hypothesis. For them it is true and always has been.

ELISABET SAHTOURIS

Gaia's Dance

The story of Gaia's dance begins with an image of swirling mist in the black nothingness called Chaos by the ancient Greeks – an image reminding us of modern photos of galaxies swirling in space. In the myth it is the dancing goddess Gaia, swathed in white veils as she whirls through the darkness. As she becomes visible and her dance grows ever more lively, her body forms itself into mountains and valleys; then sweat pours from her to pool into seas, and finally her flying arms stir up a wind-sky she calls Ouranos – still the Greek word for sky – which she wraps around herself as protector and mate.

Though she later banishes Ouranos – Uranus, in Latin – to her depths for claiming credit for creation, their fertile union as Earth and Heaven brings forth forests and creatures including the giant Titans in human form, who in turn give rise to the gods and goddesses and finally to mortal humans.

From the start, says the myth – true to human psychology – people were curious to know how all this had happened and what the future would bring. To satisfy their curiosity, Gaia let her knowledge and wisdom leak from cracks in the Earth at places such as Delphi where her priestesses interpreted it for people.

Our curiosity is still with us thousands of years after this myth served as explanation of the world's creation. And in a sense, Gaia's knowledge and wisdom are still leaking from her body – not just at Delphi, but everywhere we care to look in a scientific study of our living planet.

The new scientific story of Gaian creation has other parallels to the ancient myth. We now recognise the Earth as a single self-creating being that came alive in its whirling dance through space, its crust transforming itself into mountains and valleys, the hot moisture pouring from its body to form seas. As its crust became ever more lively with bacteria, it created its own atmosphere, and the advent of sexual partnership finally did produce the larger life forms – the trees and animals and people.

The tale of Gaia's dance is thus being retold as we piece together the scientific details of our planet's dance of life. And in its context, the evolution of our own species takes on new meaning in relation to the whole. Once we truly grasp the scientific reality of the Gaian organism and its physiology, our entire world-view and practice are bound to change profoundly, revealing the way to solving what now appear to be our greatest and most insoluble problems.

From a Gaian point of view, we humans are an experiment – a trial species still at odds with ourselves and other species, still not having learned to balance our own dance within that of our whole planet. Unlike most other species, we are not biologically programmed to know what to do; rather, we are an experiment in free choice. This leaves us with enormous potential, powerful egotism, and tremendous anxiety – a syndrome that is recognisably adolescent.

Human history may seem very long to us as we study all that has happened in it, but we know only a few thousand years of it and have existed as humans for only a few million years, while Gaian creation has been going on for billions of years. We have scarcely had time to come out of species childhood, yet our social evolution has changed us so fast that we have leapt into our adolescence.

Humans are not the first Gaian creatures to make problems for themselves and for the whole Gaian system, as we will see. We are, however – unless whales and dolphins beat us to it in past ages – the first Gaian creatures who can understand such problems, think about them, and solve them by free choice. In fact, the argument of this book is that our maturity as a species depends on our accepting the responsibility for our natural heritage of behavioural freedom by working consciously and cooperatively towards our own health along with that of our planet.

Our ability to be objective, to see ourselves as the 'I' or 'eye' of our cosmos, as beings independent of nature, has inflated our egos – 'ego' being the Greek word for 'I'. We came to separate the 'I' from the 'it' and to believe that 'it' – the world 'out there' – was ours to do with as we pleased, telling ourselves we were either God's favoured children or the smartest and most powerful naturally evolved creatures on Earth. This egotistic attitude has been very much a factor in bringing us to adolescent crisis. And so an attitude of greater humility and willingness to accept some guidance from our parent planet will be an important factor in reaching our species maturity.

The tremendous problems confronting us now – inequality, hunger, the threat of nuclear annihilation and possibly irreversible damage to the natural world we depend on as much as any of our cells depend on the wholeness of our bodies for their life – are all of our own making. These problems have become so enormous that many of us believe we will never be able to solve them. Yet just at this time in our troubled world we stand on the brink of maturity, in a position to recognise that we are neither perfect nor omnipotent, but that we can learn a great deal from a parent planet that is also not perfect or omnipotent but has the experience of billions of years of overcoming an endless array of difficulties, small and great.

When we look anew at evolution, we see not only that other species have been as troublesome as ours, but that many a fiercely competitive situation resolved itself in a cooperative scheme. The kind of cells our bodies are made of, for example, began with the same kind of exploitation among bacteria that characterises our historic human imperialism. And through the same technologies of transportation and communications first invented by those bacteria as they bound themselves into the cooperative venture that made our existence possible, we are uniting our selves into a single body of humanity that may make yet another new step in Gaian evolution possible. If we look to the lessons of evolution, we will gain hope that the newly forming worldwide body of humanity may also learn to adopt cooperation in favour of competition. The necessary systems have already been invented and developed; we lack only the understanding, motive, and will.

It may come as a surprise that nature has something to teach us about cooperative economics and politics. Sociobiologists who have told us much in recent decades about humanity's animal heritage have tended to paint us a bleak picture – calling on our evolutionary heritage as evidence that we will never cure ourselves of territorial lust and aggression towards one another, and that thus there will be no end to economic greed and political warfare. But it is the aim of this book to show that these sociobiologists have presented a misleading picture – as misleading as earlier scientists' one-sided view of all nature evolution as 'red in tooth and claw', the hard and competitive struggle among individuals on which we have modelled our modern societies.

The new view of our Gaian Earth in evolution shows, on the contrary, an intricate web of cooperative mutual dependency, the evolution of one scheme after another that harmonises conflicting interests. The patterns of evolution show us the creative maintenance of life in all its complexity. Indeed Nature is more suggestive of a mother juggling resources to ensure each family member's welfare as she works out differences of interest to make the whole family a cooperative venture, than of a rational engineer designing perfect machinery that obeys unchangeable laws. For scientists who shudder at such *anthropomorphism* – giving Nature human form – let us not forget that *mechanomorphism* – giving Nature mechanical form – is really no better than second-hand anthropomorphism, since mechanisms are human products. Is it not more likely that Nature in essence resembles one of its own creatures than that it resembles in essence the non-living product of one of its creatures?

The leading philosophers of our day recognise that the very foundations of our knowledge are quaking – that our understanding of nature as machinery can no longer be upheld. But those who cling to the old understanding seriously fear that all human life will break down without a firm foundation for our knowledge of nature in mathematical reference points and laws of physics. They fail to see what every child can see – that humming-birds and flowers *work*, that Nature does very well in utter ignorance of human conceptions of how it must work.

Machinery is in fact the very antithesis of life. One must always hope a machine, between its times of use, will not change, for only if it does not change will it continue to be of use. Left to its own devices, it will eventually be destroyed by its environment. Living organisms, on the other hand, cannot stay the same *without* changing constantly, and they use their environment to their advantage. To be sure, our machinery is getting better and better at imitating life; if this were not so, a mechanical science could not have advanced in understanding. But mechanical models of life continue to miss its essential self-creativity.

JOHN MICHELL

Feng-shui

Stories of the magic location of sacred sites are not confined to Britain, but refer to a geomantic trdition once universally known. All over the world the centres of spiritual power were discovered by means of a system which combined science, astrology and intuition. Above all, in China, not only was every sacred building magically sited, but the Chinese geomantic principles are known; for the practice of divining the sites of houses and tombs was carried on well into this century.

A hundred years ago the practice of Chinese geomancy first became generally known in the West through the complaints of European businessmen, who found inexplicable resistance to their rational plans for exploiting the country. Continually they were informed that their railways and factories could not take certain routes or occupy certain positions. The reasons given were impossible to understand, for they had no relevance, economic, social or political, to the problem of laying out an industrial network. The Europeans were told that a certain range of hills was a terrestrial dragon and that no cutting could be made through its tail. Tunnels through dragon hills were forbidden, and a proposed railway to run straight across low, flat country was rejected on the grounds that the line would spoil the view from the hills. All this was laid down by practitioners of the science of *feng-shui*, 'wind and water', obscurely explained as 'that which can not be seen and can not be grasped'.

The practice of *feng-shui* gave the landscape a quality of beauty and order totally beyond the achievement of any modern Western planner. This was because it was based not on merely secular considerations, but on a sublime metaphysical system in which scientific and poetic truth harmoniously united. The modern town and country planning expert, Professor Abercrombie, credited *feng-shui* with producing 'one of the most elaborate landscapes which has ever existed, a landscape which had to preserve certain spiritual values and also to fulfil the practical purpose of supporting a dense population'.

Geomancers, exponents of *feng-shui*, were consulted over the erection and siting of any building or tomb anywhere in China, and over the placing of any tree, post or stone which might affect the appearance and nature of the countryside. It was recognised that certain powerful currents, lines of magnetism, run invisible over the whole surface of the earth. The task of the geomancer was to detect these currents and interpret their influence on the land over which they passed. The magnetic force, known in China as the dragon current, is of two kinds, yin and yang, negative and positive, represented by the white tiger and the blue dragon. The lines of this force follow, for the most part, mountainous ridges and ranges of hills. The yang or male current takes the higher routes over steep mountains, and the yin or female flows mainly along chains of low hills. The most favourable position is where the two streams meet. The surrounding country should display both yin and yang features, ideally in the proportion of 3 yang to 2 yin. Gentle, undulating country is yin, and sharp rocks and peaks are yang. The best country is that in which the character of each part is clearly defined, but both yin and yang lines should display certain characteristics of their opposites in the country they cross.

The task which later geomancers most commonly undertook was the location of tombs. The Chinese attached great importance to the influences which played over the bodies of their ancestors, believing them to control the future course of the family's fortune. Great dynasties were said to have arisen from the particularly favourable placing of an ancestor's tomb, and the first action of the central government, when faced with revolt, was to locate and destroy the family burial mounds of the rebel leaders. Disputes between brothers over the spot where their father should be buried were common, each party hiring a geomancer to locate the site most auspicious to his own particular client's interests.

In finding a burial site a geomancer first located the main currents, yin and yang, that crossed the area where the tomb was to be sited. A spot where the blue dragon met the white tiger, where a chain of low hills ran into a mountain range, was first investigated. At such a place the power of the dragon pulse is at its height, particularly if the site is quiet and sheltered, secluded 'like a modest virgin'. Under these conditions the beneficial force is strong and active. In open country it becomes dissipated, particularly where drained by straight stretches of flowing water or by other angular lines in the landscape. The presence of railways and the straight lines of canals greatly lessens the concentration of forces in their area.

The ideal spot for a tomb is at a junction of the two currents, the blue dragon to the left and the white tiger to the right. It should face south with a hill behind and lower, picturesque country in front. The soil should be of white sand, free of ants, near the curve of a slow, meandering stream. Noisy, violent features of the landscape should nowhere be evident. If such a spot could be found, intimate and charming in all its details, this was considered perfect, particularly if the meeting of the two currents was marked by a small, grassy knoll or hollow.

Yet even here forces hostile to a particular burial might prevail.

The astrological influences had to be consulted. This was done by means of a geomancer's compass, consisting of a magnetic needle suspended at the centre of a circular disc. The disc was divided into rings, the inner ring, immediately surrounding the needle, inscribed with the eight trigrams of yin and yang, the outer rings showing the twelve signs of the zodiac, the twenty-four houses and other astrological symbols. The compass was orientated south and the influences over the man to be buried were compared with those over the proposed site. If the conjunction was favourable, the right burial place had been found.

Not only tombs were sited in this way. Every building and plantation had to occupy its correct position in the landscape. The geomancers' vision interprets the Earth in terms of the heavens. They saw the mountains as stars, the ocean and wide rivers as the Milky Way. From the great mountain ridges which conduct the main lines of the dragon power smaller currents run like veins and arteries into the surrounding country. Each of these lines has its particular astrological character, its own harmony and colour. Chinese geomancers preserved the system by which the lines could be seen and interpreted. The fleeting vision which Watkins experienced on the Herefordshire hills could be achieved at will by men who understood the secrets of terrestrial geometry.

It amazed the Chinese that materially advanced Europeans should be quite ignorant of the geomantic science, and so culturally retarded that they could see no further than the visible surface of the landscape. Many believed that the foreigners knew *feng-shui*, but for some reason were keeping their knowledge secret. It was noted that a grove of trees, planted to give shade to a Hong Kong hospital, had been placed according to the best geomantic principles, and that the richest foreigners had built their houses in a most favourable position below the finest dragon hill in the colony. Yet at other times foreigners seemed truly ignorant and gullible. They would accept as concessions the most inauspicious land in the country, flat, angular and featureless, where predictably they were subjected to flood, drought, attacks by white ants and other plagues and disasters. Moreover their doomed proposals to build railways through obvious dragon lines seemed blatantly perverse.

In China until recently, as long ago in Britain, every building, every stone and wood, was placed in the landscape in accordance with a magic system by which the laws of mathematics and music were expressed in the geometry of the Earth's surface. The striking beauty and harmony of every part of China, which all travellers have remarked, was not produced by chance. Every feature was contrived. The main paths of planetary influence, determined by thousands of years of astronomy, were discovered in the landscape, the smaller lines that ran between them reproduced in the crags and fissures of the Earth. These were the lines of dragon current or *lung-mei*. The various parts of the Earth each fell under a particular planetary influence passed down through the lines which ran above them. Besides their lunar or solar, yin or yang, characteristics, certain lines were related to one of the five planets, Jupiter, Mars, Venus, Mercury or Saturn. These planets correspond to the five materials, wood, fire, metal, water and earth. Their colours are yellow, red, blue, white and black. Other correspondences link the planets with the materials of the body, with the internal organs, and with the fortunes of men.

WILLIAM BLOOM and MARKO POGACNIK

Ley Lines

The energy network which covers the surface of Earth cannot be understood unless it is realised that the geological solid Earth is only the form (lower frequency energy state) of a more electric and subtle electro-magnetic essence (higher frequency energy state). Just as human bodies are the vehicles of manifestation for an inner, dynamic and multi-dimensional self, so the geological Earth is also but the vehicle of manifestation of a far more subtle, more dynamic and more electric inner Spirit.

Ley lines form the matrix of energy which is the *dynamic physical principle* of the geological body of Earth. Ley lines are the essential structure of the etheric body of the Earth Spirit. To appreciate this, it can be helpful to imagine Earth as having no dense physical existence, but being only a globe of interconnected lines of electric energy, a sphere made up of webs of energy.

These lines vary in length from five miles to approximately two thousand miles; they are straight, but not dead straight and may over distance undulate gently. They also vary in width and in intensity of energy. If one looks through one, as if a cross-section had been cut, a ley is hourglass shaped, its narrowest section occurring at the point of intersection with the Earth's surface. The ley exists below the Earth as much as above it.

It has the internal formation of a double vortex. This double vortex brings energy down into the geological Earth; at the same time a particular quality of energy is also radiated out from the ley line into the atmosphere.

The energy that is brought down in the double vortex is of various densities; some of these correspond to the human experiences of feeling, of emotion, of mentality, of spirit and so on. In a very real sense this vortex phenomenon is the manifestation of the *will* of the Earth Spirit to be in incarnation. The essence or the consciousness of the Earth Spirit exists at a very high frequency energy state – which if experienced directly by a human being induces a state which is often called *bliss*. The dynamism of the vortex structure of leys is the result of the *force* – or *purpose* or *will* – used by the Earth Spirit to manifest in form.

We also mentioned that the double vortex of a ley radiates a particular quality of energy. Why is this so and what is this particular quality? To answer these two questions requires an understanding of the purpose of the Earth Spirit in taking on dense physical form life at all. It parallels, of course, the purpose of human incarnation. The Earth Spirit's purpose is, through the process of time and vibratory experience, to distribute a new *quality* of energy to the fields of energy that make up her body. Human beings experience this new quality of energy in a manner that may be summed up in the two words *unconditional love*.

In a very real sense what we interpret in human experience as unconditional love is that cosmic principle which actually brings about what we recognise as life and the life force, whether in the case of an incarnating planetary spirit or a human multi-dimensional self/soul. The force of unconditional love as it incarnates in form is the indwelling cosmic fire without which there is no life – no life of growth, change, rhythm and movement.

The life force of the Earth Spirit radiates from the leys and ley centres. Without this life force radiating from the ley network, there would be no growth in any of the different natural realms – mineral, vegetable, animal or human. In some Eastern teachings this force is called *fohat* or prana. The life force of Earth which radiates from her ley network is intimately bound up with the life force of the Sun, being as they are part of the same pranic field. There is thus an exceptionally close interconnection between the Sun, the ley network of Earth and the health or life force of all the natural realms that inhabit Earth. This is why it is that throughout history people – instinctively, intuitively or self-consciously – have paid great attention to Earth's ley network. By doing so, people have been able to enhance and enrich the growth of their natural surroundings, for example their crops, as well as enhancing their own health – physical and spiritual. They have also, of course, been acknowledging their relationship with Earth.

There are two other major factors that have to be taken into account for a full understanding of the ley network.

First, Earth is not a uniformly smooth energy sphere with the same amount of energy and activity evenly spread across her. She has differentiated levels of activity and distinct centres of energy sensitivity and radiance.

Second, Earth and the Solar System are part of a far greater Galactic and Cosmic system in which there are many very intimate and sensitive energy relationships that are crucial to the existence and growth pattern of Earth.

Thus the ley network does not only carry the energy of the incarnating Earth Spirit, but the ley network is also a receiver and distributor of those other galactic energies which are relevant to the growth of Earth and her inhabitants. The most well-known of these other energies are those associated with the constellations of the Zodiac and with the other planets of the Solar System; less known, but equally vital for example, are the relationships with the stars of the Pleiades, the Great Bear and Sirius. It should, however, be noted that it is not only the ley network which is sensitive and reactive to these incoming energies; all life, both individually and in groups, and particularly human life, is also sensitive and reactive to these incoming energies.

The ley network, therefore, works in conjunction with the energy bodies of the mineral, plant, animal and human realms. The energy body of each plant or of each human, for example, is therefore involved in both the general energy system of the whole of the plant or human realm on Earth and also in the general energy system of Earth as a whole. There is thus a vital and dynamic interdependence between the parts and the whole, as the Earth Spirit carrying that new quality of energy which we call *unconditional love* incarnates through the total system. This interdependence also incorporates our Galaxy and Cosmos.

TOM GRAVES

Healing the Land

Three people sit on the ground of a Cotswold farmyard, discussing intently the work they are about to do. One of them, evidently the leader of this group, seems to be foreign, but speaks with a rich Oxford-academic accent; the other two are more obviously English. Discussion over, but still sitting on the ground, one of the three picks up what seems to be a bow, loops a stick through its string and, rocking the bow back and forth, rotates it to grind the tip of the stick against a block of wood on the ground. A wisp of smoke rises from the block, then flames as the tinder round the tip of the stick catches light. Lighting a spill from this tiny flame, the leader reaches over and lights a paraffin storm-lamp. A lamp lit by an ancient and awkward method, on a bright and sunny day.

A short while after, the three can be seen on the hillslope above the farm. One is kneeling on the ground, another is holding the lantern, and the third, the leader, has his hands raised to the sky. He *is* foreign, despite his excellent English; he is chanting in Persian, a Zoroastrian fire-ritual. But it's more than the ancient ritual, for at a signal the kneeling man hammers the stake he is holding into the ground. The short ritual comes to a close, and they move on to another of the sixty-odd points they have marked out in this valley. A complex process of Earth-acupuncture, to heal and make holy the 'atmosphere' of this small Cotswold valley.

The operation above occurred a few years ago, when I was visiting a small religious community in the southern part of the Cotswolds. It was actually the last part of a very complex piece of Earth-acupuncture, in three stages, that had taken two years to complete. The process started soon after the community had bought the farm, for they found that the place's 'atmosphere' was in such a bad state that not only was the valley devoid of wild-life, but every person staying for more than a couple of hours picked up some kind of 'stomach-bug' – whether they had drunk the water there or not. The leader of the community and another member – the Persian with the Oxford accent – were both dowsers, and I was told that they had traced the source of the trouble to a new quarry about fifty miles away. The energy imbalance this created had somehow focussed on the valley; and though the problem could not, for practical reasons, be dealt with at source, it could be dealt with by 'isolating' the valley from energies arriving from outside the immediate area, and then 'restructuring' the energies as they arrived at that point.

The first stage – the 'first aid', we could say – involved placing about twenty wooden stakes, with copper wire wound round the top of each, into the ground at various points selected by dowsing: the 'stomach bug' disappeared within days. The second stage, the repair operation, involved staking the ground in more detail, patching up gaps and loopholes: the wild-life began to return. The final 'cosmetic' stage, which was the one I saw, used copper-sheathed iron stakes to 'restructure' the energy-flow, removing the imbalance rather than simply isolating the valley from its effects. The balanced energy-flow that came into the valley brought with it deep peace and quiet – the deep silence of a cathedral. Earth-acupuncture, and a large amount of commitment on the part of the community, had changed the 'atmosphere' of the place from hellish to holy in just two years.

It was an impressive piece of work, but I'm not sure how much of the 'trimmings' of the operation were essential to its working. The community insisted that the ritual and the chanting were an essential part of the process; but since I've met dowsers doing similar work – though admittedly on a smaller scale – with just the basic 'staking', I think that while the ritual was useful and valuable 'priming' in a magical sense, it probably wasn't as essential as they believed it was. Dowsers have been using stakes to neutralise 'noxious earth radiations' from black streams for more than fifty years, in a variety of ways and forms; and their work can be seen as part of a more complex system of Earth-acupuncture that is now being developed as a means of healing the land.

The idea of Earth-acupuncture has strong roots in European tradition; and these traditions begin to make sense once we realise the interaction between people and the natural energies, and realise that most of these energies are non-physical 'codings' carried by and within physical energies, as we saw earlier. The best-known of these traditions, and the ones that tend to make 'rationalists' dismiss the concept of Earth-acupuncture without even looking at it, are those about the staking of vampires or about witches sticking pins into models of people or of land. The horror-movie images that these traditions conjure up are, to say the least, a little erroneous compared to the reality behind them: but we do need to recognise that there is a reality behind them.

The blood-sucking variant of the vampire legend we can, I think, ignore for our present purposes. But the idea of something draining away a kind of 'lifeblood' is very real, for in various forms and modes it can be seen in action around us all the time. We talk of people or places or situations that 'drain' us: a 'tiresome' person, for example, is literally a vampire in the sense of draining away physical or emotional energy. We don't deal with such people by staking them through the heart, of course (though from practical experience I know that the traditional magical 'banishing' rituals are usually more efficient at keeping them at bay than physical restraint); but extreme forms of social 'vampires' – particularly suicides or, to a lesser extent, executed murderers – were buried at crossroads, often with a stake through the heart. Church law forbade the burial of suicides on consecrated ground; this can be seen in Shakespeare's *Hamlet*, in the discussion about the burial of Ophelia. The crossroads, as an 'un-sacred' node-point in the energy matrix, was and is a more sensible place to bury such a focus of negative and destructive energy, for it should allow the dispersal of the *sha* attached to that person well away from inhabited sites. Much of the traditional lore about crossroads only makes sense when seen in this kind of energy context.

This crude manipulation of energies was almost certainly organised at an intuitive level; it's only in the last fifty years or so that Western dowsers have built up a systematic form of energy manipulation, both isolating and restructuring 'bad' energy, *sha*. The isolators and insulators used are usually physical insulation materials of some kind, such as asbestos or plastic sheeting. These are placed directly over the black stream at key points such as beneath a bed or desk, to protect the area above it. The various dowsing studies I've seen state that these do work, but only for a matter of months at most, as the insulator itself becomes 'charged' with *sha* and has to be replaced and disposed of. Isolation is at best a temporary palliative measure, and should only be used while a more permanent means of protection is being worked out.

The only permanent means of protection – or at least as permanent as can be expected when every new development alters the structure and interactions of the energy-matrix – is to re-structure the local energy network. Most dowsers use stakes or coils or similar gadgets for this, and the process resembles acupuncture, as the term 'Earth-acupuncture' implies. Like acupuncture, the principles are very simple; but the practice is anything but simple, for the right kind of stake has to be sited at exactly the right place, and even – in some techniques – at exactly the right time. Diagnosis of the problem in any given case is as complex as diagnosis in acupuncture, if not more so; at the present time there are only a handful of dowsers in Britain with the skill and experience needed to do a safe and reliable job. It's probably illegal to do it at all in the United States on the usual psuedo-scientific grounds that block the development of most unconventional medicine there. I know quite a lot of this work goes on in France and Germany, and some probably goes on in most of the countries of Europe.

From my own knowledge of this Earth-acupuncture, and going on the published case-histories of the more recent work in Britain, it seems that this staking with stakes or coils can indeed restore the energy-balance and the health of quite large areas of land. One dowser claimed that he had stabilised more than twenty square miles in one operation, but that, if true, would be exceptional: a couple of acres or so at any one time is more usual.

DOROTHY MACLEAN

Devas

At this point I might say that the term *'deva'* is a Sanskrit word meaning shining one. On the whole, I have chosen to use this word rather than the English equivalent, 'angel', which calls up stereotyped images that are more of a barrier than a help in understanding the true nature of these beings.

It wasn't until nearly ten years later that I was introduced to some of the esoteric literature on devas. However, through my own contact with them we discovered that they are part of a whole hierarchy of beings, from the earthiest gnome to the highest archangel, and are a sister evolution to the human on Earth. The devas hold the archetypal pattern and plan for all forms around us, and they direct the energy needed for materialising them. The physical bodies of minerals, vegetables, animals and humans are all energy brought into form through the work of the devic kingdom. Sometimes we call that work natural law, but it is the devas who carry out that law, ceaselessly and joyfully. The level of this hierarchy I was guided to contact was not that of the spirit of, say, a particular pea plant in our garden, but rather the overlighting intelligence, the soul essence, of all peas throughout the world.

While the devas might be considered the 'architects' of plant forms, the nature spirits or elementals, such as gnomes and fairies, may be seen as the 'craftsmen', using the blueprint and energy channelled to them by the devas to build up the plant form. It was with these beings that R. Ogilvie Crombie established communication. When Roc joined our work at Findhorn, he helped to clarify and confirm certain undefined feelings I had had about the plant world. For instance, while I could not explain why I was upset when the gorse bushes were pruned in full blossom, Roc was able to clarify exactly what was wrong through his contact with the nature spirits.

Essentially, the devas are energy, they are life force. (We humans are as well, only in our own unique way.) I was told in guidance, *You are simply surrounded by life. You are a life force moving along with other life forces. As you recognise this, you open up and draw near to these others, becoming more and more one with them, working together for My purposes.*

The devas themselves have no particular form. But in attempting to establish communication and cooperation with humans, members of the devic realms have made themselves visible in a form intelligible to humans. These forms reflect their functions. For instance, a dwarf is usually depicted with a pick-axe, denoting our human interpretation of his work with the mineral world. Angels, on the other hand, are portrayed with wings, and often as bearing something, such as a message of healing or mercy. As the devas have said, *We work in the formless worlds and are not bound or rigid in form as you are. We travel from realm to realm and are given wings to denote this movement. As we travel, our form changes, taking on the qualities of different realms. Therefore, you cannot pin us down to any one form. We deal directly with energy and that energy shapes us, is part of us, is us, until we breathe it out to where it is needed. We are limitless, free, and insubstantial.*

I have never seen any of these beings in a definite form, although sometimes I get an impression of a pattern, a shape or a colour. Once when I had the image of the Red Cabbage Deva standing in front of many vague forms, I was told, *These forms are myself and those like me as we have been and as we shall be. Although we live in the moment and are always moving, yet is our past and present with us. We are close to the inner realms where all is living. I give you this picture so that you will not see me, or any of us, as merely one of a list of static forms but will connect us up more with life. Humans are so inclined to limit and depend upon their five senses to perceive the world that they forget that we are living, changing forces* now, *outside your sense of time.*

As we became more aware of the fact that everything around us is part of the same energy in different forms, we were opened up to an entirely new way of working in the garden. The devas said, *We realise it is easy for man to think of a plant as a thing, perhaps as living, but nevertheless a thing, for he cuts himself off from the vision that sees beyond the physical, just as he cuts himself off from his own inner being which is so vast.* Taking into account the inner being of plants, we began to realise that the garden must be known from within as well as from without, that it must grow spiritually as well as physically.

To a deva, the garden is not an assembly of various forms and colours but rather moving lines of energy. In describing our garden they said they could see the forces from below gradually being drawn up and blending with those coming down from them in great, swift waves. Within this field of energy, each plant was an individual whirlpool of activity. *We do not see things as you do, in their solid, outer materialisations, but rather in their inner life-giving state. We deal with what is behind what you see or sense, but these are interconnected, like different octaves of the same melody. What we see is different forms of light.* Years later, when I read about Kirlian photography, which records the luminescence given off by matter, I felt this related to the subtler forces of which the devas speak.

The devas stressed the importance of our learning to see the true reality, as they do, so that we might with the power of our directed thought not only affirm the perfection of each plant but actually lift

181

it to a higher level. *By thinking in terms of light, you add light to that already existing. Hence, you speed up growth and enhance beauty, you see truth and link up with God's perfection.* The intention of the devas in introducing us to their way of seeing was not to detract from the beauty of the world as seen by human eyes, but to enhance it by expanding our awareness into a broader and truer perception.

6

Practical Implications

Ina May Gaskin
Deborah Rozman
Joseph Bharat Cornell
Phyllis Kystal
Christopher Day
Roger Harrison
Donald Keys
Danaan Parry and Lila Forest
Arnold Mindell
Michal J. Eastcott

Introduction

The worst accusation that can be levelled at the New Age is not that it is stupid or romantic or for the psychologically gullible, but that it is narcissistic and a waste of time. New Agers, comes the accusation, do nothing but study their navels. And if they are not studying their navels, they are studying *invisible worlds – ho ho!* And, to be honest, I have met folk in the movement who do nothing at all, but think that they are doing a lot.

My own background, and that of many people in the movement, includes a high degree of political and social awareness; a large proportion of New Agers work in the caring professions. In particular, understanding the dynamics of human potential and of Gaian interdependence, there is a powerful thrust in the movement to better the conditions and quality of life for all people and beings on the planet. We are inescapably bound together and the professed ethics of the movement are compassion, caring and unconditional love. In a sense one can say that the New Age movement includes all the attitudes of the green movement, but that its spiritual drive and its trust in human nature and in the future gives it a more hopeful dynamic.

There is a central spiritual idea which has practical implications. It states that as we are all interconnected, both tangibly and invisibly, it is crucial how we behave in our own lives. Political action, creating peace, creating a socially just world, all begin at home. The woman or man who leads a loving, decent and generous life, with a sensitive awareness of the domestic, work and wider environment, is a most powerful influence for global peace and improvement. The notion is, for example, that our moods and thoughts affect global reality. To live daily life in a way that demonstrates integrity and love is perhaps the greatest challenge for all of us. Our power to live such a life and radiate its effect into the world is supported and amplified by the use of meditation and other spiritual practices.

In the final section of this book I have arranged the extracts so that they begin with childbirth and children and then pass on to wider and more 'adult' implications.

The opening contribution is from the sixties classic, *Spiritual Midwifery*. There are then two extracts which relate to children's education, the first by Deborah Rozman on meditation, the second by Joseph Cornell on Nature. We then move into adolescence with an exercise from Phyllis Krystal showing how a teenager can cut the energy ties that bind him/her to a parent.

Then into adulthood and a passage from Roger Harrison telling how New Age ideas can be used in business, commerce and organisational transformation. This is followed by three extracts which touch on global ecology and planetary politics. The first is from Donald Keys who founded Planetary Citizens; the second from Danaan Parry with Lila Forest, who founded the Earthstewards Network; and the third is from Arnold Mindell, applying group therapeutic techniques to community and global conflict.

The section then concludes with an extract from Michal Eastcott on an approach to meditation which invokes and radiates a blessing to the world.

INA MAY GASKIN

Spiritual Midwifery

A Husband and Wife Form a Single Energy Unit

Some couples exchange energy by loving, and some do their main energy exchange by fighting. One couple I know got together in an interesting way. They noticed that whenever they got near each other, they usually ended up in an argument. After this had happened a few times, they figured out that they must be pretty attracted to each other. They seemed to like to exchange energy with each other, even if it was by hassling. They soon noticed that their arguments were of no consequence, so they decided they would try exchanging energy in a friendlier way and see what that was like. They eventually decided to get married.

In Some Relationships, One Partner will be in the Habit of Short-changing the Other in Energy Transactions

At one birthing, the mother's first, the husband was a big help to her. During a rush he would squeeze her back, trying to rub in exactly the right place for her and keeping his full attention on her to the very end of the rush. After a rush, he would smooch her, give her a lot of love and encouragement, and she wouldn't acknowledge that he had said anything to her. It was uncomfortable because the way she was being with him left the energy unbalanced. He had been giving her his best, and she hadn't acted like it was good enough to be noticed. He was so obviously feeling her labour with her and trying to share her load in any way that he could that she needed to give some energy back to make it feel right. I thought at the time that it must look to him like maybe she regretted having got familiar enough with him to have got pregnant. When I mentioned this (I tried to do it humorously), she laughed, and then she let him know that I hadn't been far off in my guess, and then she let him know that she loved him and that it was okay. From then on, they did fine. He helped her a lot, she accepted his help, and they had a nice baby girl not long afterwards.

At another birthing, just before the birth of the baby, the lady would tell her husband that she loved him, feeling the energy of the baby very strong and wanting some graceful way to channel it, and he would just nod – wouldn't tell her that he loved her too and give her back as much as she had just given him. The midwives told him that it wasn't fair to be stingy about the energy that way, that this was the same energy that was trying to get his child born. They told him that he was really lucky to have such a nice lady, and encouraged him to have a good time at this birthing since it was one of the highest experiences that he would ever have. He loosened up and their baby was soon born.

Inhibition can Block Birthing Energy

If I suspect that inhibition is slowing down the progress of labour, I pay attention to the situation for a while, and observe the couple go through a few rushes. I look to see if this couple really loves each other. At the same time I am watching them, I am trying not to impose my own presence on them so much that they don't have any room to be together. Sometimes I will see that the husband is afraid to touch his wife's tits because of the midwives' presence, so I touch them, get in there and squeeze them, talk about how nice they are, and make him welcome. That way he can be uninhibited and loving at the same time. One of the strongest things that a man can do to help his lady during their birthing is to let her know he loves her in all the ways that he can. *A marriage should be reliable, fun, and uninhibited.*

Stephen taught us in the beginning that stimulation of the ladies' breasts had a powerful connection with bringing about contractions of the uterus. Our group of midwives had known this and used it as a tool for two or three years before we heard that the medical community, in doing experiments, had discovered that there is a powerful endocrine hormone called oxytocin that is produced by the pituitary gland, which can be prompted to do this by stimulation of the breasts. We had been using this in starting labour in the woman, or, where labour had begun, in speeding it up. We prefer to do this by pleasanter means than an IV drip.

One time I was delivering a single lady whose cervix was fully dilated, but she wasn't able to move the baby. Her pelvic measurements were ample, but she couldn't get herself gathered together so that all her energy was working the same way. Usually it is possible to teach a mother how to push if she is pretty free of subconscious. She can usually learn in a few tries how to get all that energy focused into pushing. But sometimes, no matter how many times you go through it with a lady and demonstrate and do it with her, she always seems to move her leg or something at just the time when the energy is building. She moves that way, or forgets and lets out her breath or does something that you know she could be doing better. When I have a case like this, I usually begin to suspect there is some kind of subconscious that is tying up the energy. I have noticed that it is often sexual subconscious if the energy is blocked once the cervix is already dilated.

So in this case I started talking about it and since she was a single lady, I asked her about what the baby's father was like and what her relationship with him had been. It turned out that she didn't like him too much – she thought he was good-looking, but she didn't really like him too much. As she talked about it, and everybody in the room heard what she had to say about him, it seemed to free up a lot of energy that she had tied up inhostile feelings about him, and she could feel better about her baby being half that guy's genetic makeup. He wasn't going to have anything to do with the raising of the child, but she needed to feel okay about the part of the baby that was him.

I remember a similar situation with a married lady who had already had one baby with her husband. All through their relationship they questioned whether they ought to be together. Then they got pregnant again. They split up and got back together several times during the pregnancy and finally they just agreed not to do it together. During her labour, she had to come to peace about having his baby. The baby didn't want to come out until she felt okay about the regrets over what had gone on so far.

When someone says, 'I love you' and means it, it opens up his throat – it literally does it. And when the throat opens up so does the cervix. I've been checking a lady's dilation at the same time she'd say that, and I could feel a distinct difference in her tissue, in how stretchy she was, that was exactly synchronous with her saying, *'I love you.'* It made me really understand that words are vibrations and that some combinations of words have greater power than others. 'I love you' is very strong.

One thing to remember is not to babble away all your energy by talking about insignificant or irrelevant things while the birthing is happening.

Sometimes labouring mothers get amazingly beautiful during a rush; you can see the prettiest one of that lady that you ever saw. These are very important moments to look for. Just to appreciate the way somebody is being tends to manifest it; nothing needs to be said.

One of the single mothers who came to the Farm to have her baby was very unsatisfied with how she looked. At the time she came to us, she had a large patch of pimples on each cheek, and she would spend quite a bit of time looking critically at herself in the mirror, which didn't tend to help her complexion any. (What you pay attention to, you get more of.) I was present during part of her labour, when she was approaching transition. She was being very brave, and as I looked into her eyes during a rush, I would see that her pimples tended to fade whenever she could stay on top of the energy during a rush. If she would start to lose control a little bit and tighten up her face, the redness would come on again and the pimples would look exaggerated. By the time her son was born, she had managed the energy well enough that her pimples were about half as red as they had been at the onset of labour, and when I saw her again a few days later, her face was completely healed. Instead of looking in a mirror and not liking what she saw, she had been looking in her son's eyes. He wasn't critical a bit. He had that pure vision that newborns have, and he just loved her.

I remember an interesting birthing. The mother was a single lady who was about six feet tall and not really comfortable about being that big. She had this prim, proper, nicey-nice way about her that was a hang-up to the energy when she started having her first child. I arrived at the birthing when she was about four or five centimetres dilated. She was handling her rushes pretty well in that she wasn't complaining, but I noticed right away that her skin was not very fine-textured as is usually the case when a lady is running this much energy. Usually the facial skin looks very subtle and delicate; and you can see an amazing subtlety of expression. But her skin was more red and coarse-looking, and the level of expression was not too delicate – her face moved in bigger chunks at a time. Then, when she got to where she was almost fully dilated, she got very nauseous all at once. She turned green and had to throw up right away and had a hard time doing it. (It is interesting to notice how easily and gracefully somebody pukes, as this can tell you something about their very most basic attitudes. If a person has a hard time throwing up, to where it takes a very strong rush of nausea before she can do it and she gets a very revolted look on her face, not doing it as naturally as a dog or a new baby does it –it is because of conditioning, and it's best if you can point out the direction of this conditioning and help free her of it.) So this lady barfed a long time and went through all the colours of green that she could. There were a lot of secretions that day. After she was done throwing up and got to feeling all right about it, she started having a sense of humour and said, 'This was not exactly what I had in mind that I would be doing at my birthing. I thought I was going to be having this fine spiritual experience.' Here she was on her hands and knees throwing up all over the place on a hot summer day, etc. While all this was going on, I was noticing some very distinct changes in her appearance. She began looking rosy, and amused, and her face looked a lot more subtle and real. Her mouth looked very pretty, and I thought she was having her spiritual experience, even if it didn't fit her preconceptions.

Throwing up dilated her cervix the rest of the way, and she had a beautiful boy after a very short second stage. All that barfing freed her up so that she was ready for anything, and that's the attitude that a birthing mother needs to have.

DEBORAH ROZMAN

Meditating with Children

Harmoniously balanced, universally centred, happy, calm, creative children.

These class sessions will be a definite integrating factor in the lives of the children involved. A divine self-image is mirrored to them through the form, vibration and atmosphere of the class. Wholesome attitudes about life, human relations, use of energies, effective ways of expressing feelings about and with each other and working out differences – *which work to further the evolutionary process* – are the goals of each class period. With the prime objective of the classes being to instil a definite experience of unity and balance between the inner subjective worlds and outer objective worlds, the result will be a definitely increased ability of each child to cope, to understand and to express.

In the classes we consciously link the inner and outer worlds through meditation, a going within and self-observation, discussing our experiences, and expressing our awarenesses in activities. This process enables the children to develop a continuity of awareness between what goes on inside the body and what goes on outside the body. All activities are structured for the direct purpose of expressing and understanding the subjective self and for developing self-direction and self-realisation. Through following the class formats, the children's concentration, self-initiative, intuition, memory and imagination receive definite stimulation. By offering techniques to help children consciously become aware of being 'whole' they are less likely to get caught in the traps of material identification and the problems caused by being embroiled in the glamours and illusions of those who do not know themselves and the world they have evolved. Being whole and unified we have defined as a definite experience of unity between that which lies within and that which lies without. This unity manifests itself as an ever-inclusive awareness of Self, revealing the nature of cause and effect as it activates energy in daily life. As much as possible the children are educated (the true meaning of education is 'to lead out') to expand their awareness in terms of wholes, to identify and relate themselves through this unifying process to gradually revealed expanded patterns of Being and expanded states of awareness beyond the logical, linear and time-bound patterns presently imposed in education. Visual aids and the examples of great individuals whose awareness has transcended the normal mind patterns (the great scientists, poets, philosophers and mystics and saints) are particularly helpful tools for realising these objectives. Children learn about essence through imaging, imitating and identifying.

Spaceship Meditation

Imagine there is a spaceship inside of your head. Step inside your spaceship. Now, go all the way up in your spaceship, out of the top of your head past billions of stars, up, up, up, up . . . (pause) . . . observe what you see, now go all the way down in your spaceship . . . down, down, down, down, . . . (pause) . . . now go all the way up, up, up, up, higher and farther this time . . . now go all the way to the left . . . farther and farther, now go all the way to the right . . . farther, farther, and farther . . . now all the way straight in front of you, farther, farther, farther, farther . . . (pause) . . . now all the way behind, go farther and farther back, on and on, farther and farther . . . (long pause). Now, come back slowly to the centre and back into the top of your head and now you are inside your head again. You have travelled over and through the entire universe. Open your eyes, look around you. What did you see in your universe? Discuss with each other. (Adapt this meditation to visit a star, a planet, the centre of the sun, etc.)

Balloon Meditation

Feel a balloon inside your spiritual eye. Now we are going to blow up our balloons. But these balloons are very special. They never burst, they just keep expanding and expanding and expanding. Feel your balloon expand, blow it up in your mind a little bigger, and bigger, and bigger, feel it getting so big that it is bigger than your head and is expanding everywhere . . . Feel it bigger than this room, feel it bigger than the city, bigger than the country, bigger than the oceans, bigger than the whole world . . . (long pause) . . . now blow it up once more so that it is bigger than the whole Universe and all the stars and the planets and the sun are inside your balloon too, and imagine that every idea and every thought and every feeling is inside the balloon.

Personal Account by Primary Teacher, Stephanie Herzog (Elementary school teacher, Scotts Valley Public Schools)

I began using meditation in the classroom the day after Deborah Rozman spoke at our school district inservice. I started the children with the simple exercise: relaxation, breathing and concentration on a star between their eyes while concentrating on having a good day and doing well in all that they were doing. Due to fear of parent criticism, I call it centring and concentrating our energies. We centre five minutes in the morning and ten minutes in the afternoon. If the children come in over-active from any recess we centre before beginning work. I told parents who work in my classroom as volunteers that the centring was a relaxation exercise for increasing the children's concentration. These parents accept what I am doing in a positive way and participate with us.

A wonderful thing is happening in my classroom which I feel is a direct result of meditation. I seldom have to discipline the children. They have increased in self-direction. There is a peaceful-mellow feeling or atmosphere in the room and it is a pleasure to be in the atmosphere. I feel a group awareness is evolving. The children seem closer to one another and care more for each other. They seldom fight, and if they have a disagreement are often able to resolve it themselves. The 'I don't like boys, or I don't like girls' attitude, which has always been prevalent in my primary classrooms over the past seven years and which discussion could not eradicate, is disappearing through meditation. Boys and girls are interacting more. This change of consciousness is apparent but slow.

I have noticed a definite change in the playground which I attribute to meditation. Previous to meditation some of the boys in my classroom were functioning on the playground as a sort of gang, causing problems for other students. Now, without any direction from myself most of my boys (and some of my girls) play soccer or football at recess. They taught one another how to play the games. They organise their own teams, play the games, referee the games all on their own, with a minimal amount of angry feelings. It amazes me to watch them. I never thought this age child (7–8 yrs) could learn to interact in such a way. I watch but seldom supervise. They are proud to play in my presence.

I encourage the children to meditate on their own. Some have related experiences of doing better in sports. Some have fallen asleep doing it. We need to discuss what they are practising on their own more. I have noticed recently when we are all quiet together as a group that a nice feeling of peace comes over and into me. I have always had some problem in the classroom in keeping the children quiet while I am giving directions. Since meditation I am finding that the children are very attentive when I speak. It is so delightful! Each day flows smoothly. I also find I am beginning to speak more to the inner parts of the children.

I try to open my heart by doing the meditations and yoga every morning and lunch apart from the children as well as with them. The difference is amazing. I find that to the extent I allow myself to become uncentred, anxious or scattered, the children become anxious and noisy. They pick up my energy and send it back. I become more uncentred – and it all snowballs. Now I try to stay centred realising I can only do so much in a day.

The meditations using the imagination, such as the balloon meditation, have been most successful. The children love them – and simply shine with energy and quiet excitement afterwards. I tell the children that we are using the same imagination that we write stories with, or paint with, except we are doing it in our minds. The children are asking to write creative stories about their experiences, so painting and writing after this type of meditation is our next step. I am glad the suggestion came from them.

One experience from meditation that was beautiful to me was in relation to a child's mother who was talking to me about some difficulty she was having with her husband. As she was expressing her concern her son walked in. He said, 'Mom, the trouble with you is that you don't centre yourself.' She asked him to show her how which he did *beautifully*, and a wonderful communication happened then between the three of us. I had not known that the meditations had affected him so much since he had always seemed somewhat resistant to them.

JOSEPH BHARAT CORNELL

Sharing Nature with Children

In Ohio some years back, a naturalist at an outdoor education camp led a group of children on a very special hike. I was a participant rather than a leader that day, and I still enjoy my memories of the outing. Our guide created dramatic, contrasting experiences for us that ensured that all of us would have deep, new, personal contacts with the natural world.

Most of the children had never been in an evergreen forest in their lives, and we were going to one of the few pine forests in southern Ohio. (This stand of pines was planted many years ago as part of an arboretum, a place where trees are scientifically studied.) The children were excited, and our naturalist-guide channelled their high energy skilfully to create a moving experience of the forest.

She first took us to a Christmas-tree farm, where she announced with a flourishing sweep of an arm and a twinkle in her eye, 'This is the pine forest.' Groans and disappointed shuffling of feet – the trees were barely taller than the children.

She then blindfolded all of us and led us through a sunny deciduous forest. Pretty soon we heard a stream and she said, 'There's a narrow bridge here, so you'll have to cross one at a time.' The first child started across, then shrieked with nervous laughter. The rest of us waited uneasily, not knowing what was ahead.

My turn came and I groped my way forward, taking a first cautious step on to the bridge. Aha! No wonder there were squeals – the bridge swayed dizzily from side to side, and bounced up and down at the same time. Between the creaks and groans of ropes and wood, I heard water rushing along far below. At the other side I was greeted by a flutter of small hands; the naturalist had let the children take off their blindfolds to watch me cross. I now removed my own blindfold and saw a safely built suspension bridge, its handrails polished from much use.

We replaced our blindfolds and struck out on the trail again. After a while the sound of our footsteps changed; we heard no more crackling leaves, only a soft, muffled crunching as we walked. Then there was a dark shadow all around us and we sensed a deep quiet – fewer bird sounds, and no rustling of leaves in the wind. A child broke the silence: 'Where are we?'

The naturalist said, 'Lie down on your backs and try to feel what is special about this place.'

We lay for a long time experiencing the deep, restful quiet. Finally, the naturalist told us to take off our blindfolds. Shooting skyward were countless magnificent pine trees. My spirits rose with them, and I was overwhelmed with admiration and awe – I had never seen a forest this way before. The children were completely stunned. Finally, we sat up and looked around at each other, quietly sharing our amazement with appropriate expressions. On our own we wandered through the forest, touching the trees and gazing up into the forest cathedral.

It takes a happy combination of setting and receptivity to have a really deep experience like this. That's what the games in this chapter are for: to bring us that fresh and mysterious contact with other members of the natural world.

Earth Windows

The forest looks fresh and interesting, when you see it from a brand-new angle. In this game, the children lie still on the forest floor, absorbed in watching and listening to swaying trees, fluttering birds, and the rushing wind. Through holes in its leafy ceiling, silent clouds peek into the children's woodsy room. Animals may come very close because the children are quiet and hidden.

Have everyone lie down and begin thinking of himself as part of the Earth, looking skyward. Cover each child's body with leaves, sticks and pine needles – clear up to the sides of his head. Leave only the face exposed, and use enough leaves and sticks to give him a feeling of being down inside the Earth. Now place leaves (pine needles work best) over the children's faces, patchwork-fashion. Make sure the leaves are free of dirt, and tell the children to close their eyes as you arrange this final bit of covering.

Tell the children you'll give a signal when it's time to come back; this will help them stay under the leaves longer without getting restless. You should give the signal before they become restless. Surprisingly, I've found that twenty minutes is usually not too long.

In a large group, work quickly and have the children help bury each other. Work in one direction, away from those covered first. Then when the first-covered emerge, you can steer them away from the others who are still enjoying the forest quiet. Any individuals or pairs who are likely to talk and disturb those around them can be buried some distance away from the others.

Children will be much more agreeable to the idea of being covered with soil and leaves if they've been digging or crawling on the forest floor just before the game begins. It's important also to say something in advance about the bugs that may crawl over them. Play this down! You may want to let the children first handle various bugs, allowing the bugs to crawl over them. This is often a lot of fun – the children lose their early-learned prejudices against insects, and begin to appreciate these fascinating little creatures. Encourage them to stay calm while lying under the leaves and being crawled upon; ask them just to feel what the bug is doing, so that they can tell the others about it afterwards.

Earth Windows gives an experience of the forest through the forest's own eyes.

Heartbeat of a Tree

A tree is a living creature. It eats, rests, breathes and circulates its 'blood' much as we do. The heartbeat of a tree is a wonderful crackling, gurgling flow of life. The best time to hear the forest heartbeat is in early spring, when the trees send first surges of sap upwards to their branches, preparing them for another season of growth.

Choose a tree that is at least six inches in diameter and has thin bark. Deciduous trees are generally better for listening to than conifers, and certain individuals of a species may have a louder heartbeat than others. Press a stethoscope firmly against the tree, keeping it motionless so as not to make the interfering noises. You may have to try several different places on the tree trunk before you find a good listening spot.

Children will want to hear their own heartbeat. Listen also to the heartbeats of mammals and birds – the variety in sounds and rhythms is fascinating.

PHYLLIS KYSTAL

Cutting the Ties that Bind – Puberty

After the person is relaxed, I suggest that we both imagine a triangle erected between us, explaining its function if that has not already been done. I have the person take a place at point B on the base, with me at the other end at point A, joined by a line representing the mutual trust we have for each other as working partners. Then we both visualise an antenna reaching up our spines, out from the top of each of our heads, meeting at a point in space at the apex of the triangle, which we call the High C, High Consciousness or God–self. The High C is the innate wisdom within all of us, where we are all one.

We then take time to ask that each of us be guided from that mutual High C, so that the right questions and directions will come to the one who is directing and that the person in the relaxed state will receive and be ready to handle whatever he needs to see, feel, know or experience at that particular time.

This method has proved to be foolproof over the years and we have never had occasion when someone with whom we were working got out of his depth, or was faced with any memory, fault or old trauma that was too much for him to handle.

I then explain that the person is not to worry if this first time he sees nothing, as in that event I can easily slip into the reverie state myself and describe what I see, and then direct him according to how I am guided from within. Even if that is difficult, I make it clear that I can, if so directed, take over, watch and describe the impressions I am receiving and do whatever I am prompted to do to help on his inner level. This seems to take all the anxiety and pressure off those who may be worried that they will not be able to visualise.

Next, I ask the person to visualise the two circles of the Figure Eight which are already familiar from the two-week daily practice periods, and then invite into the circle opposite the one he is in the parent from whom he is about to separate. I tell him to explain to the parent that the ritual about to be performed will free both of them so that each will be able to live his own life as a separate individual and will no longer be pulled this way and that by the actions of the other via the cords which still bind them together. I then encourage the person to see if he can see the ties between him and his parent, and to tell me at which parts of the body on each person the cords are attached. Most people seem to be able to visualise this fairly easily and some are really shocked at what they see. I warn the person not to be disturbed since what he sees will show us how best to help the relationship.

It is not at all unusual for the parent of the opposite sex to be joined to the child between the sex organs, telling us a great deal about their relationship and showing us where they will need to work if they ever hope to have a good relationship with someone of the opposite sex.

Some people find only one link while others discover several, depending on the closeness, either positive or negative, of the relationship. We have had a few cases where the connection was so strong that the two were like Siamese twins. In these situations, it was impossible for the person desiring to be free to see clearly and it was out of the question to expect him to perform the 'surgery' himself. In this case the person directing the session must be willing to perform the operation for him, urging him to participate as much as possible.

When the ties have been located, I ask for a description of the size and texture and, here again, I have heard literally hundreds of different descriptions, all symbolic of the relationship and often astonishingly revealing. There have been velvet ribbons, nylon thread, fishing lines, wire, rope, chains, metal bars, and many, many other types of cords.

When the nature of the ties has been determined, I tell him to ask to be shown the appropriate instrument with which to sever or detach the bonds, and again the selection is surprisingly varied. Scissors, all kinds of knives such as kitchen and hunting knives, swords, and daggers, light rays, laser beams, fire, acid, saws, to mention but a few, are forthcoming.

I usually suggest that the first cut be made in the middle of the bond and then each end removed from each person's body where it is attached. Frequently I have to help remove the end from the person doing the detaching if it happens to be on a part of the body which is hard for him to reach or is too sensitive for him to dare to tackle on his own with any confidence of success.

As each end is removed, I suggest placing the right hand (if the person is right handed, otherwise the left hand) over the place where it was removed on either body, with the other hand behind it to create a force field. Then we ask that a healing force flow down from the High C into his hands and into the wound left by the cutting.

The ties are then placed in a pile at the feet of the person working and, when they have all been detached, he asks to be shown the best method of destroying them, thus preventing them from returning to continue the old pattern.

Most people choose to burn or bury, dissolve with acid, or hurl the bonds into the sea or a fast-flowing river. Frequently, people are so anxious to be finished with such ties that they cannot think of enough to do to be sure they are definitely destroyed, often deciding to bury the fire in which they have burned them and then jumping up and down on the site to erase all evidence of it. This has, at times, developed into something like an Indian war dance, which I then suggest should become an expression of the person's relief at being finally free. I encourage them to let go and express this freedom in any way they choose.

After they are satisfied that everything has been done to erase all trace of the old ties, I suggest they thank the parent from whom they have just been separated for providing the means for them to enter the world in a human body, and thus be able to learn whatever was necessary in this life.

Next the person performs a ritual in which he asks forgiveness from the parent and forgives the parent for any hurts that have been inflicted on him, consciously or unconsciously. This is often very hard for the person to do, especially in a case where there are hard feelings between him and the parent. It is essential that the forgiving be done as it is part of the process of becoming detached and whole. Lack of forgiveness can forge the links all over again in a negative way.

I usually start by having the person first ask the parent for forgiveness, as this part of the ritual seems to be, for most people, slightly easier: many people suffer from a load of guilt and this presents the person with an opportunity to relieve himself of the burden. I suggest that he allow specific things to come to mind for which he would like forgiveness and either to verbalise them or silently mention them, one at a time. If he chooses to be silent, I ask him to let me know when he has finished, to the best of his knowledge. I also tell him that anything more coming up later can always be handled at that time. We find that this opportunity to ask forgiveness is most welcome and frees the person from the haunting sense of guilt and regret which people are so often left with, particularly after the parent has passed on.

The next step is to forgive the parent for any hurts or wrongs inflicted, either consciously or unconsciously, on the one seeking release. This is by far the harder task for most people and, in some cases, they find it impossible to attempt.

At such times, I suggest that even though the person cannot find it in his heart to forgive this parent, he can ask the High C, or God-force within him, to send forgiveness from the top of the triangle between us down through himself and across to the parent. This is almost always acceptable even by those who know they need to forgive but cannot bring themselves to do so on their own. Again, I suggest that they allow specific episodes to enter their minds where

197

forgiveness of the parent is needed to set them both free from the negative emotions which bind people just as strongly as positive ones.

Finally, the parent is asked to leave the scene and go on his way to lead his own life, now free from the constant emotional tug of the child. This request does not necessarily mean that there will be no further contact between them; indeed, most people find that, on the contrary, the relationship becomes much less emotionally charged and more satisfactory.

We always suggest an appropriate parting, preferably with a blessing. Sometimes it is indicated that a triangle be visualised between the parent and child connecting them both to the High C instead of to one another. We have been shown that this visualisation is the most helpful thing anyone can do for another person, and we call it 'running the triangle'. We often do this ourselves when we receive a call for help (even before the person has been told anything about it) to connect him to the High C as quickly as possible.

One further step is taken to complete the release. This is a cleansing process, which is designed to wash away all old conditioning and habit patterns. This process is a preparation for working on habits separately, which will be discussed in the next chapter. Sometimes the release is immediate, but it can also take a longer time to become evident.

I usually suggest that the person look around his inner scene for a body of water, such as a stream, pool, ocean, or waterfall. He is then instructed to remove all his clothes, to leave them in a pile on the ground and, taking a large leaf or smooth stone, to enter the water and wash himself thoroughly. This will remove unwanted negative habit patterns or attitudes picked up from parents, and he should recall them from the lists he has already compiled of his parents' negative attributes. When he is satisfied that he has cleansed himself of them, he is told to run up and down to dry himself off, jumping and leaping to express his freedom. When he is dry, I hand him a fresh loose robe or gown of a neutral colour to wear until he grows a new set of attributes of his own, or, if prompted from within, I lead him to find his own new garment. Then I ask how he would like to destroy the old clothing which ties him to his childhood reactions. Most often he will decide to burn his old clothes and, as in every other part of the work, I am often amazed at some of the elaborate methods people will choose to destroy them.

The most important part of the work is the person's own active participation, which alone can reach through to the subconscious mind. The more emotion involved, the deeper the subconscious is impressed with the new message, and thus, the sooner the message will be put into effect. Most people are delighted at the opportunity to rid themselves of their old unwanted habits and find no problem becoming emotionally involved in the process.

I always warn the person that for the next three days after the session he can expect to experience mixed emotions, such as mourning or sadness mixed with relief, but that he need not worry as this is quite usual and will soon pass. If the warning is not given, and the person does go into a depression or some similar change or mood, it may come as a shock and throw doubt on the whole experience.

It is also advisable to tell the person not to talk about his experience with anyone for at least three days, as the emotional energy needs to be contained to give it a chance to stabilise, solidify and become a reality. Talking about it too soon can allow the energy to leak away, especially if the person to whom the experience is described happens to be sceptical and expresses doubt. This reaction is infectious and becomes like a blight on the still delicate new growth within the person who has just worked.

We then both thank the High C for directing the session and I give verbal suggestions to bring the person back to full awareness of his physical body, which I remind him has been given a healing treatment during the time we were working on the inner level. I suggest that he wriggle his toes, bend his knees, move his hips, arch his back, and stretch his arms, all reminiscent of a dog or cat stretching the whole body upon awakening from sleep.

I then emphasise the day's date and that he is in my workroom and that he can now sit up slowly, remove the scarf from his eyes, return to full conscious awareness, and begin to function freely after his recent release.

Then I explain that it is advisable after cutting the ties, particularly those connected to parents, to write an unmailed letter to the parent expressing his release. This letter bypasses the conscious mind of the person to whom it is addressed but reaches his subconscious. It is best written as soon after the cutting ceremony as possible when strong emotions aroused by the ritual are usually still present. The more emotion with which the letter is written, the deeper the effect it will have on both the one writing it and on the one to whom it is addressed, since emotion is the energy which is needed to carry the message to the subconscious level of the mind. The letter should be a repetition of the statement made during the ritual that each person is now free to live as a separate individual. It should not include anything negative, such as criticism or blame, and should concentrate only on the freedom both will now begin to experience. I have seen some dramatic results when this has been done with strong emotion.

I recall one case where a son who had had no contact with his parents for several years, suddenly and without knowing the reason, called them long distance on the phone after his mother had gone through the ceremony of cutting the tight connection which she had seen still existed between them, and had written the follow-up unmailed letter.

Another young man, also without knowing why he was doing it, called to tell his parents that he loved them. He had never been able to say this before. This occurred after his father had detached cords from him and set him free to live his own life.

There are many cases of parents changing their old attitudes to their grown children when the latter have cut the binding ties. Their reports always refer to a cessation of tension and to a more flowing relationship. In addition to this easing of tension, people mention that it has become much easier to talk than ever before and to see one another for the first time as people and not just as relatives.

If the person has been reared by people other than the natural parents, he should be helped to release from these after cutting the ties to his own parents. The method is almost identical to that described above except that, instead of thanking the parents for supplying entry into a physical body, it is more appropriate to thank them for assuming the responsibility for his care in place of his parents. For other members of the family who have had partial influence on the growing child such as grandparents, the wording of the ceremony can be adjusted and adapted appropriately.

CHRISTOPHER DAY

Architecture and Environmental Design as a Healing Art

Yet silence is something we need to have access to, for while noise is stressful silence is healing.

Where in the world can we go to find this sort of silence? And for those who can afford the expense, how much noise does travelling there cause? One place to go is within oneself. Many seek inner silence through meditation, but it is not easy to keep inner noise at bay. But if we are to design healing environments we need to create qualities of holy silence that are accessible for all, not just for globetrotters and mediators but especially for those who lack the outer or inner means.

Even if we can't *define* silence, we can recognise it. Gentle, unobstructive, calming, life-supporting, holy sounds allow us to be quiet within: eternal sounds, sounds of the breath of air, the quiet endlessness of water – definitely not sounds of the ephemeral moment however calming. Cows chewing the cud and bumble-bees droning are calming, almost soporific, but they are not eternal. Silence, tranquillity and the eternal have a lot to do with each other.

It's even harder to define silent architecture but likewise easy to recognise it. There is dead silent or living silent architecture. To create living silent architecture we need to understand and work with the essential qualities of living silence: the gentle, the unobstructive, the tranquil, the eternal, the life-supporting, the holy.

As a foundation of tranquillity we need balance. This often means focus and axis. Symmetry is rigid, rigidity excludes life. Balance is life-filled and breathes from one side to the other. Balance is also a matter of scale and proportion. Rooms can be quite small – monks' cells were often little more than the space to lie and stand in. The smaller a room is, the more modest, plain, ascetic and quiet it can be – furniture is an intrusion. Such a room is for a specific purpose, but not a silent place *within* the stream of daily life. If the proportions, textures, light and other qualities are not just right, a small room is a trap, a larger one can often get away with it although you can start to rattle around, and its silence can begin to feel empty. Too large a space can be too awe-inspiring. The human being is too insignificant beside the power of architectural scale. Those cathedrals that are places of silence (and there are not so many, for more are places of awe) are not the largest ones, their scale reduced by the way they are built of tiers of elements. The gestures of the romanesque ones tie them down firmly to the earth. Imagine such a cathedral plastered and painted uniformly – in simplicity its size would be too strong – certainly it would not be silent!

Proportion determines whether places can be at rest or whether they have a directional dynamic and the feeling that goes with it. Awe, expectation or soothing can be produced with upward, forward or all-round horizontal emphasis. Proportions at balance reflect balance in the human body and induce a mood of balance in the soul.

Proportions that are too high, too wide, too long – like lines that are too dynamic or spaces that are too strongly focal – risk being too compelling. I want to leave the occupant free. I try to be careful, therefore, not to have too strong an emphasis. Indeed for a place of silence I try to underplay the architecture generally so that it is not intrusive. Simplicity, enshrined in the modern movement, is often experienced by non-architects as boring. Some buildings need to be less simple, some more so. Places of silence need to be simple – how can reverent simplicity be achieved without boredom?

I approach simplicity like this: the space can generally be entered and focused axially but slight variation from one side to another, slight ambiguities in form and, most particularly, living lines (flare at the base of the walls, curved qualities in the almost straight and straight in the curved and so on) give the space a quality of life – so too with straighter, but not colliding lines does the texture of wood, even if its colour variation is muted by stains or lazure veils. This life is further enhanced by the light. Where the windows are placed, how they are shaped, how the light is quieted – for instance divided by glazing bars reflected off splayed windows or filtered through vegetation – can enhance the interplay between daylight, sunlight and reflected light which is so crucial to the mood of a room.

Light needs texture to play on. Again I am looking for a life-filled, but unobtrusive, gentle texture. I commonly use hand-finished render. This can bring gentleness, life, conversational softening of changes in plane and – because of the absolute necessity that the plasterer is aesthetically involved – soul is impregnated into the room. This certainly is not the only material, nor is it everywhere appropriate, but where it is it is one of my favourites. Being applied to block-work and requiring more sensitivity than skill, it has the additional advantage of being cheap and well-suited to gift work or self-build.

I've been in spatially simple rooms which lack any life in their texture. Smooth-plastered, smooth-painted rooms, even the wood-work gloss painted. To be alone, quiet, in such a room is to be in a prison. You *need* a radio, hi-fi or television for company to fill the empty space, to bring a kind of life. I aim to make rooms in which you do not need these supports, rooms that will be alive with sunlight or candlelight, birdsong outside or with grey dawn, twilight and silence.

Texture-less rooms need wallpaper or colour schemes to give interest, to paint a superficial individuality upon their surface. I use colour for a different function, so different that when a client says, 'I have these curtains, I want a colour scheme to go with them,' I am at a loss to know what to do: I use colour to create a mood. Yet often, for silence, the indoor colour I use is white. White, justifiably, has a bad reputation; it's the colour people use when they can't think of anything else. But it is the colour I use when I don't *want* anything else, when I want silence. Some people think white is not a colour, but the right white (there are many – think of the difference between lime wash, emulsion and gloss paint, not to mention all the different colours of white) can sing! White is the mother of all the colours – it has in it all the moods that each individual can develop as an individuality – white can be calm, life-filled, joyous, timeless, whereas blue can only be calm and risks being cold or melancholic; orange can be full of life, welcoming, but risks being too forceful, even discordant; yellow can be joyous but risks being too active; I have never seen more eternal qualities than in Vermeer's paintings, yet brown risks being too heavy, dark, oppressingly entrapping.

However, where the room or window shape is rectilinear with smooth surfaces and sharp arises, I would certainly not use white – it would be altogether too hard. In such a room white would emphasise any noise. Research on colour and perceived noise does indeed show white rooms to sound loudest. When we use it we therefore need to be particularly attentive to qualities of shape, texture and light or indeed it will seem noisy. The quietest colour for a room has been found to be purple. In ancient times purple was not a colour anyone could use, its use on clothing restricted to a certain spiritual rank. Even today, less sensitive to the 'beings of colour' as we are, it doesn't seem quite appropriate for everyday use; a purple kitchen doesn't feel quite right.

I use particular colours when I wish to emphasise a particular mood. Red can bring warmth, stimulation, passion and aggressiveness. With all colours, associative qualities such as coolness with blue are bound up with physiological effects upon the organs and metabolism. Yellow for instance can bring light to a sunless room; it can also bring vitality and cheerfulness. Green is calming and refreshing; it is the colour of surgical gowns and actors' 'greenrooms'. The meditation room is to be lazured in bluish purple.

In therapy, coloured light has been shown to be more effective than pigments. Coloured windows only feel at home in specific sorts of place (such as churches) but coloured light can be achieved by reflection. Opaque colours are forceful and dominating, translucent lazure is therefore both more acceptable and more effective than opaque pigment. Brick tiles and timber with dark rich weavings bring warmth. We even designed a theatre to be painted inside in grey (not a flat grey but one made up of thin veils of red, blue, green); this was also to be a focal, unobtrusive space, but not a place of silence!

Similarly I try to make silent, sacred rooms *plain*. These rooms need to be somehow above any more specific mood. When the circular meditation chapel was nearing completion it looked so attractive inside with its exposed radial rafters that many people wanted them left like that. I felt that they created a warm cosy atmosphere with noticeable architecture, appropriate for a living room perhaps, but not for a chapel, especially not for the silent, spirit-renewing focus of a retreat centre. I offered to pull the ceiling off if people didn't like it: fortunately I didn't have to.

In the same way that colours can be too individual so can material. The difference is that certain materials are the right materials for the place and it doesn't feel right – or may not be practical – to use other ones. In some countries brick, stone or timber is the only suitable choice and I have experienced wonderfully sacred places in diverse materials. Generally there needs to be very few different materials. Often I use only three: walls and ceiling of the same finish, running without break into each other and unified by a single uninterrupted colour; wooden doors and windows, unpainted but possibly stained or translucently lazured, and a texturally inviting floor of a colour to warm reflected light – usually wood, brick, tiles or carpet. Unity of materials and colours has a quietening influence and for that reason they need to have sufficient life in them or the whole place will slide into lifelessness.

The shapes, forms and spaces need therefore to have gentle movement. The static resolution of the right angle lacks life. Dramatic or dynamic forms and gestures have an excess of force. To have both movement and stability, gesture needs to answer gesture in a life-filled, harmonic conversation – not repetition but resolution, transforming what the other says so that it is just right for its particular location, neighbours, material and function. Quiet harmony is the product of a quietly singing conversation.

Perhaps the most essential quality is timelessness. A painting can be timeless, so can a building. Obviously the painting has to avoid anything that finds its resolution in time outside the moment – like someone kicking a ball. The same with a building. This doesn't only mean qualities which are both traditional and modern at the same time; it also means resolution of the sculptural forces – of gesture, of gravity, of structural and visual tension. Dead things are stable, immovable, but they are left behind by time. The eternal lives in every moment.

ROGER HARRISON

Leadership and Strategy in Business

Conscious evolution does add one very powerful concept which is missing or understated in much contemporary writing about leadership and high-performing organisations. It is the concept of *attunement*, meaning a resonance or harmony among the parts of the system, and between the parts and the whole. As the concept of alignment speaks to us of *will*, so that of attunement summons up the mysterious operations of *love* in organisations: the sense of empathy, understanding, caring, nurturance, and mutual support.

Love, what a closet word it is in organisations! Far better to talk openly of those old shibboleths, sex, money, and power, than to speak of love. This is the true male chauvinism in business: the discrimination against women masks the deeper fear of love.

Yet love is far too powerful ever to be truly exorcised. We find it everywhere if we but look. Love is evoked by beauty and by quality in the products or services we produce. It is present in the comradeship of co-workers, in the relationship of mentor to protégé, in the loyalties between people which transcend personal advantage. Love is found in the high ideals of service and contribution which are articulated in the published values of many corporations. It speaks through our dedication to workmanship and excellence of performance.

There is a mystery in words. When we call the love we find in our organisations by other names than its own, it loses its power. I suspect we are reluctant to name love because to do so will release that power, and we do not have forms and processes with which to channel it. Love has its demonic side, too, and we are perhaps not wrong to be wary of it. We do speak, somewhat gingerly, about caring, open communication, consideration, and the like. Not about love.

When we do think about love and organisations, we are apt to see love as a disruptive force, destructive of order and good business judgement. Images come to mind of managers making personnel decisions on the basis of affinity and friendship or setting prices based on the needs of the customer. Of course, people do sometimes make business decisions by consulting their hearts, but it is seldom admitted, and there are certainly no business school courses on how to do it.

New Age organisations, by contrast, attempt more often than not to invoke the power of love in their decision-making. They have developed forms and processes for effective decision making: group meditation to enable members to 'go inside' and consult their hearts, asking themselves what they are 'called' to do, and other similar approaches.

Alignment and attunement are both processes for achieving *integration* and unity of effort among the differentiated parts of a system. The idea of organisation alignment is getting a good press of late through the awakening interest in the role of superordinate values, top management leadership, and the characteristics of high-performing systems. I believe we also have much to learn of attunement. Alignment channels high energy and creates excitement and drive. It evokes the demonic. Attunement is quieter, softer, receptive to the subtle energies which bind us to one another and to nature. It tames and balances the demonic by opening us to one another's needs and to our own sense of what is fitting and right, what is the 'path of the heart' which best expresses our higher selves.

Without attunement and without evoking the power of love in our organisational lives, I think we shall not find peace, but only ceaseless striving.

* * *

The new leader is seen as having a caring, respectful, and positive attitude towards people, and a willingness to share power. He or she is more open and non-defensive regarding his or her own faults and vulnerabilities than former leaders, and less likely to use fear, domination, or militant charisma than before. The picture is one of a personally secure and mature individual who can articulate the values and high principles which give organisational life meaning, but who is more humble and receptive than we normally expect visionary leaders to be. Perhaps this conception of leadership is best expressed as *stewardship:* leadership as a trust which is exercised for the benefit of all; the leader as serving the followers, guided by a vision of the higher purposes of the organisation. Thus, the organisation is seen as animated by the sense of its own higher purpose. The leader focuses the attention and consciousness of the members on those purposes. But the leader also knows that the parts have legitimate purposes of their own which are not completely expressed by the purposes of the whole, and he or she facilitates the attunement processes by means of which organisation members can come to know, respect, and care for one another's needs and individual purposes. The flow of human energy is not one way, from the members to the organisation, but the uniqueness of each part is also preserved and nourished by the whole.

In the past, leaders we call 'great' have generally been very strong, ruling through fear and respect, and/or very charismatic, releasing and focussing the demonic for their followers. Our concept of leadership is clearly different. Our 'new leader' avoids the use of fear and arbitrary authority without being soft or avoiding conflict. He or she is a visionary, but the demonic thrust which is implicit in the charismatic style is balanced and tamed by a nurturing receptivity. The leader brings healing and harmonising influences which we can only call love into the organisation.

* * *

A radical leap is required to move from our normal habit of thinking of organisational purposes as defined internally to thinking of an organisation in terms of planetary purpose. Seen from the planetary point of view, the organisation exists only as part of a larger reality, supported and nurtured by the larger system on which it depends. Its purposes are not solely determined or decided by itself, but are 'given' by its place in the larger system. Organisation purpose is not simply decided by its members but is rather to be *discovered*. The process of discovery is partly internal to the organisation, involving an inner search for values and meaning. It also has an external aspect, that of discovering meaning through the transactions of the organisation with its environment. Viewed in this way, a primary task of the organisation is the discovery of its place and purpose in the larger system. Every event in its history can be viewed as part of a lesson, the meaning of which is to be intuited by the organisation's members.

Adopting such a point of view requires a fundamental change in one's orientation to goals and to the success and failure of one's plans. We can begin, in Kipling's words, to 'meet with triumph and disaster, and treat those two imposters just the same'. If one's orientation is to learning, then failure carries just as much information as success. In fact, failure may be more valuable, because in our failures are embedded Nature's messages about required changes.

★ ★ ★

From the point of view of conscious evolution, then, strategic planning is a search for meaning, rather than a search for advantage. It is an intuitive process in which the goals and activities of the organisation are examined against the criteria of the heart: does this task enliven the doer, giving value and meaning to life? Do we still experience satisfaction in the attainment of this goal? Do we strive joyously, or with desperation? Do we feel that we are net contributors of value in our work in the world?

In approaching strategy from the point of view of purpose, our aim is definitional, rather than positional in a market domain. Our endeavour is to forge a shared view of reality which will serve the organisation members as a base for day-to-day decision-making and which will direct the leadership thrust of the dominant coalition.

The activity is definitional in that we are attempting in a variety of ways to penetrate the forms of the organisation in its internal and external relationships in order to discover its essence. Our belief is that when the forms (systems and structures) and processes (doings) of the organisation flow from its essential qualities (being), the organisation will become energised and integrated and will be effective in dealing with its environment.

The questions we ask in order to determine the essential qualities of the organisation are simple, though the process of answering them may be difficult.

First we may ask, who are we, and what are our gifts? What are our distinctive competences; what have we to contribute which is unique or different? What special knowledge do we have? What do we value? What do we believe in?

We may also ask of ourselves, what are we called to do? What needs do we see in the world which we are moved to meet? What activities have 'heart' for us? What do we love doing?

We may examine our 'core technology', those processes we use to transform inputs into outputs. How does the core technology link us to those parts of the environment which supply us with our inputs and receive our outputs? What do these key domains in our environment need from us, and what do we need from them?

We may ask ourselves what other messages we are receiving from the environment, from governments, publics, and special interest groups. Do these tell us more about our mission or calling in the world?

DONALD KEYS

Planetary Citizens

The transition of the world to a peaceful planetary society awaits the transformation of nations, which depends directly upon change in citizens – transformation in each cell of the body planetary. Unless and until enough individual cells – particularly 'leadership' cells – achieve a global vision and a sense of shared identity, the nations will continue to be afflicted with the disease of selfish separatism, acting like roving dog packs on the decks of Spaceship Earth, endangering us all.

The humanisation and the sacralisation of planetary affairs thus can be achieved only through you and me – through our actions, based on our inner identification with the oneness, the soul of humanity. You and the world are not separate; the world will achieve only if you achieve. A higher order relationship, with higher order demands and rewards: are you ready and willing to manifest it in your life? Where do you stand with respect to other cities, states and nations? At a personal level, of course, we all have likes and dislikes concerning other people. At a more essential level of relationship, can you discover that all beings everywhere are equally related and equally precious? Ask yourself, 'Have I developed a sense of bonding, of kinship, of identification with the needs, the aspirations, the dreams of humans throughout the planet? What are the limits of my inclusiveness?' To put it in other words, how big is your heart? How big have you allowed it to become? We set the limits upon ourselves, for the universal Heart is unbound and by nature all–inclusive. Where do you stand in relation to this, your deeper being?

These are practical questions. The answers can disclose your attitudes and help you to assess the present level and quality of your actions on behalf of human unification. These answers can also indicate your self-imposed limitations. The human spirit may have limitless potential, but we condition our responses and accept a seriously limited notion of our capacities. If we lack skills necessary to accomplish new goals, then we cannot suddenly acquire them in the next moment. In the realm of awareness and inclusiveness, however, fundamental human change can occur in the twinkling of an eye. With practice we can learn how to recognise and how to reject false beliefs, negative thinking, distorted images and self-imposed limitations. We then come to see that it is we who have given them power over us and that we can withdraw and redirect that power. With practice this process of change can occur from moment to moment. From it proceeds everything worthwhile: a clearer vision, creative ideation, more inclusive attitudes, and finally, motivation to overcome lethargy and to acquire the skills necessary to implement our vision.

An inward journey, then, is consistent with our outer goal; our part in the process of world–building, of realising a preferred human future and manifesting a New Age goes hand in hand with our inner expansion, our deeper realisation, our *Intronautics!* There is a remarkable connection between developing a planetary awareness and moving closer to our inner source. With inner seeking comes universal awareness and identification with all lives.

The next step for planetising humanity is our process of emancipation, the passage from limitation and narrow preoccupation. The transformation of society awaits the transformation of the self – of enough selves, at least, to tip the balance. What we need for planetary emergence is the next appropriate step for each person where he or she is. All people can take the step across the threshold of planetary awareness. All can learn the commonality and communality of human needs, wishes, desires and dreams.

When the transformed seeker becomes a knower, then he or she becomes a powerful force for human unification. The very being of such a person manifests it, telegraphs it, radiates it throughout the global network of subtle human connectedness and, to a tiny degree, will elevate the whole.

We need enactment in practical, everyday terms from everyone. First, to fulfil basic human needs, not in acts of demarcated charity, but in a natural identification with our other extended selves. Can we rest if 'we' are hungry, diseased or cold? Can our sleep be peaceful, our days serene, when two-thirds of the race cannot see beyond the bone-weary struggle for immediate survival? Can we remain uninvested in human salvage, or in upgrading the conditions of life? We will not be whole until the planet is whole; we will not be healed until humanity is healed.

DANAAN PARRY and LILA FOREST

Earth Stewards

The skies are filled with great white geese migrating homeward after winter's southern sojourn. Soon they will return to their ancestral mating marshes high in the Canadian wilderness. Are these wondrous beings thinking about which bearing to fly, or worrying about being off course? It is I, watching them, who hold such thoughts, not they. For they possess an instinctual knowing that I have long ago surrendered so as to develop the faculty with which I ponder their being 'on' or 'off' course. They are at one with the world in which they fly, and they do not wonder why.

Early in the development of humankind, we too felt our oneness with all that is, as we naturally and unconsciously lived each moment in harmony and balance. As do the few remaining aboriginal humans today, we wandered in the spirit, being given that which was needed, and feeling our symbiotic, psychic connection with every living thing. The concept of 'reverence for Nature' would have been ridiculous, since, we *were* Nature, not apart from it. Although a unique species, we still retained the connection to all that is.

As each kind of living thing evolved so as to express its unique gift within the whole, humankind began to develop its gift, that of being conscious of its-*self*. For us, the task was to evolve to the point where we could integrate the paradox of being: at the same moment separate and yet connected, unique and yet one.

And so, through thousands of years of evolution, we have journeyed far from our original state of *being*, from our surrender to our oneness with all. We have foregone our intuitive knowing nature, while our physical bodies and our minds have developed their uniqueness, their separateness, so as to fully experience all that there is to experience.

And while this has been quite perfect in terms of the necessary development of the 'separateness' pole of the paradox, still we must remember that our task as conscious beings is not only to *experience* uniqueness but also to stay conscious of our Oneness with the All.

As we look at the state of our physical world today, we see the effect of our lack of remembering. When we forget that we must manifest our total connectedness with all beings at the spirit and heart levels while we manifest our uniqueness at the physical level, then an imbalance occurs. And because of our ability to create our reality, this imbalance can bring us to a point of ultimate separation of poles, to a point of destruction of our unique life forms.

This lower form of return to oneness is not in harmony with the unfolding plan of which we are a part. The higher path, which is available to us if we choose to accept it, is a return to oneness through conscious evolution. That is, we have within our range of alternatives, that of evolving to a point of Conscious Oneness. This is the completion of the circle, except that it is now a spiral.

To choose the spiral path of upward consciousness evolution rather than the circular path of locked-in movement from oneness-to-separateness-to-devastation-to-oneness, all in an unconscious manner, we must accept the challenge that we ourselves have set before us. That challenge is to remember. We must remember who we really are, in the midst of acting out who we arranged to be. This is the paradox of oneness and separateness.

Each of the unique manifestations of the One has a role in this unfolding drama of spiralling evolution. Our role, no more nor less important than any other, is to develop and use our consciousness-of-self as a tool for service. Humankind is unique among all beings primarily in that we are conscious of our consciousness.

From this awareness has come the concept of Planetary Stewardship, as a vehicle for the full use of our unique gift. One definition of Steward is '. . . one of the servants on a passenger ship'. Planetary Stewardship may be defined as those servants on Spaceship Earth who have accepted the responsibility of employing their expanded consciousness in the service of the whole. Stewards own no-thing, yet they care for all things. Planetary Stewards are those humans who are beginning to remember that we are here not only to experience our uniqueness, but also to utilise that uniqueness in the service of Oneness. From oneness, through a time of separation, and now an evolution to the point of *conscious* oneness – this is the path

211

of stewardship. When we see ourselves as stewards, carers, lovers of our planet, and not as owners and masters of it, then shall there be lasting satisfaction from our labours.

ARNOLD MINDELL

Global Therapy

At a seminar on conflict resolution for The Colorado Institute for Conflict Resolution and Creative Leadership (CICRCL), I introduced a war game to give people an experimental grasp of global conflict. This experiment turned out to be the most educational shock I have yet had about war. The theory I wanted to test and was able to prove was: no one wants conflict; we try to forget it, thereby inadvertently propagating a war for which we are unprepared. The one-hundred-member study group decided to process the US conflict with Iran that was happening in the Persian Gulf at that time, 4 October 1987. The game was set up as follows: six people standing in a line represented the US leaders, and six standing in an opposing line, the Iranians.

Behind these two groups were another two groups of twenty people who were not allowed to speak during the proceedings, but were encouraged to make noises representing the collective opinion, behind the leaders. The rest of us sat on the sides and watched.

There were no further instructions about what should happen. The longer the US and Iranian leaders debated, the louder the two background groups representing collective opinion became. By making so much noise, they boisterously pressed their leaders closer and closer to confrontation. Finally and out of the blue, as the two front lines of the groups moved closer to one another, some unknown participant ran forward, yelling above the noise that he would drop a bomb. No one paid attention to him in the midst of the chaos and so he dropped the bomb, made a huge noise and the 'world' blew up. The groups confronted and intermingled as the bomb went off, playing out the national collectives which had driven the countries to war as the rest of the world stood by and watched.

After the World had Ended

Surprisingly, after the 'bomb' had exploded, everyone simply lay on the floor, 'dead', strewn haphazardly on top of each other. The room was absolutely quiet. No one spoke. After what seemed hours, several voices began whispering, asking what had happened. Instead of discussing the game in the large group, the field broke up and each worked individually and internally on his or her most difficult conflict by writing a dialogue between the different sides of the conflict. Using the idea of Jung's active imagination, the participants tried to slow down the internal escalation of their own conflicts in order to process all sides.

The next morning, we were surprised to learn that in the night there had been a real battle between the US and Iran in the Middle East. I have frequently seen such synchronicities, in which a group event mirrored an outer event. Are such events evidence of the non-local behaviour of global fields?

In any case, several people spoke that morning about their war-game experience and many questions were asked. Why was there such a love of murder? Why did everyone, soldiers and pacifists alike, get so excited about playing war? A few of the pacifists who had participated in the game were shocked, and courageously admitted that they had been excited by the game's violence and killing, an excitement which they had never experienced before. Of course, this was just a game. Yet, why was it thrilling to be so angry and aggressive? There are innumerable reasons for aggression, some of which have already been discussed. But another reason worth thinking about is that we forbid ourselves to be angry in our personal lives.

Since anger and murder are allowed on a national basis it becomes a thrilling relief to be allowed to be angry and kill in the name of the flag. The world encourages murder and the altered states of aggression and pain in the name of nationalism. These states are forbidden to us as individuals. This is one of the reasons why we so often find ourselves at war. Even those in the game who believed in their sanity had to question their actions and behaviour.

★　★　★

Our assumptions here are that the world we live in is partly organised by transpersonal fields within and around us. These fields are physical and psychological. The field is organised by various forces, such as gravity, electromagnetism, weak and strong nuclear forces, and dreaming, a hitherto unrecognised power. The field has often been imagined as an anthropos figure whose development is suicidal or growth-oriented. The majority of myths portray the field as having a mind of its own, one which is awakening.

Modern concepts such as Jung's collective unconscious and Sheldrake's morphic field, as well as ancient ideas from Taoism, Buddhism and Christianity, agree on one thing: the world we live in has the potential to be a wise dreamer. But modern group work indicates that this wisdom does not operate overtly unless the field we live in is made conscious to us all. Only when all of its parts are represented and appreciated, when group edges are recognised and investigated, does the field manifest its wisdom. Until now, however, our global awareness of this field has been minimal. The vast majority of the population ignore their own and the world's problems. Most of us think that the world's problems have nothing to do with us. We believe that acute crises will be solved by people and forces outside us.

But global consciousness is increasing, too. Though we notice an increasing attempt to solve our problems with causal solutions, there is also a growing awareness that the most powerful leadership in a group is the ability to follow the processes trying to happen. The old belief that power resided in one individual is now being differentiated by new field concepts. Global consciousness is relieving; it understands that we don't all need to be conscious group facilitators all the time. We can relax too! But when we feel that the time has come, we must learn how to follow the group's escalations and de-escalations, both of which always seem to create a new centre, a community, enriching and exciting for all.

Global consciousness seems to break old communication patterns. Any form of process–oriented group work brings the electricity back to our fading interest in community life. That, of course, does not take much. But there are many times when group processing is more exciting and more productive than the murder and struggles of war! Group work done with awareness brings us closer to one another. It gives us the chance to know the 'authorities' and our 'opponents' and also to get in touch with the energy and role of the 'terrible enemy' in ourselves. In this moment, the old static and apparently irreconcilable opposites, the persecuted and persecutor, begin to melt.

I have been astounded again and again to find that people locked into frozen conflict desire, more than anything, to live in a global community. The tragedy of chronic conflict lies not only in the unabating violence and hatred, but in the repression of our need for oneness. We all search for a 'home' and are waiting for our sense of immediate family to extend to people of all races and nationalities. After working with thousands of people everywhere, I am forced to conclude that behind our racism, fear and resistance to those who are different, lies our hope for closeness.

The Numinous Community Core

Community rituals such as New Year's Day, Christmas, Thanksgiving, Solstice Festivals, Passover, and Carnival are attempts to get to the numinous core of the field we live in, a centre to which we all relate. But rituals are not enough. They are programmes which give us security and hope, and which attempt to remind us of the wondrous or divine background of our world. But they also tend to reduce our interest in finding the numinous centre of life right here and now, in the everyday problems we feel, hear about and suffer from.

Rituals need to be rediscovered and created daily in the heart of our world problems. Think of the experiences mentioned in this book. Think of how the war game ended in a powerful silence, or of how the conflict between blacks and whites was resolved in a mutual experience of love and trust. I recall processing a conflict in a large growth centre which began with almost physical violence and ended with sensitivity and love.

I remember facilitating a language conflict between German and English speakers which brought up anger and resentment between the groups about the Holocaust. I recall with amazement how the group came to a momentary resolution when one single German woman stepped forward and wept in pain because of what had happened during World War II. An American Jewish woman came forward and knelt in front of her, hugging her legs as she wept, and the two spontaneously created a statue of a goddess and her worshipper.

I have frequently seen unhappy, unstable individuals disturbing huge groups through their behaviour, and then being relieved of their torture when the group integrated their madness by becoming more lively. True, some of these groups strayed far from their status quo while integrating their disturbers. These groups showed that momentary and unusual states of chaos heal the instability of the individual while creating a true community. The group went through phases of becoming a mob and suddenly a community, finding its centre in the spiritual experiences mirrored until then only in the individual's maddest dreams.

Most of the large group experiences I have witnessed have been with normal, everyday people. Each of these groups was able to find non-ordinary states of reality, and to create numinous cores, transforming the group into a community.

Where Is It All Going?

Having seen so many of these experiences forces me to make a hypothesis. Groups, communities and even our local relationship conflicts all have one thing in common. The boredom, tensions, cold war, open conflicts, aggression and madness which amaze, hypnotise and terrify all of us *are* unconscious attempts to reveal and discover the powerful and exciting, electric and holy heart of the dreambody we live in.

How else can I explain what I recently saw in Zurich, a city governed by a religious and work ethic, a very conservative and reserved city? A large group of people had come to hear me talk about our society's addiction to the status quo. We convened in a circle after the lecture. When the participants were asked what they saw in the middle of the room, some said they saw a large flower, others imagined children playing, one saw a huge stuffed animal and all laughed.

The group decided to give form to this last fantasy by playing it out. More and more individuals rose from the circle and began to join together and created a huge, cuddly stuffed animal which slowly 'moved' around the room and cuddled the others still sitting. Out of a momentary chaos, a new world had appeared, one in which the inside cuddled the outside, and people connected through their need to love and touch.

That night, Zurich became a huge body realising a momentary dream of relatedness, giving everyone the feeling that life was still worth living.

But people all over seem to strive for this numinous community core, even though old rituals are apparently dying out. I was shocked to discover how the tribal shamanistic healing rituals in Africa are disappearing as bush life is replaced by Western or rather, cosmopolitan civilisation. But the powerful spirit which creates community experience and which once gave us all a reason for living seems indestructible.

It is true that the remaining few per cent of our planet still living in a coherent tribal community will soon become extinct as the twenty-first century begins, and yet ancient forms of shamanistic ritual continue. I'll never forget how surprised my audience in Nairobi was to hear that they were not the only ones still interested in witch-doctors but that many people in northern California either consider themselves to be healers or else have recently been healed by one! Lifestyles change, but the search for the numinous both for ourselves and our communities continues with unrelinquished passion.

MICHAL J. EASTCOTT

Blessing the Planet

It is often easier to meditate in the company of others and group meditation has an extra value, a 'plus' factor beyond the sum total of each individual's contribution. This is because, when meditating in a group, we each bring our own quota, yet are also able to stand on the groundwork which has been built by our fellows. The vibration they are establishing, the impulse of their forward going are aids to our progress also, and meditation with others, if it is united on a common theme, can be extremely helpful and a powerful medium for creative and invocative work.

This brings us, finally, to the service of Blessing. As with the creativity of meditation, so its benediction also has a two-way flow and blesses both the one to whom it is directed, or who is held in its aura, and the one who meditates. When we succeed in offering the right receptive medium and invocatory vibration, the beneficence of the Soul is ours; healing, strengthening, 'spiritualising' forces pour in and through the channel we create. These can be radiated in the measure in which they are received, indeed, we radiate what we are and have in us whether we know it or not. Therefore, some part of our meditation must reach out to others and to our environment, must spread its quality and benediction.

But we can do more than that. We can deliberately radiate the spiritual forces with which we make contact, can channel them – act as 'transmitting stations'. We may hardly be able to send them out with a 'switch-on' efficiency, but we may have more pervasive power than we are aware of, and shall be able to bless, strengthen, heal, lift, according to the channelship that has been built.

This should be remembered as one of the great goals of meditation. Not only can we – and must we – turn to the Soul, our spiritual Mentor, for guidance, instruction, strength and all we need for our own benediction, but we can become agents for the storehouse of the Spirit, intermediaries able to bring some measure of the treasures of the kingdom of heaven to earth for mankind. We can, in fact, set up an 'agency' for whatever kind of treasure we choose; love, wisdom, joy, compassion, light, goodwill – there is no scarcity of these holy things at their 'source', and no dearth of need for them in the world. The only lack lies in ourselves, in the human inability to call upon them adequately and channel them truly in our lives. The gates of heaven are never closed.

But all the same, we must be under no illusions that we can work miracles. We are only infinitesimal units in a vast arena of what is still unregenerate substance. We are but tiny points of energy in the sea of mankind. This recognition and acknowledgement is a necessary humility, an essential to keep our work true and clear and unclogged by glamour and false notions of what we can do.

Yet, at the same time it is important to realise that as dedicated individuals we can be a definite force for good. Each of us is a part of the current that will eventually become a spiritual tide. And we need never forget, when faced with the difficulties, disheartenments and disillusions that beset us inevitably from time to time, that we are literally the substance of that new tide and on our resilience its flow depends.

Another point it will profit us to remember is that not only have we the strength of comradeship on the outer planes with those, like-minded and co-dedicated, who are seeking to achieve the same ends, but on subjective levels our prayer, thought, invocation, brotherhood of spirit gather into an immense world power.

★ ★ ★

Since we must always share our blessings, radiate our God-hood, perhaps the best ending to this study of meditation is the following formula which can be used to send out the gifts of the spirit to the world. It is based on the Buddhist 'Blessing of the Four Divine States', and through it we align ourselves with these divine qualities and then, using all our meditative powers, build a channel for each of them in turn and send them out to bless and redeem.

It is a method that is quite simple, but it may be used to meet any particular need in the world as well as generally and pervasively. It need take only a few minutes, yet if we do it each day, joining with the thousands working the same way, how much spiritual energy is being conducted into mankind's aura to lift and heal? This is one of the mysteries we cannot know yet, but it is also one of the inspiring thoughts that entice us onwards, stimulate our efforts and encourage us ceaselessly to try to walk as Souls.

Blessing of the Four Divine States

Having made a rapid alignment along the usual lines, visualise the Earth as a globe bathed in light. Standing as a transmitter of the qualities invoked and endeavouring to send them especially to places of particular need, say, aloud if possible:

Love to all beings—
   North—South—East—West—Above—Below
Love to all beings.
    (Pause for a few moments of silent radiation.)

Compassion to all beings—
   North—South—East—West—Above—Below
Compassion to all beings.
    (Radiation)

Joy to all beings—
   North—South—East—West—Above—Below
Joy to all beings.
    (Radiation)

Serenity to all beings—
   North—South—East—West—Above—Below
Serenity to all beings.
    (Radiation)

      So let it be.

Afterword

I wake up and wash. I light a candle and then meditate. I walk to work aware of the contours of the Earth beneath the concrete of the city. I greet each situation as an event in my education. I am aware of the energy of the people I meet and the invisible dance between us. I seek to hold myself grounded and loving, and yet be genuine and empowered.

I play and fight with my family, and they play and fight with me. And we talk and challenge and grow together.

I light a candle again, meditate and go to bed to sleep and work in my dreams.

I teach and I learn.

I am breathing so that I can be present and authentic.

It is very hard. It is also very graceful.

The New Age movement may disappear altogether. But the renaissance of our instinctive spirituality, and all the approaches to support it, is growing.

Notes on Contributors

Roberto Assagioli is the founder of Psychosynthesis, the most influential of the transpersonal schools of psychology. A medical doctor and psychiatrist, Dr Assagioli was also a student of Alice Bailey and helped found the Meditation Group for a New Age. His books include *Psychosynthesis* and *The Act of Will*.

Alice A. Bailey is considered by many people to be the most influential twentieth-century writer on spiritual and occult philosophy. She wrote some books on her own but her major output was as the secretary of the Tibetan teacher Djwhal Khul. Alice Bailey also founded the Lucis Trust and the Arcane School.

William Bloom, the editor of this anthology, is a New Age teacher and author working mainly out of St James's Church, Piccadilly, and the Findhorn Foundation. His books include *Meditation in a Changing World* and *Sacred Times*.

David Bohm is Professor of Theoretical Physics at Birkbeck College, London University; he has also taught at Berkeley, Princeton and Haifa. His books include *Causality and Chance in Modern Physics*, *The Special Theory of Relativity* and *Wholeness and the Implicate Order*.

Eileen Caddy co-founded the Findhorn Foundation, the New Age educational community in north-west Scotland. Her many books of channelled spiritual inspiration have been a comfort and guide to many thousands of people.

Fritjof Capra is the leading figure in pointing out the similarities between modern physics and Eastern mysticism with his best-selling and much-translated *The Tao of Physics*. He is currently doing research in high-energy physics at the Lawrence Berkeley Laboratory and lecturing at the University of California. He is also the author of *The Turning Point*.

Ken Carey is the founder and administrator of Greenwood School, based on the principles of experiential education, in Missouri. His channelled books include *The Starseed Transmissions* and *Return of the Bird Tribes*.

Joseph Bharat Cornell is Director of Earth Sky: Sharing Environmental Awareness, a non-profit environmental group in California dedicated to imparting an awareness of the natural world to all who seek a deeper understanding. His work with children and his book, *Sharing Nature with Children* have been very influential.

Ram Dass was a Harvard academic who 'turned on, tuned in and dropped out' in the 1960s to become one of the most important contemporary spiritual teachers. His books include the classic *Be Here Now* and *Journey of Awakening*.

Christopher Day trained as an architect and sculptor. His background inspiration includes the work of the German esoteric philosopher, Rudolph Steiner. In addition to designing buildings, Christopher Day runs a consultancy on the development and rescue of places, both buildings and landscape. He is the author of *Places of the Soul – Architecture and Environmental Design as a Healing Art*.

Michal J. Eastcott was a student of the Tibetan teacher Djwhal Khul and co-founder of Meditation Group for a New Age. Her books include *The Silent Path*.

Marilyn Ferguson is the editor of the *Brain/Mind Bulletin*, an advisor to *Revision Journal* and the author of *The Brain Revolution* and *The Aquarian Conspiracy*.

Ina May Gaskin is one of the founders of the Tenessee New Age community, The Farm, where one of the major areas of focus has been spiritual approaches to pregnancy and birth. Her classic book, *Spiritual Midwifery*, has been a major influence.

Shakti Gawain is a transpersonal psychologist and workshop leader living in California. She is the author of the best-selling *Creative Visualisation*.

Tom Graves is Britain's best known and most influential dowser, working through teaching and writing. He was trained as a graphic designer and for many years ran a successful computer typesetting business. He combines a thorough awareness of modern technology with a deep respect for ancient wisdom traditions. His many books on dowsing include *Needles of Stone*.

Liz Greene has a background in transpersonal psychology and is Britain's most well-known and influential transpersonal astrologer. Her many books include *Relating: An Astrological Guide to Living Together*.

Willis W. Harman is director of the Center for Study of Social Policy at the Stanford Research Institute and professor of engineering-economic systems at Stanford University. His books include *An Incomplete Guide to the Future*.

Roger Harrison is a management consultant working internationally. His work with chief executives and top management teams includes personal counselling, executive development, strategic thinking, organisation design and the management of change.

Louise L. Hay is a central figure in popularising many of the concepts of spiritual and New Age healing, through lectures, tapes and workshops. Her books include the bestselling *You Can Heal Your Life* and *Heal Your Body*.

Barbara Marx Hubbard is a futurist, writer, lecturer and teacher. She has been a key figure in networking and mobilising the American New Age movement, training individuals and groups. Her publications include *The Evolutionary Journey*.

C.G. Jung is one of the most influential thinkers and writers of this century. Originally working alongside Freud, Jung expanded psychoanalytic theory to include the deepest mysteries of psychology and spiritual development. His collected works run to many volumes; his books addressed to the general public include *Man and his Symbols* and *Modern Man in Search of a Soul*.

Donald Keys co-founded and is President of Planetary Citizens. He is a past Director of SANE and the International League of Human Rights, and worked for many years as a consultant to UN delegations and committees. His books include *The Abolition of War: Neglected Aspects* and *Earth at Omega: A Charter of Personal Possibilities*.

Phyllis Kystal is a spiritual teacher with a particular focus on the techniques of practice occultism which serve psychological transformation. Her book, *Cutting the Ties that Bind*, is one of the sanest and most useful introductions to practical inner work.

Stephen Levine is a poet and teacher of meditation who has worked extensively with the dying. He is director of the Hanuman Foundation Dying Project and acts as a consultant to hospital and meditation groups. His books include *Who Dies? An Investigation of Conscious Living and Conscious Dying.*

James Lovelock is an independent scientist who cooperated with the NASA space programme and since 1974 has been a Fellow of the Royal Society. He is also visiting professor in the Department of Cybernetics at Reading University. He is responsible for introducing the contemporary idea of *Gaia*, that the Earth is a living self-regulating organism. He is the author of *Gaia – A New Look at Life on Earth.*

Dorothy Maclean co-founded the Findhorn Foundation, the New Age educational community in north-west Scotland. She was instrumental in reawakening an intelligent awareness of the fairy and angelic kingdoms, particularly in relation to cooperation in gardening and horticulture.

Corinne McLaughlin, with her husband Gordon Davidson, co-founded the Sirius Community in Massachusets and the School of Spiritual Science. Together they wrote *Builders of the Dawn*, an overview of New Age communities.

Abraham H. Maslow was one of the pioneers of humanistic psychology. He taught at Brooklyn College and was Chairman of the Department of Psychology at Brandeis University. From 1967 to 1968 he was President of the American Psychological Association. His books include *Towards a Psychology of Being, The Farther Reaches of Human Nature* and *Religions, Values, and Peak-experiences.*

John Michell was educated at Eton and Cambridge. He is a student of traditional knowledge and the mysterious, and has been a central figure in the Earth Mysteries movement. He has a particular focus on Earth energies and the sacred mathematics of temple and church architecture. His books include *The Earth Spirit* and *The View Over Atlantis.*

Arnold Mindell is a key figure in the field of dream and body work. An analyst in private practice, he is also the founder of the Center for Process-oriented Psychology, Zurich and Portland. His books include *Working on Yourself Alone, City Shadows* and *Working with the Dreaming Body.*

Richard Moss is a medical doctor who underwent a deep mystical experience since when his life has been dedicated to spiritual teaching and facilitating transformative experiences. His books include *The Black Butterfly* and *The I That Is We*.

Caroline Myss was a successful American publisher who discovered that she had a remarkably accurate talent for intuitive diagnosis and psychological interpretation. She now works, teaches and writes to expand the horizons of contemporary medicine. With her colleague, Norman Shealy, she is the author of *The Creation of Health – Merging Traditional Medicine with Intuitive Diagnosis*.

Leonard Orr is the founder and head of Rebirthing, the therapeutic breathing technique which releases deep patterns of stress from the human body and psyche. He wrote *Physical Immortality* and, with Sondra Ray, *Rebirthing in the New Age*.

Danaan Parry is the founding director of the Holyearth Foundation and the Earthstewards Network. He is a specialist in theoretical and practical conflict resolution working in industrial and international relations.

M. Scott Peck is a practising psychiatrist who integrates modern psychoanalytic and therapeutic insights with a spiritual approach. His book *The Road Less Travelled* is widely recognised as the wisest and most useful New Age book yet published on personal relationships.

Marko Pogacnik is Yugoslavia's leading landscape sculptor working with art and the esoteric tradition of healing landscape. His work has been exhibited internationally and his books include *A Hidden Pathway through Venice* and *Die Erde Heilen*.

Sondra Ray is a leading international rebirther and founder of the Loving Relationship Trainings. She is the author of many books including *I Deserve Love* and *Ideal Birth*.

Jane Roberts channelled the *Seth* books. She was also an accomplished, insightful and amusing writer in her own right. The *Seth* books are considered by many people to be the most insightful books on transpersonal psychology currently available.

Gabrielle Roth is an innovative exponent of experimental dance and theatre, working to open people to their own creative power. She is the author of *Maps to Ecstasy – Teachings of an Urban Shaman*.

Deborah Rozman is a teacher and educational consultant working in California, with a particular focus on integrating New Age with mainstream educational approaches. She is the author of *Meditating With Children – The Art of Concentration and Centering*.

Peter Russell is a writer and management consultant combining the scientific, spiritual and psychological approaches. His book, *The Awakening Earth*, is considered by many to be the most accessible introduction to New Age thinking and the new paradigm.

Elisabet Sahtouris is a biologist, philosopher and writer. She is co-director of the International Institute for the Environment and the author of *Gaia: The Human Journey from Chaos to Cosmos*.

Rupert Sheldrake is a biologist, writer and teacher who is a seminal figure in expanding the contemporary boundaries of scientific knowledge. He received his doctorate and taught at Cambridge. His books include *A New Science of Life, The Presence of the Past* and *The Rebirth of Nature*.

David Spangler is a writer and lecturer who has been a central influence in the New Age. He coordinated the first educational programmes of the Findhorn Foundation and started the Lorian Association. He is the author of many books including *The Laws of Manifestation* and *Revelation – Birth of a New Age*.

Starhawk is a white witch and the most influential New Age exponent on the religion and techniques of the Goddess and Wiccan. Her books include *The Spiral Dance* and *Dreaming The Dark*.

Sir George Trevelyan is considered by many to be the father figure of the British New Age movement. He founded the Wrekin Trust, which specialises in running courses and workshops. He is an inspiring lyrical speaker and the author of many books.

Marion Woodman is a Jungian analyst working in Toronto. She is the author of four widely acclaimed books on the psychology and attitudes of modern women: *The Owl Was a Baker's Daughter: Obesity, Anorexia Nervosa and the Repressed Feminine; Addiction to Perfection, The Pregnant Virgin* and *The Ravaged Bridegroom*.

Roger J. Woolger is a graduate of Oxford University and a Jungian analyst working in the USA. He has been instrumental in creating a clear theoretical and practical framework for understanding past life experiences in the context of therapy. He is the author of the influential book, *Other Lives, Other Selves.*

Alan Young was an English lawyer who became vice-president of one of America's largest corporations. He took early retirement and then began a new career as spiritual healer and teacher. He is the author of *Spiritual Healing – Miracle or Mirage.*

Bibliography

1 What is the New Age?

Barbara Marx Hubbard, 'The Evolutionary Journey', *The Evolutionary Journey – A Personal Guide to a Positive Future*, Evolutionary Press, 1982, pp.9–14, 61–3

Marilyn Ferguson, 'The Aquarian Conspiracy', *The Aquarian Conspiracy – Personal and Social Tranformation in the 1980s*, Paladin/Granada, 1982, pp.30–34, 124–7

Peter Russell, 'The Emergence of a Social Super-organism', *The Awakening Earth – Our Next Evolutionary Step*, Routledge, 1982, pp.54–5, 80–6

Willis W. Harman, 'Metanoia', *An Incomplete Guide to the Future*, Norton, 1979, pp.32–4

Alice A. Bailey, 'The Way of the Disciple', *A Treatise on White Magic*, Lucis Press, 1974, pp.326–36

David Spangler, 'Revelation – Birth of a New Age', *Revelation – Birth of a New Age*, Findhorn Foundation, 1977, pp.99–100, 149–50

Sir George Trevelyan, 'Spiritual Awakening in Our Time', *A Vision of the Aquarian Age*, Coventure, 1977, pp.15–18, 21–2

Starhawk, 'The Rebirth of the Goddess', *The Spiral Dance*, Harper & Row, 1989, pp.198–200, 207–12

2 Inner Voice

Liz Greene, 'The Planetary Map of Inner Potential', *Relating – An Astrological Guide to Living with Others*, Aquarian Press, 1986, pp.23–9

C.G. Jung, 'Foreword to the *I Ching*', *I Ching or Book of Changes*, Arkana, 1989, pp.xxii–xxiv, xxxviii–xxxix

Ram Dass, 'The Energies of Meditation', *Journey of Awakening*, Bantam, 1985, pp.145–7, 192–4, 200

Corinne McLaughlin, 'How to Evaluate Channelling', *How to Evaluate Psychic Guidance and Channelling*, Sirius, 1987, pp.2–5, 8–13

Agni Yoga, 'The Heart of the Aum', *Heart*, Agni Yoga, 1982, pp.7–12

Eileen Caddy, 'The Earth and All Humanity Made New', *The Spirit of Findhorn*, Fowler, 1977, pp.31–3, 38–9

Ken Carey, 'The Starseed Transmissions', *The Starseed Transmissions*, Uni Sun, 1988, pp.1–2, 9–12

A Course in Miracles, 'Time and Reincarnation', *A Course in Miracles*, Arkana, 1985, pp.57–8, 228–33

Jane Roberts, 'The Dream World', *The 'Unknown' Reality*, Prentice Hall, 1979, pp.450–458

3 Healing

Richard Moss, 'An Invitation to Radical Change', *The Black Butterfly*, Celestial Arts, 1987, pp.1–2, 62–3

Jane Roberts, 'Cellular Awareness', *The Nature of Personal Reality*, Prentice Hall, 1974, pp.144–8

Caroline Myss, 'Redefining the Healing Process', Norman Shealy & Caroline Myss, *The Creation of Health – Merging Traditional Medicine with Intuitive Diagnosis*, Stillpoint, 1988, pp.130–7, 171–2, 236

Alice A. Bailey, 'Esoteric Healing', *Esoteric Healing*, Lucis Press, 1961, pp.2–5, 32, 40–2

Alan Young, 'Techniques Used by Spiritual Healers', *Spiritual Healing: Miracle or Mirage?* DeVorss, 1981, pp.16–22

Louise Hay, 'Disease and Thought Patterns', *Heal Your Body*, Eden Grove, 1984, pp.1–2, 5–8, 10–11

Shakti Gawain, 'Creative Visualisation', *Creative Visualization*, Bantam, 1985, pp.5–7, 75–7

Stephen Levine, 'Healing into Life and Death', *Healing into Life and Death*, Anchor/Doubleday, 1987, pp.28–34

4 Human Potential

M. Scott Peck, 'Love', *The Road Less Travelled*, Rider, 1989, pp.i, 84–5, 89–92

C.G. Jung, 'Archetypes, Shadows and the Anima', *The Archetypes and the Collective Unconscious*, Routledge, 1971, pp.3–5, 7, 20–8

Abraham H. Maslow, 'Peak-experiences', *Religions, Values and Peak-experiences*, Penguin, 1987, pp.19–20, 59–68

Roberto Assagioli, 'Psychosynthesis', *Psychosynthesis*, Viking Press, 1973, pp.21–30

Marion Woodman, 'Reclaiming the Body', *The Pregnant Virgin*, Inner City Books, 1985, pp.55–61

Gabriel Roth, 'Your Father, Your Lesson', *Maps to Ecstasy*, Crucible/ Aquarian, 1989, pp.108–119

Leonard Orr and Sondra Ray, 'Rebirthing', *Rebirthing in the New Age*, Celestial Arts, 1983, pp.72–6, 78–9, 83–4, 115–18.

Roger J. Woolger, 'Past Lives', *Other Lives, Other Selves*, Bantam, 1988, pp.10–19

5 Gaia

Fritjof Capra, 'The Tao of Physics', *The Tao of Physics*, Flamingo/ Fontana, 1989, pp.229–35

David Bohm, 'Implicate Order', *Wholeness and the Implicate Order*, Ark/Routledge, 1988, pp.147–50

Rupert Sheldrake, 'Morphogenetic Fields', *A New Science of Life*, Paladin, 1988, pp.75–7, 82–4, 95–6

James Lovelock, 'Gaia', *Gaia*, Oxford University Press, 1982, pp.3, 5–7, 9–11

Elisabet Sahtouris, 'Gaia's Dance', *Gaia – The Human Journey*, Pocket Books, 1989, pp.23–6

John Michell, 'Feng-shui', *The New View Over Atlantis*, Thames & Hudson, 1983, pp.59–62

William Bloom and Marko Pogacnik, 'Ley Lines', *Ley Lines and Ecology*, Gothic Image, 1985, pp.4–7

Tom Graves, 'Healing the Land', *Needles of Stone*, Granada, 1978, pp.222–6

Dorothy Maclean, 'Devas', *The Findhorn Garden*, Findhorn Press/ Harper and Row, 1975, pp.57–60

6 Practical Implications

Ina May Gaskin, 'Spiritual Midwifery', *Spiritual Midwifery*, The Farm, 1978, pp.442–6

Deborah Rozman, 'Meditating with Children', *Meditating with Children*, University of the Trees, 1977, pp.5–6, 78, 82, 146–7

Joseph Bharat Cornell, 'Sharing Nature with Children', *Sharing Nature with Children*, Ananda Publications, 1979, pp.17–23

Phyllis Kystal, 'Cutting the Ties that Bind – Puberty', *Cutting the Ties that Bind*, Sawbridge, 1986, pp.28–34

Christopher Day, 'Architecture and Environmental Design as a Healing Art', *Places of the Soul*, Aquarian Press, 1990, pp.139–45

Roger Harrison, 'Leadership and Strategy in Business' in 'Leadership and Strategy for a New Age' in John Adams (ed.), *Transforming Work*, 1984, pp.101–3, 105–7

Donald Keys, 'Planetary Citizens', *Earth at Omega*, Branden Press, 1982, pp.98–100

Danaan Parry and Lila Forest, 'Earth Stewards', *The Earthstewards Handbook*, Sunstone, 1987, pp.77–9

Arnold Mindell, 'Global Therapy', *The Year 1*, Arkana, 1989, pp.115, 118–20, 136–9

Michal J. Eastcott, 'Blessing the Planet', *The Silent Path*, Rider, 1975, pp.147–9, 151–2

Further Information

If you would like a fact sheet of addresses and contacts for New Age education, please send a stamped addressed envelope to:

Alternatives
St. James's Church
197 Piccadilly
London W1V 9LF

A New Age video-music production produced and directed by Peter Donebauer is available from:

Diverse Production Limited
Gorleston Street
London W14 8XS
Tel: 071-603 4567

Running time: 40 minutes
Price: £9.99

Abstract images and music similar to the opening titles of the broadcast programmes form a '20th century moving mandala' unique to the video medium.